The Place of Michael Oakeshott in Contemporary Western and Non-Western Thought

Edited by
Noël O'Sullivan

imprint-academic.com

Copyright © this collection Imprint Academic, 2017

Individual contributions © the respective authors, 2017

The moral rights of the authors have been asserted.
No part of this publication may be reproduced in any form
without permission, except for the quotation of brief passages
in criticism and discussion.

Published in the UK by
Imprint Academic, PO Box 200, Exeter EX5 5YX, UK

Distributed in the USA by
Ingram Book Company,
One Ingram Blvd., La Vergne, TN 37086, USA

ISBN 9781845409265 Paperback
ISBN 9781845409272 Hardback

A CIP catalogue record for this book is available from the
British Library and US Library of Congress

Contents

Contributors	iv
1. Noël O'Sullivan Introduction	1
2. Douglas Den Uyl The Myth of Politics	20

3. Natalie Riendeau
   The Role of Legend in Oakeshott's Political Thought:
   The Practical and Historical Past
	41

4. Terry Nardin Oakeshott as a Moralist	56

5. Timothy Fuller
   Historicism and Political Philosophy:
   Reflections on Oakeshott, Collingwood, Gadamer and Strauss
	73

6. Edmund Neill The Nature of Oakeshott's Conservatism	90

7. David Boucher
   The Depoliticization of Politics:
   Crisis and Critique in Oakeshott, Schmitt and Koselleck
	107

8. Wendell John Coats, Jr. Michael Oakeshott as Philosopher of 'the Creative'	123

9. Noël O'Sullivan
   Constitutionalism, Legitimacy and Modernity
   in Michael Oakeshott and Leo Strauss
	142

10. Chor-yung Cheung Oakeshott, Hayek and the Conservative Turn of Chinese Liberalism	160
11. Gurpreet Mahajan Oakeshott in India: At Home or Out of Place?	180
Index	195

Contributors

David Boucher FRHistS, Professor of Political Theory and International Relations, Cardiff University.

Chor-yung Cheung, Assistant Head and Senior Teaching Fellow, City University of Hong Kong.

Wendell John Coats Jr., Professor of Government, Connecticut College, New London, CT.

Douglas J. Den Uyl, Vice President of Educational Programs at Liberty Fund, Inc.

Timothy Fuller, Lloyd E. Worner Distinguished Service Professor and Professor of Political Science, Colorado College.

Gurpreet Mahajan, Professor of Political Science, Jawaharlal Nehru University, New Delhi.

Terry Nardin, Professor of Political Science, National University of Singapore and also Yale-NUS College.

Edmund Neill FRHistS, Lecturer in Modern History, New College of the Humanities.

Noël O'Sullivan, Emeritus Professor of Political Philosophy, University of Hull.

Natalie Riendeau, PhD in Political Theory (Cardiff University), independent scholar and Senior Policy and Research Analyst for the Government of Canada.

Noël O'Sullivan

Introduction

Since Michael Oakeshott never courted public recognition in any sphere of life, he might have looked askance at being elevated to a special place on the academic pantheon by the recent publication of two 'Companion to Oakeshott' volumes.[1] Be that as it may, the event is an opportunity to ponder on the continuing rise of his star in both Western and non-Western contemporary thought. Although there are many possible explanations, it is intriguing to speculate about how Oakeshott himself might have assessed his contribution, had he been willing to entertain the topic. Perhaps the best hint is provided by a radio broadcast he gave on the central place of myth in every civilization (Oakeshott, 1975).

Although we usually think of civilization as something 'solid and external', Oakeshott said, in reality it is 'a collective dream', the substance of which 'is a myth' (Oakeshott, 1975, p. 150). By myth, he explained, he did not mean a mere flight of fancy but 'an imaginative interpretation of human existence, the perception (not the solution) of the mystery of human life' (Oakeshott, 1975, p. 150). As such, myths may be more or less coherent and profound.

Turning to the myth that inspires our own civilization, Oakeshott observed that although this 'springs from many sources' extending back to the ancient world, it is mainly indebted to medieval Christianity, 'which no subsequent experience or reflection has succeeded in displacing from the minds of European peoples' (Oakeshott, 1975, p. 151). According to this myth, which owes much to the teaching of St. Augustine (Oakeshott, 1975, p. 58),[2] the human race

---

[1] Podoksik, E., ed., *The Cambridge Companion to Oakeshott* (Cambridge: CUP, 2012). Franco, P. and Marsh, L., eds., *A Companion to Michael Oakeshott* (Penn State UP, 2012).

[2] Oakeshott, M., *Hobbes on Civil Association* (Oxford: Blackwell, 1975), p. 58, where Oakeshott described the *Leviathan* as 'the first great achievement in the long-projected attempt of European thought to re-embody in a new myth the Augustinian epic of the Fall and Salvation of mankind'.

sprang from the creative act of God, and was as perfect as its creator. But, by an original sin, mankind became separated from the sources of its happiness and peace. This sin was Pride, the perverse exaltation of the creature, by which man became a god to himself ... But while corrupted man pursued his blind desires, an enemy of himself and of his kind, divine grace set a limit to human self-destruction, and promised a restoration of the shattered order, an ultimate salvation. This, briefly, is the myth that gave coherence to the [European] dream. (Oakeshott, 1975, pp. 151-2)

In order to appreciate the strengths and weaknesses of a myth, Oakeshott said, it is necessary to turn to literature rather than philosophy, since philosophy lacks the gift of imagination that characterizes the most profound literary and poetic expressions of myth (Oakeshott, 1975, p. 151). The task of great literature, he emphasized, is 'not to break the dream, but perpetually to recall it, to recreate it in each generation, and even to make more articulate the dream-powers of a people'.[3] On very rare occasions, however, philosophy itself may display such profound imaginative power that it rises to the level of literature, as Oakeshott believes was the case in Hobbes's *Leviathan* (Oakeshott, 1975, p. 150). More usually, the philosophic achievement is not so much 'an access of imaginative power' as an 'increase of knowledge' which makes the myth more intelligible, but not more inspiring (Oakeshott, 1975, p. 151).

In the modern world, Oakeshott warned, the future of every myth is increasingly endangered by what he described as the 'perverse genius' of the scientist, who is not content to live within a dream or myth but tries instead to destroy it. Although the scientist likes to present this destructive aim positively as waking from the dream into the real world, he fails to realize that if he succeeds we should not only 'find ourselves awake in a profound darkness, but [that] a dreadful insomnia would settle upon mankind, not less intolerable for being only a nightmare'.[4] In a subsequent retelling of the story of the Tower of Babel, Oakeshott expressed the fear that even if the modern myth survived the scientific project, it might nevertheless be reduced by a world bent upon prosperity to an impoverished instrumental vision of endless human gratification, accompanied by political ideologies which treat the rule of law as at best a device for implementing goals that provided

---

[3] Oakeshott, M., 'Leviathan: A myth', in *Hobbes on Civil Association* (Oxford: Blackwell, 1975), p. 150.
[4] Oakeshott, M., 'Leviathan: A myth', in *Hobbes on Civil Association* (Oxford: Blackwell, 1975), p. 151.

little protection for individual freedom.⁵ The misfortune of the modern world, in other words, is to have adopted what a sympathetic commentator has termed a 'counterfeit myth' which endangers civilization and individual freedom alike by deluding us about 'the kind of community to which we belong and the sorts of persons we are'.⁶ The delusion, in David Boucher's summary of Oakeshott's interpretation, is that we now think of society almost entirely as an economic enterprise, and of the activity of ruling as management. Our greatest need, accordingly, is to reformulate the counterfeit myth in a way compatible with freedom and its principal condition, *viz.* the rule of law and the maintenance of civil association.

From this standpoint, Oakeshott's contribution to contemporary thought may be viewed as a sustained endeavour to revise the inherited European myth in ways that would make it both more coherent and more able to counter the dominance of the counterfeit version.⁷ Before examining his principal revisions, however, the general nature of the link Oakeshott made between myth and politics must be noticed. This is explored in the chapters by Douglas Den Uyl and Natalie Riendeau.

For Den Uyl, Oakeshott's primary concern is with myth in its specifically political form. In this form, Den Uyl argues, myth performs the vital task of grounding Oakeshott's distinction between authority and power, which is fundamental not only to his ideal of civil association but to the entire modern tradition of theorizing about it from Hobbes onwards. Myth can perform this task because it is displayed above all in 'moral imagination', which is Oakeshott's term, Den Uyl writes, for 'a type of imagination that generates within us a sense of commitment or obligation, moral or otherwise ... because we find it compelling in itself'. For Oakeshott, Den Uyl concludes, obligation is thus the product of artifice expressed in moral imagining, and it

---

5   Oakeshott, M., 'The Tower of Babel', in *On History and Other Essays* (Oxford: Blackwell, 1983).
6   Boucher, D., 'Schmitt, Oakeshott and the Hobbesian legacy in the crisis of our times', in Dyzenhaus, D. and Poole, T., eds., *Law, Liberty and State: Oakeshott, Hayek and Schmitt on the Rule of Law* (Cambridge: CUP, 2015), p. 149.
7   There are short but valuable discussions of Oakeshott's view of myth, as well as comparisons of his view of myth with that of Carl Schmitt, in Bhuta, N., 'The mystery of the state concept, state theory and state making in Schmitt and Oakeshott'; Boucher, D., 'Schmitt, Oakeshott and the Hobbesian legacy in the crisis of our times'; Dyzenhaus, D., 'Dreaming the rule of law', all in Dyzenhaus, D. and Poole, T., eds., *Law, Liberty and State: Oakeshott, Hayek and Schmitt on the Rule of Law* (Cambridge: CUP, 2015). See pp. 10-37, 123-52 and 234-60, respectively.

is on the tenability of this contention that Oakeshott's defence of the distinction between authority, which obligates, and power, which merely obliges, ultimately depends.

As Den Uyl observes, the main philosophical challenge to this distinction is Spinoza's naturalistic philosophy, according to which authority is reducible to power. Examining Oakeshott's response to this challenge, Den Uyl focuses on Oakeshott's emphasis on the poetic aspect of moral imagining. All activity, including political activity, has a poetic dimension, but this is ignored by Spinoza's desire to give an entirely scientific account of politics. But what, precisely, does Oakeshott mean by poetic activity? The poetic dimension arises, in Oakeshott's own words, when 'images in contemplation are merely present' and 'provoke neither speculation nor inquiry about the occasions or conditions of their appearing but only delight in their having appeared'.[8] In so far as the political has a poetic dimension, Den Uyl's thesis is that this dimension is precisely what Oakeshott's concept of political myth is intended to highlight. In short, for Oakeshott 'the poetic in politics is myth', and it is the existence of myth which grounds authority by making it irreducible to power. It is this fact which explains why Oakeshott believes that the characteristically modern tendency to purge the political of any poetic or mythical dimension has disturbing implications for the future of civil association, since it is only that dimension which prevents the gradual reduction of politics to an affair solely of power.

Den Uyl's analysis of the part played by myth in underpinning the distinction between authority and power central to Oakeshott's theory of civil association is complemented by Natalie Riendeau's contention that Oakeshott's formal ideal of civil association is only fully intelligible in the broader context of his conviction that it is 'legends of political life [that] allow humans to make themselves at home in the world, to know who and where they are … and to project themselves into the future' (Riendeau, 2014).[9] As Riendeau emphasizes in this book, however, relocating Oakeshott's formal analysis of civil association in the broader context of legend as the key to political identity creates a major tension in his political thought. Specifically, the tension is between his 'thin' analysis of the logical postulates of civil association, on the one hand, and his historical treatment of the constitutive part played by

---

[8] Oakeshott, M., 'The Voice of Poetry in the conversation of mankind', in *Rationalism in Politics and Other Essays* (Indianapolis: Liberty Press, 1991), p. 509.

[9] Riendeau, N., *The Legendary Past: Michael Oakeshott on Imagination and Political Identity* (Exeter: Imprint Academic, 2014), p. 48.

myth and legend in the actual creation and maintenance of civil association, on the other. Expressing the tension slightly differently, although the bond of civil association is 'the continued recognition of the authority of rules as rules', those rules are only part of what Oakeshott believes is necessary for living together. As the ancient Romans above all realized, harmonious living together is only possible when a political identity is 'intimately linked to, and ultimately ensured by, political legends and the legendary past' (Ch. 3, p. 55, in this book). What Oakeshott admires in particular about the Roman genius for myth creation is that it was 'their poets, and not their gods, [who] were the creators of a legend of political life which has never been surpassed in its ability to endow a society with its sense of identity' (Riendeau, 2014, p. 47).

The vital role Oakeshott assigns to legends in the constitution of political order and social solidarity means, Riendeau suggests, that they perform a 'weak foundationalist' role in his political thought, despite his rejection of foundations in the stronger sense of 'prior claims about unquestionable or sacred or natural premises' (Riendeau, 2014, p. 46). Weak foundationalism is well illustrated by Roman history, in which a shared 'political imaginary' was carefully constructed in the form of a poetic narrative centred upon the original foundation of the city (Riendeau, 2014, p. 47). In this respect, Riendeau notes, Oakeshott's political thought has something in common with Hannah Arendt's stress on the importance of foundational myths, although his weak foundationalism does not necessarily refer to an act inaugurating a new beginning but simply to a narrative that makes sense of an established tradition of political behaviour (Riendeau, 2014, p. 47).

In the light of Oakeshott's sympathy for the role of myth and legend in the constitution of civilization, it may well be wondered whether he is more accurately seen as a moralist in search of ultimate meaning than as a philosopher *proprio nomine*. On this issue, Terry Nardin defends Oakeshott's philosophical status by insisting on a distinction between Oakeshott as a 'theorist of morality' and as a 'practical moralist' (Ch. 4, p. 56, in this book). Neglect of this distinction, Nardin holds, has obscured the fact that, as a theorist of morality, Oakeshott has always remained committed to the strictly philosophical task of analysing the logical postulates implicit in moral experience, rather than to the practical moralist's task of advising about conduct. When this distinction is borne in mind, Nardin observes, Oakeshott's perspective is undoubtedly a philosophical one, although one which can also, Nardin concedes, 'be read [if we wish] as a moral one' (Ch. 4, p. 71, in this book). If we choose to adopt the moral perspective, however, that should not be allowed to blur the vital distinction Oakeshott makes between philosophy and moralism.

What revisions, then, did Oakeshott believe the modern European myth required in order to make it more coherent and viable? Four principal ones may be identified in his writings as a whole, of which he credited Hobbes with the first and most important, simply adopting it himself. This revision consists of Hobbes's elimination from the inherited myth of the story of the Fall of Man. Oakeshott commended Hobbes for this revision because the story of the Fall encouraged the utopian belief that man might one day be restored to perfection by purging the social order of power and conflict. He also praised Hobbes for replacing the perfectionist view of man with a profoundly sceptical one that emphasized man's 'littleness, his imperfection [and] his mortality, while at the same time recogniz[ing] his importance to himself' (Oakeshott, 1975, p. 154).

Subsequently, Oakeshott modified his interpretation of Hobbes. Pride, which Hobbes often viewed negatively as an enemy of peace and justice, now assumed a positive dimension when Oakeshott identified a line of argument in Hobbes according to which, Oakeshott maintained, 'the just disposition is still recognized to be an endeavour for peace and what is sought is still the emancipation from the fear of violent and shameful death at the hands of other men, but the desired condition is to be attained, not by proud man ... surrendering his pride and becoming (by covenant) tame man, but by the moralization of pride itself'.[10] Now, he credited Hobbes with something more than removing the story of the Fall from the Western myth. His achievement, rather, was the identification of a distinctively individualistic impulse in the emergent European character expressed philosophically in Hobbes's rejection of the old 'Rational-Natural' mode of cosmological thought, for which the human good was determined independently of man's choice, in favour of a vision of life in terms of 'Will and Artifice', for which human existence becomes an open-ended adventure in self-creation. The good, in other words, is autonomy as such, and the end is knowing how to belong to oneself.[11] Whether Hobbes actually subscribed to this vision of man, rather than to the more craven view of men as impelled by fear of death to confer absolute authority on the

---

[10] Oakeshott, M., 'The moral life in the writings of Thomas Hobbes', in *Rationalism in Politics and Other Essays* (Indianapolis: Liberty Fund, 1991), p. 339. See also p. 341 for pride in the Augustinian tradition more generally, from which Oakeshott maintains that Hobbes took his own conception.

[11] Oakeshott, M., 'The moral life in the writings of Thomas Hobbes', in *Rationalism in Politics and Other Essays* (Indianapolis: Liberty Fund, 1991), p. 339.

Leviathan with which he is more commonly credited, is a contested issue.¹² What seems clear, however, is that Oakeshott was able to exploit a tension at the heart of Hobbes's thought arising from the fact that, in Irene Coltman's words, 'At the centre of the *Leviathan* there is a statement of love and honour, instead of [order and] justice.'¹³ Coltman is referring to Hobbes's admiration for the poet Sidney Godolphin (1610-1643), to whose brother Sir Francis Godolphin he dedicated the *Leviathan* following Sidney's early death in the civil war in the Royalist cause. Why, it may be asked, did Hobbes esteem Sidney Godolphin so highly?

The answer may partly be found in a poem by Sidney Godolphin that suggests a kinship with Hobbes's view of life as an endless series of desires and imperfect satisfactions:

> *Vaine man born to noe happinesse*
> *but by the title of distresse,*
> *alleyed to a capacitie*
> *of Joy only by miserie:*
> *whose pleasures are but remedies*
> *and best delights but the supplyes*
> *of what he wants; who hath noe sense*
> *but poverty and Indigence.*¹⁴

The main reason for Hobbes's esteem, however, was that in Hobbes's eyes Godolphin was one of the few naturally virtuous human beings not primarily motivated by the fear of death but by an aristocratic sense of honour. This is evident in the second sentence of the Preface to the *Leviathan*, where Hobbes wrote of Godolphin that

> there is not any vertue that disposeth a man, either to the service of God, or to the service of his Country, to Civill Society, or private Friendship, that did not manifestly appear in his conversation, not as acquired by necessity, or affected upon occasion, but inhaerent, and shining in a generous constitution of his nature.

As Irene Coltman remarked, it was precisely because Hobbes 'loved Godolphin for not needing the horrors of *Leviathan*' that his devotion 'was morally, if not politically, as subversive as any liberal doctrine. He [Hobbes] knew that the best thing was not his orderly and peaceful

---

12 See for example Müller, J.-W., 'Re-imagining Leviathan: Schmitt and Oakeshott on Hobbes and the problem of political order', in Tralau, J., ed., *Thomas Hobbes and Carl Schmitt: The Politics of Order and Myth* (London: Routledge, 2011).
13 Coltman, I., *Private Men and Public Causes* (London: Faber and Faber, 1962), p. 191.
14 Quoted in Coltman, I., *Private Men and Public Causes* (London: Faber and Faber, 1962), p. 188.

commonwealth but his gentle and courageous friend.'[15] Because Godolphin, as a man of honour, could stand by his word even when doing so placed his life in danger, he was recognized by Hobbes as being able to be a 'first performer' in the state of nature: that is, one who could keep his promises even when there was as yet no sovereign to enforce them.

Hobbes's admiration for Godolphin was shared by Oakeshott. Whereas Hobbes emphasized that Godolphin belonged to a minority of 'magnanimous natures', however, and was therefore not a possible model on which to base political theory, which realism required must be based instead on the fear of death that motivated the majority of men, Oakeshott tended to make Godolphin's aristocratic character a moral and cultural precondition for his ideal of civil association, ignoring Hobbes's scepticism about the propriety of approaching political theory in such a way. Although Oakeshott's moral esteem for the aristocratic values of men like Godolphin commands sympathy, his political revision of the modern myth on that basis seemed doomed from the outset to produce the hostility to mass democratic societies evident in, for example, his essay on 'The Masses in Representative Democracy' and the disillusion with modernity at large he subsequently expressed in 'The Tower of Babel'.

Oakeshott's second revision concerns the concept of agency or selfhood upon which Hobbes relied, which Oakeshott found neither 'satisfactory [n]or coherent'.[16] In fact, the deficiency Oakeshott seized upon was not peculiar to Hobbes but was characteristic of the concept of selfhood found in both pre-modern and many modern theologians and philosophers. This was a tendency to think of the self as divided into two parts, one material and the other rational or spiritual. No satisfactory account was provided, however, of how the two parts are connected to each other. Closely related to this dualist conception of the self is the equally problematic issue of the relation between subject and object—that is, between the agent and the world. In the pre-modern period this was not found disturbing since it was simply taken for granted that the agent's being is continuous with the external world, which is itself rational or spiritual. In the modern period, however, Descartes opened up a gap between the agent as knower and the world as object of knowledge which subsequently found elaborate philosophical expression in Kant's doctrine that the external world can never

---

[15] Coltman, I., *Private Men and Public Causes* (London: Faber and Faber, 1962), p. 191.
[16] Quoted by Müller, J.-W., in Tralau, J., ed., *Thomas Hobbes and Carl Schmitt: The Politics of Order and Myth* (London: Routledge, 2011).

be known as it is in itself since it is always interpreted through categories inherent in the mind. The agent, in other words, always wears conceptual spectacles which can never be removed. The fear of many modern philosophers, in consequence, has been that we are condemned to subjective idealism of some kind, since we can never step past our ideas to the world of things themselves.

For Oakeshott, both the pre-modern dualist view of man and the modern subject–object dualism are mistaken. Instead of dividing the self into two different parts, he adopts a monolithic concept according to which the self is reflexively constituted, in the sense that its existence is entirely self-interpreted. In other words, the self is never acted upon by a separate quasi-material part composed of passions, feelings and sense perceptions. Similarly, the modern dualism of subject and object is rejected by Oakeshott because the self never encounters a world entirely separate from it. This does not mean that we are always cut off from reality but only that a world completely separate from thought would lack all determinacy and hence could not exist. By way of clarification, Oakeshott explains that because all experience is determinate or, in his own phrase, 'modal', the task of philosophy is not to escape from thought but to identify the precise nature (or postulates) of the modality involved, which may be practical, historical, scientific or aesthetic but can never be purely subjective since each kind of modality contains within it its own criterion of reality. Nor is experience purely relative. It is, rather, conditional, being defined by its modality.

Because experience is always interpreted, Oakeshott's conception of the self is essentially active, standing in direct opposition to the passive one of thinkers who view it as merely responding to external stimuli. This active conception of the self is especially evident in what Oakeshott alluded to as the 'poetic' character of human activity, which is alternatively described by John Coats as its 'creative' nature.[17] Coats's chapter has the special merit of situating this creative conception of the self in the wider context of the Western cultural heritage as a whole by tracing the lineage of Oakeshott's thought to the Hebraic strand in it, rather than the classical Greek one. In Coats's words, 'the general drift and outline of Western philosophy and political philosophy ... from the late medieval period onward' can be interpreted as

> an increasingly explicit argument between the cosmological, ontological and ethical assumptions of ancient Greek rationalism and the implied assumptions of the Judaic and Christian biblical inheritance over the

---

[17] See Coats, W.J. and Cheung, C.-Y., eds., *The Poetic Character of Human Activity: Collected Essays on the Thought of Michael Oakeshott* (Plymouth: Lexington Books, 2012).

issue of 'the creative' in cosmology, history and conduct, to the increasing favour by late modernity of the latter ... Oakeshott's is an important twentieth-century voice echoing for the most part [the Judaic and Christian] perspective of 'the creative' *versus* the Greek rationalist side of the debate. (Ch. 8, pp. 123-4, in this book)

As other Oakeshott scholars have remarked, his sympathy for the Judaic/Christian stress on creativity links Oakeshott's philosophy in particular to that of existentialists like Jean-Paul Sartre (Farr, 1998).[18] It is worth noticing, however, that Oakeshott's conception of the creative self never sought to break completely with the inherited religious myth by offering a purely secular vision of the human condition since it remained tinged throughout his life by Christian imagery. This is especially evident in the survival of his sympathy for Augustine's image of human beings who, like the pilgrims endowed with free will in their legally constituted 'pilgrim city', are 'adventurers' in a somewhat similar legally constituted civil association (Oakeshott, 2003, p. 243). Like Augustine's pilgrims, Oakeshott's adventurous selves all recognize themselves and each other

> in terms of wants rather than slippery satisfactions, and of adventures rather than uncertain outcomes. This is a disposition to prefer the road to the inn, ambulatory conversation to deliberation about means for achieving ends ... and since men are apt to make gods whose characters reflect what they believe to be their own, the deity corresponding to this self-understanding is an Augustinian god of majestic imagination who, when he might have devised an untroublesome universe, had the nerve to create one composed of self-employed adventurers of unpredictable fancy, to announce to them some rules of conduct, and thus to acquire convives capable of 'answering back' in civil tones with whom to pass eternity in conversation. (Oakeshott, 2003, p. 243)[19]

What is especially notable amongst the surviving Christian images in Oakeshott's latter day version of Augustinianism is an equivalent of the central concept of salvation, now reformulated as the quasi-existentialist task of constructing a self or soul of one's own and living according to it (Oakeshott, 2003, p. 241). In this sense, Oakeshott once wrote, '*Memento vivere* is the sole precept of religion; and the religious man knows how easy it is to forget to live' (Oakeshott, in Fuller, 2003).[20] What is no less notable, and might have greatly surprised Augustine himself, is the positive rejection by Oakeshott of any concept of sin,

---

[18] Farr, A., *Sartre's Radicalism and Oakeshott's Conservatism* (London: Palgrave, 1998).

[19] Oakeshott, M., *On Human Conduct* (Oxford: Clarendon, 2003), p. 243.

[20] Oakeshott, M., 'Religion and the world', in Fuller, T., ed., *Religion, Politics and the Moral Life* (New Haven: Yale UP, 2003), pp. 27-38.

since it is vital for the adventurer not to be dismayed by his or her imperfections (Oakeshott, 2003, p. 241).

Oakeshott's third revision of the myth consisted of injecting a deeper sense of the historicity of experience. Historicity had two dimensions. One was a sense of rootedness in tradition which he regarded as the only remedy for the rationalism that has inspired the ideologies that have dominated European political life since the Enlightenment. In this perspective, Oakeshott's revision of the myth took the form of what was in effect a restatement of the Aristotelian conception of practical reason, in opposition to the abstract deductive rationality that has inspired a style of politics characterized by the pursuit of ideals arrived at independently of concrete experience. The second dimension of Oakeshott's treatment of historicity took the form of identifying the logical postulates of a specifically historical mode of experience in which the contingency of human identity and historical events are fully acknowledged without destroying the explanatory power of history. This does not arise through finding laws or regularities in the past, but through identifying the way in which contingencies 'touch' together to provide a coherent whole in much the same way, Oakeshott said, that the stones in a dry wall touch together.

Oakeshott's concept of historicity is most readily intelligible, Timothy Fuller suggests, when it is related to that of three other twentieth-century philosophers, *viz.* R.G. Collingwood, Leo Strauss and Georg Gadamer, whose interpretations of historicity range from Collingwood's embrace of historicism to Strauss's critique of it. Oakeshott and Gadamer, Fuller argues, occupy a middle ground between those two positions. With Gadamer, Oakeshott shares in particular the belief that all practical thought about ethical and political issues is inevitably rooted in tradition, which means that normative theorizing that entails an *a priori* dismissal of the existing order is inevitably a mixture of folly and delusion. This belief, which is evident in Oakeshott's critique of rationalist politics, is echoed in Gadamer's desire 'to confront the will of man, which is more than ever intensifying its criticism of what has gone before, to the point of becoming a utopian, or eschatological consciousness, with something from the truth of remembrance; with what is still and ever again real' (Gadamer, 1988, p. xxvi). In Oakeshott's case, however, acknowledgement of the historicity of experience does not necessarily lead to wisdom, in the form of deeper self-knowledge. It leads only to the awareness that history is an autonomous intellectual discipline with its own criteria of relevance.

It will be evident from the reference to Gadamer's rejection of modern voluntarist optimism that historicist sympathies tend to nurture sceptical conservative sentiment in politics. Although this is true in Oakeshott's case, his conservatism is so deeply tinged with individualist and constitutional sympathies that some recent writers have claimed that he is more properly seen as a liberal than a conservative thinker. The debate about the propriety of describing him as a conservative is the subject of Edmund Neill's chapter. Like all modern ideologies, Neill observes, conservatism has taken a wide variety of forms. Although Oakeshott did indeed flirt with anti-modernist versions of it, Neill argues that what distinguishes his mature conservatism in late works like *On Human Conduct* is a distinctively modernist position which does not simply accept whatever tradition bequeaths, or yearn for a past golden age. Instead, Oakeshott's conservatism embraces a form of pluralist individualism that celebrates the unprecedented opportunities for self-development and self-expression brought by the decline of the corporate, communal and hierarchical medieval world. But how sustainable is this modernist version of conservatism?

Philosophically, Neill argues, Oakeshott's position is dependent on a highly sceptical account of the self according to which it is difficult for agents to apprehend the ends of other agents, let alone the sentiments in which they pursue those ends. Although Oakeshott admits that an attenuated form of intersubjective understanding is possible, human agents are largely thrown back on the resources of tradition. This view, Neill remarks, 'can certainly be queried, even if it is not completely implausible'. Politically, Neill adds, Oakeshott's position has been queried 'both [by] those on the Left who seek to advocate greater pluralism than Oakeshott envisages in his work, and [by] those on the Right who feel that the authority of the state is under attack, and that Oakeshott's position offers an insufficient defence of this'. Overall, Neill argues, Oakeshott's position has the resources to withstand such criticisms, despite the fact that Oakeshott himself was sometimes a little reticent about doing so explicitly.

Oakeshott's fourth revision of the myth involved an attempt to give the modern Western concept of the limited state more precision than has hitherto been conferred on it. What was unusual about his enterprise was that it involved a radical rejection of the age-old Western quest for a rational ground for law and ethics in favour of a sceptical alternative theory according to which the source of legal and moral obligation consists simply in the acknowledgement by those obligated of the authority of the laws and moral constraints by which they are bound. In this respect Oakeshott's sceptical move from reason to authority as the ground of obligation echoes Hobbes who, in the fifth chapter of *Leviathan* (entitled 'Of reason') confined the role of reason to studying the consequences of actions and pursuing the logical implications of conceptual definitions. Having prepared the way by indicating that reason cannot ground morality, Hobbes completed the shift from reason to authority as the source of obligation to law in chapter sixteen, where he introduced a crucial distinction between a 'natural' and an 'artificial' person. A natural person is an individual viewed in his private capacity; whereas an artificial person is the holder of an office which confers a representative capacity that enables him to obligate those who acknowledge his jurisdiction in the course of acting on their behalf.

Implicit in Hobbes's distinction between natural and artificial personality is the claim that understanding the politics of a state based on the rule of law requires the distinction between authority and power already touched upon in connection with Douglas Den Uyl's chapter. Further aspects of the distinction are explored by David Boucher. Two issues in particular are discussed, of which the first is David Boucher's exploration of perhaps the most important objection now commonly made to Oakeshott's political thought. This was recently summarized by Jan-Werner Müller when he argued that Oakeshott 'depoliticizes' politics by replacing politics by an apolitical concept of conversation that is neither in nor about politics.[21] In response to the depoliticization charge, Boucher brings out the complexity of the issue at stake by locating it within a debate between Carl Schmitt and such followers of his as Reinhart Koselleck, and Oakeshott. On the one hand is Oakeshott's desire to tie the political proper to debate amongst the members of civil association about the desirability of the rules and policies they deem to be required for its maintenance. On the other is the claim of Carl Schmitt and thinkers influenced by him, such as Reinhart Koselleck, that the political is not about civil association but about the ability to make the decision which distinguishes friend and foe, since it is upon this that political unity depends. For Schmitt, that is, political legitimacy is not about constitutional government through the rule of law but about power and the ability to protect those subject to it.

Boucher makes clear that the two radically different concepts of the political that divide Oakeshott and Schmitt reflect two diametrically opposed responses to the pluralism of modern societies: while Oakeshott embraces modern individualism, Schmitt rejects it as a potential formula for anarchy and accordingly defends a form of

---

21 Müller, J.-W., 'Re-imagining *Leviathan*: Schmitt and Oakeshott on Hobbes and the problem of political order', in Tralau, J., ed., *Thomas Hobbes and Carl Schmitt: The Politics of Order and Myth* (London: Routledge, 2011), p. 75.

collectivism. Two of the most interesting features of this debate, Boucher observes, concern very different interpretations of the relations between the state and the rule of law, and the interpretation of Hobbes. In the case of the state, Oakeshott regards its claim to sovereignty as inseparable from the rule of law, whereas Schmitt regards the rule of law as a major obstacle to political unity. In the case of Hobbes, on Oakeshott's interpretation he is the first great modern philosopher of individualism, law, authority and moral obligation, whereas, for Schmitt, Hobbes is the first great theorist of power, decisionism, collectivism, security and prudential reason.

Although for Oakeshott the rule of law provides the moral basis of the state in so far as it is a civil association, his analysis of the relationship between morality and law seems to conflate a formal analysis of the logical postulates of the rule of law with a substantive conception of its moral content in the treatment in particular of the concept of *ius*.[22] More precisely, although Oakeshott maintains that law in civil association is formal, he adds that it is only authentically formal when what he terms '*jus*' is intrinsic to it (Oakeshott, 1983, p. 159). At first sight, this requirement does not seem to jeopardize the formal nature of law since by it, Oakeshott writes, he means only that law must observe such formal principles as 'non-instrumentality, indifference to persons and interests, the exclusion of *prive-lege* [i.e. exemption from legal obligation] and outlawry, and so on' (Oakeshott, 1983, p. 159). The problematic nature of *jus* emerges, however, when Oakeshott writes that 'to deliberate the *jus* of *lex* is to invoke a particular kind of moral consideration' which can only be discerned by a 'prevailing educated moral sensibility capable of distinguishing between the conditions of virtue, the conditions of moral association ("good conduct") and those which are of such a kind that they should be imposed by law ("justice")' (Oakeshott, 1983, p. 160). But who possesses the 'educated moral sensitivity' which, Oakeshott adds, is necessary in order to distinguish between *jus* and 'whatever moral idiocies there may be around' (Oakeshott, 1983, p. 160)? And who is to define what 'moral idiocy' is? Oakeshott's insistence on the relation between morality and the rule of law, then, seems to entail reliance on the substantive consensus of enlightened moral elite, and therefore cannot be developed solely in terms of the logical postulates entailed by the rule of law. This reliance, needless to say, is especially problematic in view of the moral

---

[22] In the following paragraph I have drawn on some comments about *ius* previously published in an article on Oakeshott in *Cosmos and Taxis*, vol. 2, issue 1, 2014.

diversity of modern Western societies, which makes it difficult for such an elite even to be identified.

Since a major recent development in Oakeshott scholarship has been the spread of interest in his political thought to non-Western thinkers, what remains to be considered is whether Oakeshott's reinterpretation of the European myth has any relevance beyond the West. At first sight, non-Western interest may seem strange in view of the fact that it has plausibly been maintained that 'the country [Oakeshott] is addressing is England, and he has little directly to say to other countries' (Gamble, in Nardin, 2015, p. 96).[23] It may seem even stranger in view of the fact that Chinese thinkers themselves have emphasized the Chinese preference for a rationalist style of politics since this alone, they believe, can free them from the long-established Chinese tradition of authoritarian rule (Zhang, in Nardin, 2015, p. 146). In addition, the primary Confucian concern is with moral perfectionism, rather than with the ideal of civil association that dominates Oakeshott's thought, and the perfectionist ideal points indeed towards an enterprise type of politics that Oakeshott regarded as incompatible with freedom (Sungmoon Kim, in Nardin, 2015, p. 166). It is hardly surprising, then, that in his essay for the present volume Chor-yung Cheung suggests that it is the more rationalistically inclined Hayek, rather than Oakeshott, who commands most interest among Chinese liberal sympathizers with the Western ideal of the limited state. Hayek, he notes, is favoured because 'he is never short of a plan', which is a major attraction for Chinese liberals seeking to respond to political crises in China and, more generally, to the challenges of modernity. Hayek's sympathy for planning, in short, means that is he is 'naturally easier [for the Chinese] to understand than the sceptical Oakeshott' (Ch. 10, p. 177, in this book).

Despite the reservations of non-Western thinkers about Oakeshott's political scepticism, there are nevertheless certain aspects of his thought which have a positive appeal for them. At the most general level, as Chor-yung Cheung has observed elsewhere, there is in particular a convergence between the importance of conversation in the Confucian ideal of education and Oakeshott's fondness for conversation as the crown of civilized achievement (Cheung, 2012).[24] At the political level, Oakeshott's ideal of civil association resonates with Chinese liberals'

---

[23] Gamble, A., in Nardin, T., ed., *Michael Oakeshott's Cold War Liberalism* (New York: Palgrave Macmillan, 2015), p. 96.

[24] Coats, W.J. and Cheung, C.-Y., eds., *The Poetic Character of Human Activity: Collected Essays on the Thought of Michael Oakeshott* (Plymouth: Lexington Books, 2012), p. 59.

ideal of a limited state, even if they do not share Oakeshott's concern with constitutional legitimacy. In particular, non-Western thinkers have been attracted by the political moderation and rejection of exclusionist politics they associate with civil association (Bi Hwan Kim, in Nardin, 2015, p. 186).[25]

Turning to the reception of Oakeshott in India, Gurpreet Mahajan notes in her chapter that, as in the case of China, Indian intellectuals committed to Indian independence disliked Oakeshott's hostility to rationalist political thought and commitment to tradition. This scepticism, she suggests, helps to explain why Michael Oakeshott was not, and has not been, an important influence in India, despite the fact that the writings of earlier members of the British Idealist school such as T.H. Green and Bernard Bosanquet had attracted a great deal of attention there. In addition, Mahajan writes, Oakeshott's ideal of civil association appears to conflict radically with the Indian constitution itself, since this was designed to create an enterprise association devoted to realizing social and economic equality and, more generally, social justice for all. Nevertheless, there are 'several other dimensions of the Indian political imagination, its history and traditions, where one can find "intimations" (to use Oakeshott's term) of civil association'. From the twentieth century onwards, in particular, commitment by the Indian political elite to creating a democratic and independent India echoed Oakeshott's anxieties about the enterprise mode of relationship. In particular, Mahajan concludes, Indian democracy can learn from Oakeshott's insistence that in a free society

> it is more important to focus on *how* a government acts rather than *what* it does. In a growing economy where the government is pushing for greater deregulation, liberalization of the economy and withdrawal of the state from different sectors, there is a steady clamour for less and less government. This excessive preoccupation with the quantum of government action and the extent of its intervention needs to be moderated by the Oakeshottian understanding of what matters more when it comes to government action. Less government is not by itself enough. One needs to back it with rule of law, on the one hand, and an emphasis on *how* the government acts, on the other ... These are some aspects of public and political life in India which can be enriched through an engagement with Oakeshott. (Ch. 11, p. 192-3, in this book)

In brief, what emerges from non-Western interest in Oakeshott's model of civil association is that attempts to apply it beyond the Western context inevitably tend to treat it as a merely instrumental device for accommodating diversity and promoting liberal reform, whereas for

---

[25] In Nardin, T., ed., *Michael Oakeshott's Cold War Liberalism* (New York: Palgrave Macmillan, 2015), p. 186.

Oakeshott himself the basis of the civil model is ethical. It is ethical in the sense that it is constitutive of the political identity of individualists for whom the authority of a formal rule of law enables them to acknowledge obligation, rather than mere power, in the non-voluntary membership of the state. More relevant to non-Western concerns, as Chor-yung Cheung has noted in *The Quest for Civil Order* (2007), is Ernest Gellner's sociological and functional concept of civil association which disconnects the civil model from the Western ideal of individual freedom and treats it simply as a means for integrating post-traditional societies fragmented by modernization (Cheung, 2007, pp. 13–50).[26] Gellner himself, it should be added, emphasized that even his cross-cultural conception of the civil model is applicable mainly to East Asian societies and was not optimistic about applying it to Islamic culture (Gellner, 1994).[27]

Conclusion

What then has Oakeshott's revision of the European myth achieved? In no case, it should be emphasized, did Oakeshott claim novelty for his revisions: his achievement consists, rather, in the rigour of his reformulations than in the imaginative originality of the enterprise itself. And, in practice, the actual course of events in the European cultural and political world has created an ever widening a gap between the hopes that inspired Oakeshott's revised myth and reality. Oakeshott himself was indeed intensely aware of this in his later writings, in which his growing despondency found expression in an essay on 'The Tower of Babel' (Oakeshott, 1983).[28] In that essay, Oakeshott no longer identified the primary threat to civil association with the growth of ideological politics which had dominated his thought in the interwar and early postwar decades. Nor was he now primarily worried about the enterprise state. What troubled him was, rather, the emergence of an all-pervasive instrumental mentality which he believed had come to pervade the whole of modern life and effectively marked the end of the inherited myth. So far as any remedy for this destructive mentality is possible, it can only be the restoration to modern Western culture of the sense of play which characterized it in different form in the ancient Greek and medieval worlds, but has now been almost completely

---

[26] Cheung, C.-Y., *The Quest for Civil Order* (Exeter: Imprint Academic, 2007).
[27] Gellner, E., *The Conditions of Liberty* (London: Penguin, 1994).
[28] Oakeshott, M., *On History and Other Essays* (Oxford: Blackwell, 1983). In the following paragraph I have drawn on a previously published essay in 'Michael Oakeshott on civil association', in Franco, P. and Marsh, L., eds., *The Essential Oakeshott* (Penn State UP, 2012).

eliminated in the modern technological age. Oakeshott's belief in the constitutive role of play in civilization, it may be noted, was one he shared with the Spanish philosopher Ortega y Gasset and the Dutch historian Huizinga, both of whom maintained liberal democracy, to the extent that it requires civil association, cannot survive in a culture devoid of any sense of play.[29] Unfortunately, what mainly seems to happen is that while opportunities for entertainment increase, culminating perhaps in the egotistical fantasies facilitated by virtual reality technology, there is little sign of play in Oakeshott's sense influencing contemporary Western culture.

If we turn from the political to the academic world, however, the continuing relevance of three in particular of Oakeshott's revisions of the Western myth can scarcely be in doubt. The first is his reflexive theorization of agency in *On Human Conduct*. The second is his exploration of the postulates of historical understanding. The third is his restatement of the nature of practical reason and the implied critique of the neo-Kantian mode of normative political theorizing dominant during the past half-century. Oakeshott's critique has been echoed in contemporary debate in, for example, Raymond Geuss's sustained indictment of the widespread tendency to treat political theory as a branch of applied ethics, in which independently premeditated ideals (to use Oakeshott's own phrase) are used to pass moral judgement on the existing social order. As Geuss notes, when the study of politics is conducted in this way, such crucial issues as the historical origins of the existing social order and the actual values of its members; the constitutive role of law in liberal democratic citizenship; the existing distribution of power and, above all, the difference between power and authority, are all issues that are marginalized or even eliminated. For those concerned about this situation, Oakeshott's revisions of the Western myth remain significant.

References

Bhuta, N. (2015) The mystery of the state concept, state theory and state making in Schmitt and Oakeshott, in Dyzenhaus, D. & Poole, T. (eds.) *Law, Liberty and State: Oakeshott, Hayek and Schmitt on the Rule of Law*, Cambridge: Cambridge University Press.

Boucher, D. (2015) Schmitt, Oakeshott and the Hobbesian legacy in the crisis of our times, in Dyzenhaus, D. & Poole, T. (eds.) *Law, Liberty and State: Oakeshott, Hayek and Schmitt on the Rule of Law*, Cambridge: Cambridge University Press.

---

[29] See Ortega y Gasset, J., *The Revolt of the Masses* (London: Unwin, 1961) and Huizinga, J., *Homo Ludens* (London: Paladin, 1970).

Cheung, C.-Y. (2007) *The Quest for Civil Order*, Exeter: Imprint Academic.
Coats, W.J. & Cheung, C.-Y. (eds.) (2012) T*he Poetic Character of Human Activity: Collected Essays on the Thought of Michael Oakeshott*, Plymouth: Lexington Books.
Coltman, I. (1962) *Private Men and Public Causes*, London: Faber and Faber.
Dyzenhaus, D. (2015) Dreaming the rule of law, in Dyzenhaus, D. & Poole, T. (eds.) *Law, Liberty and State: Oakeshott, Hayek and Schmitt on the Rule of Law*, Cambridge: Cambridge University Press.
Dyzenhaus, D. & Poole, T. (eds.) (2015) *Law, Liberty and State: Oakeshott, Hayek and Schmitt on the Rule of Law*, Cambridge: Cambridge University Press.
Farr, A. (1998) *Sartre's Radicalism and Oakeshott's Conservatism*, London: Palgrave.
Franco, P. & Marsh, L. (2012) *A Companion to Michael Oakeshott*, Pennsylvania: Penn State University Press.
Franco, P. & Marsh, L. (2012) *The Essential Oakeshott*, Pennsylvania: Penn State University Press.
Gellner, E. (1994) *The Conditions of Liberty*, London: Penguin.
Huizinga, J. (1970) *Homo Ludens*, London: Paladin.
Müller, J.-W. (2011) Re-imagining *Leviathan*: Schmitt and Oakeshott on Hobbes and the problem of political order, in Tralau, J. (ed.) *Thomas Hobbes and Carl Schmitt: The Politics of Order and Myth*, London: Routledge.
Nardin, T. (ed.) (2015) *Michael Oakeshott's Cold War Liberalism*, New York: Palgrave Macmillan.
Oakeshott, M. (1975) *Hobbes on Civil Association*, Oxford: Blackwell.
Oakeshott, M. (1983) *On History and Other Essays*, Oxford: Blackwell.
Oakeshott, M. (1991) *Rationalism in Politics and Other Essays*, Indianapolis, IN: Liberty Press.
Oakeshott, M. (2003) *On Human Conduct*, Oxford: Clarendon.
Oakeshott, M. (2003) Religion and the world, in Fuller, T. (ed.) *Religion, Politics and the Moral Life*, New Haven, CT: Yale University Press.
Ortega y Gasset, J. (1961) *The Revolt of the Masses*, London: Unwin.
Podoksik, E. (ed.) (2012) *The Cambridge Companion to Oakeshott*, Cambridge: Cambridge University Press.
Riendeau, N. (2014) *The Legendary Past: Michael Oakeshott on Imagination and Political Identity*, Exeter: Imprint Academic.
Slomp, G. (2011) *Thomas Hobbes and Carl Schmitt: The Politics of Order and Myth*, London: Routledge.
Tralau, J. (ed.) (2011) *Thomas Hobbes and Carl Schmitt: The Politics of Order and Myth*, London: Routledge.
Tudor, H. (1973) *Political Myth*, London: Macmillan.

Douglas J. Den Uyl

The Myth of Politics

Michael Oakeshott's legacy to modern political thought is nothing if not insightful. Although described by himself and others as a 'conservative', Oakeshott defies typical ideological labelling. His conservatism does not guide his reflections, but rather his reflections get summed up in the label 'conservative'. But such a label hardly gives one a clue as to what one will find within his writings. The insights found therein do not fall along typical conservative lines, bearing instead a unique quality of reflection that prevents the reader from predicting Oakeshott's conclusions ahead of time. As a consequence, the usual things said about political matters are not the usual descriptions found in Oakeshott. It is this quality of Oakeshott's work that I want to exploit here in one particular way. The focus of what follows will be on the basis for artifice[1] in politics and how that foundation may help ensure a successfully functioning civil association. The role of artifice is central to Oakeshott's discussion of civil order, for it is connected to an important distinction between power and authority. The problem of artifice grows out of a problem I have addressed elsewhere on why Oakeshott preferred Hobbes over Spinoza. I shall rehearse some of my earlier conclusions again below as a way of helping to understand a dimension of artifice that I believe is at least implicit in Oakeshott's conception of politics. It is a dimension increasingly being ignored, at least partly as a result of a 'Spinozistic' understanding of politics. Our journey will begin, however, from a seemingly distant starting point—namely, with Oakeshott's brief

---

[1] Today 'artifice' tends to refer to a clever device or trick of some sort. Oakeshott uses the term in contrast to what is natural. The distinction is one of contrasting art and nature. However, a work of art must 'lie in nature' and for Oakeshott that seems to be will and imagination. Our focus below is mainly on imagination which we argue can compel the will in ways which serve our thesis here. Civil authority is itself a work of art, but its authority may be strongly rooted in the imagination. For Oakeshott's account of artifice, see Oakeshott, M., *Hobbes on Civil Association* (Indianapolis: Liberty Fund Inc., 1975), pp. 27–9.

description of myth. That starting point will, however, also serve as our point of conclusion.

Myth and Politics

In a volume of essays entitled *Hobbes on Civil Association* there is a radio talk given by Oakeshott with the title '*Leviathan*: A Myth'.[2] Besides presenting Hobbes's great work *Leviathan* as 'philosophical literature' and a 'work of art', Oakeshott makes a few remarks about myth generally and about myth as connected to Western civilization — remarks no doubt inspired by Oakeshott's understanding of *Leviathan* itself. We are told that civilization is at root a 'collective dream' and that the substance of that dream is 'a myth, an imaginative interpretation of human existence, the perception (not the solution) of the mystery of human life'. In the case of *Leviathan*, Oakeshott argues that Hobbes plays off of the central myth of Western civilization, namely the myth of the Fall whose lessons centre around the sinfulness of pride and the pervasiveness of sensuality or desire. *Leviathan* both modifies the myth while continuing it. There is in *Leviathan* no fall, as in the original story, but rather the possibility of a rise through agreement with our fellows. That agreement both dampens pride and gives order to our inherent sensuality. We can appreciate any modifications of the myth offered by *Leviathan* because we are thoroughly familiar with the myth to begin with. And while pride and sensuality are not the impetus for a fall in *Leviathan*, but rather the occasion for a rise, they nonetheless reflect matters central to the human condition just like the traditional myth.

Whatever the status of *Leviathan*, to claim that civilization is a dream, and myth its expression, certainly is cause for pause, if for no other reason than the inherent idealism of such a claim. Indeed, the typical opponent of myth, namely science, is itself described 'as a dream that [the scientist] is awake'. Science may be involved in a project of 'destroying all myth', but for Oakeshott science does not escape being a part of the dream. Science then, it would seem, is part of the dream but not part of the myth. By the same token, the myth seems to be independent of science and something to which science feels compelled to respond. It is tempting to say that in the modern world the myth is that science can replace myth.[3] Oakeshott's main point,

---

[2] Oakeshott, M., *Hobbes on Civil Association* (Indianapolis: Liberty Fund Inc., 1975), pp. 158–63.

[3] The cessation of myth by science is described by Oakeshott as a 'dreadful insomnia' with the qualities of a 'nightmare'. Noël O'Sullivan notes that for Elie Kedourie the 'secularist' trend in politics has had the same impact upon

though, is that myth is larger than science. It not only competes with science as a way of understanding our world, but it also defines *for* science what science itself must ultimately address if it is to be successful in displacing myth. In the abstract, then, if myth ceases, so does science, but the reverse does not hold. In this way, myth is more fundamental than science. Myth also has an additional poetic quality that we shall discuss more below, which science ostensibly does not. But if science can and does take on such a quality, it too becomes, to that extent, myth.

Part of our own story here is to take Oakeshott seriously and regard *Leviathan* as philosophical literature. That will mean eventually that something deep in the nature of politics is itself 'literature'. In this regard it is, as we shall see, Spinoza's task to replace the mythical dimensions of *Leviathan* through a pure science of power. The Spinozistic onslaught is difficult to withstand, but if it is possible, *Leviathan* possesses the quality with which to do so. But we are getting ahead of ourselves.

Myth is not extensively well defined in Oakeshott's talk, and it is not a term typically discussed in his works.[4] We do know that for Oakeshott the purpose of literature in civilization is not to break the dream and the myth that accompanies it, but to 'perpetually recall it'. Consequently, literature retells the story of the myth in various ways. If the literary qualities are also philosophical, as in *Leviathan*, we are instructed as well as reminded. The myth to which Oakeshott is referring in his talk as being central to our civilization is the myth of the Fall, where the Pride of mankind, as original sin, separates us from our Creator. In the separation from God we fall into our own sensuality. The perfection of God's creation is thus sullied and we are distanced from the happiness we once knew within that perfection. *Leviathan* still points to that same distance and its causes, but calls forth some means we have taken to mitigate the effects of our pride and sensuality. *Leviathan* instructs by suggesting how the political serves this

---

revelation as Oakeshott's account here of science upon myth. See, O'Sullivan, N., 'Philosophy, politics and conservatism in the thought of Elie Kedourie', *Middle Eastern Studies*, Vol. 41, No. 5, Sept. 2005, p. 713. Myth and revelation are not mutually exclusive alternatives, and the value of their presence in politics as something other than pure rationalism is part of Oakeshott's point and our point here. Besides myth being more in keeping with Oakeshott, it seems to me that the mythical dimensions of any revelation are what is relevant here.

[4] An examination of the indexes of Oakeshott's major works does not, for example, turn up the term 'myth'. If he uses it, it is not enough to compel an indexer's attention.

mitigation. It seems fair to say, therefore, that Oakeshott sees the myth as inevitably linked to the political, not only because *Leviathan* is so linked, but also because the political, like the myth itself, is a fundamental feature of human existence and would thus utilize myth in its own self-understanding.

Leviathan does not begin with paradise from which is precipitated a fall. Rather, Hobbes's state of nature turns out to be quite the opposite. But as Oakeshott points out, what is recalled in Hobbes's myth that conforms to the traditional one is our mortality and how that is affected by our pride and sensuality. In this original 'state of nature' it is not the 'transitoriness of his satisfaction that hinders a man's happiness, but the constant fear that death may supervene and put an end to satisfaction by terminating desire'. Since one of our fears in this regard is how others may hinder the pursuit of our desires, we mitigate the problem by coming up with an agreement, that is, a political way or governing our desires. And as Oakeshott also notes, pride and sensuality 'are the poles between which, according to our dream, human life swings'. *Leviathan* is another means by which that message is conveyed and remembered.

Over the many years since Hobbes's *Leviathan* first appeared, so called 'social contract theory' has been criticized as being ahistorical and false to the understanding of how human beings come to live together. Yet if the story of the social contract is considered myth rather than history or science, its historical or scientific validity is of little importance. What is important is what that myth reminds us of with respect to human life and its prospects. The pride and sensuality that are so central to the traditional myth are the dispositions both driving us away from and towards one another. The general myth, then, gets transformed into a political myth (the agreement among the social contractors) as a way of mitigating the extreme propensities of our basic dispositions. Moreover, in Oakeshott's interpretative hands, this general myth is presented less as a solution to a problem than it is as a reminder of the tenuous character of any such 'solutions', precisely because of the universality and ceaseless character of these very human dispositions. We are more easily reminded of such things when we understand the degree to which politics is an artifice. It is much harder to see the point if politics is, as in Aristotle, construed as simply natural. However true that may be, both the fragility and distinctiveness of the political are masked by the all pervasive and ineradicable character of whatever is considered 'by nature'. The social contract story by contrast reminds us forcefully that however natural the political may be, there is a critical component of it that is artifice, and that the authority of this artifice is somehow derived from the myth it invokes. The problem then is making room for what is not 'natural' in politics. That is a problem to which we now turn where the naturalism of Spinoza is pitted against the artifice advanced by Hobbes.

Hobbes and Spinoza

As mentioned earlier, I want to point to some of the discussion and conclusions I presented elsewhere[5] about Spinoza and Oakeshott as a means to contributing to our discussion here. The problematic of the earlier piece was to explain why Oakeshott, who seemed to have an early youthful enthusiasm for Spinoza, seldom mentions him, and never with the same admiration and extent that he does with Hobbes. I discard immediately the notion that Spinoza was, for Oakeshott, simply a footnote to Hobbesian ideas. Rather, Oakeshott treats him as a different and separate sort of thinker, albeit one he largely rejects in favour of Hobbes. The main basis for the rejection of Spinoza is that Oakeshott takes Spinoza as seeing the state to be a kind of enterprise association as opposed to Oakeshott's favoured civil association, which Hobbes apparently manifests.[6] Here I want to claim that the difference between the two thinkers centres around Spinoza's naturalism.[7] As I am using the term here, naturalism is the view that all apparently second-order creations can be reduced to first-order natural causes. Naturalism would be, then, a direct threat to the role and authority of artifice as central to understanding the political.

In seeing Spinoza's naturalism in comparison with Hobbes, one of the most central ideas of Spinoza that separates him from Hobbes is Spinoza's claim that, 'the individual's right of nature does not cease in the political order' (TP III, 3). For Spinoza our right of nature is strictly equated with the power we possess: 'he has as much right against other things in nature as he has power and strength'(TP II, 4). 'Other things in nature' includes other human beings, so unlike Hobbes, where a civil association brought about by a social contract is what delivers us from

---

[5] Den Uyl, D.J., 'Spinoza and Oakeshott', in Abel, C. and Fuller, T., eds., *The Intellectual Legacy of Michael Oakeshott* (Exeter: Imprint Academic, 2005), pp. 62–85.

[6] It is often typical when looking at this history of political philosophy to think of Hobbes and Spinoza as the same kind of political thinker in that both seem to reduce politics to power and human purposes to desires alone. Oakeshott is thus offering a relatively unique insight in seeing these thinkers as being quite different.

[7] I am not interested here in whether Oakeshott's understanding of Spinoza is accurate or not. Some of that issue is taken up in my essay. Our concern here is the nature of certain ideas as Oakeshott employs them rather than the accuracy of his interpretation of any historical figure.

war into peace, political life for Spinoza is simply a certain configuration of power relations. There is, in other words, a shift for Spinoza in the *pattern* of power relations between the 'state of nature' and the political order, but no change in the nature of the relationship involved. It is all just configurations of power, and what pretends to be otherwise can be reduced to it. In a very important sense, nature just is power for Spinoza,[8] so the political would be 'natural' for Spinoza as well. Spinoza is also a kind of absolutist in politics, so he envisions the political order as a condition where the sovereign holds the citizens sufficiently in his power to check any deviances from the sovereign will (TP III, 3, 5). His theory in general, however, is simply that the ebb and flow of politics is nothing other than the ebb and flow of power. With right and power being equivalent, there is no movement out of a state of nature to a political condition.[9] There are rather endless tussles of power within some sort of corporate body or bodies; and any promises or allegiances made thereby are held together solely by the powers that keep them in force (TP II, 12, 18).

With Oakeshott's Hobbes the matter is essentially different. Some important aspect of the very nature of political life is an artifice, a creation of will whose function is to mediate and order relations among those who have agreed to be citizens of one corporate body. In other words, the 'civil condition is an artifact' according to Oakeshott (HCA, 49). Neither thinker sees the political order as a means to perfection, but Hobbes/Oakeshott see it as a humanizing force, whereas for Spinoza the political order is more of a way of stabilizing power as a means to thereby producing even more power. However motivated by passions and inclinations human beings are in Oakeshott's Hobbes, there comes a point where will with reason kicks in, at least to recognize the need for an agreed upon social arrangement and the consequences of doing without one. As Shirley Letwin notes, this is done without the aid of nature.

> The moral of Hobbes' novel account of the human predicament is that if men hope to agree on anything, they must come to do so without the help of any natural pattern, standard, criterion, sanction, or model.[10]

In Spinoza by contrast there need be no 'agreement' — only the conquest and submission of wills, however devoid they may be of rationality.

---

8   See, e.g. E4 Def.8.
9   There is actually no 'state of nature' for Spinoza (though he will use the term, e.g. TP II, 18) because individuals are too weak as individuals to live in such conditions (TP II, 15).
10 Letwin, S.R., *On the History of the Idea of Law*, edited by Noel B. Reynolds (Cambridge: Cambridge University Press, 2005), p. 94.

Hence all is nature and only nature. As such, no artifice is created in Spinoza, only various modes of force and submission. No doubt the differences between these thinkers have much to do with how they look at individuals and the motivations for their conduct.

Although Oakeshott notes that Hobbes 'is the first moralist of the modern world to take candid account of the current experience of individuality', he adds that 'it is clear also in Spinoza' (Letwin 1993, p. 22). The two thinkers, however, have different notions of individuality. Spinoza's individuals are simply particular modes of being as defined in metaphysical terms. In that regard, they are thus essentially the same, being defined as expressed instances of a greater whole. Oakeshott says of Hobbes, however, that Hobbes presents us with a 'unique human individuality' (HCA, 84). What appears to be unique about the individuality as Hobbes conceives of it is the presence of some sort of creative dimension. Oakeshottean individuals make themselves into individuals. That process is essentially absent in Spinoza's account where individuals are more the product of forces than the originator of them. The creative dimension in Hobbes's individuals is the basis for the sort of morality that is relevant to politics—namely the protection of that very individuality itself. Moreover, it is this individuality that gives rise to the artifice of politics. Again, Shirley Letwin expresses the point well:

> We must then recognise that the morality that can sustain the kind of individualism and the idea of law that Westerners have learned to value rests on the conception of rationality as a creative faculty rather than as a pipeline to certainty. The important novelty in this morality that is crucial for understanding the idea of law is that each man is assumed to possess individuality not in spite of, but because of his rationality. His individuality is not accounted for by a 'core' of passions or urges beating against a corset imposed by 'reason' or 'society.' To say that human beings possess individuality means that all are the makers of their own thoughts, that they are capable of shaping a personality, and that they are responsible for what they become ... The fundamental fact about the human world is not the omnipresence of conflict, but the potentiality for unlimited variety.[11]

By contrast with Oakeshott and Hobbes, it is not too far off to suggest that for Spinoza political actors are indeed 'accounted for by a "core" of passions or urges beating against a corset'.[12] While politics for Spinoza

---

[11] Letwin, S.R., *On the History of the Idea of Law*, edited by Noel B. Reynolds (Cambridge: Cambridge University Press, 2005), pp. 329-30.

[12] Spinoza, of course, allows for the possibility that one can be 'free' and escape the push and pull of passive desires. That is the point of the last

is best described by the ebb and flow of passions and urges, for Oakeshott/Hobbes we can conceivably fashion an order among ourselves that will protect our potential for 'unlimited variety'.

The political order generally is for both Hobbes and Spinoza an extension of their conceptions of human nature and the meaning of individuality. But as hinted at above in Letwin's comments, how law is conceived is a function of this conception of individuality as well. Richard Friedman notes that Oakeshott ends up assimilating Hobbes to his own views about law.[13] The Oakeshott view holds that genuine law is less a command on what to do than it is an expression of patterns of practices that are given a central role in determining appropriate or acceptable conduct through the creation of a sovereign authority who interprets and promulgates those practices. The 'artifice' then largely comes through the authority that gets conferred in the political process—an authority that is not given by nature or anything else for that matter. As Terry Nardin points out,

> The rule of law is a mode of association grounded on recognition of the authority of laws, not on their alleged worth, rationality, or justice … Law can answer the need for agreed principles only if it is authentic law—law, that is, whose authority as law is established apart from its moral propriety or consequential desirability.[14]

The important point to note about the central character of the principles of agreement that gain expression through law in a civil association is that these principles are virtually *sui generis* and not the consequence of, or impetus for, some other process outside of itself. Because of the various pursuits of power, actual political practice may mask this essential component, but in so far as there is any politics left as Oakeshott wants to conceive it, the *sui generis* nature of the organizing

---

books of his *Ethica* and other writings as well. However, such free persons seem to have little to do with the functioning of political orders.

[13] Friedman, R., 'Michael Oakeshott and the elusive identity of the rule of law', in Abel, C. and Fuller, T., eds., *The Intellectual Legacy of Michael Oakeshott* (Exeter: Imprint Academic, 2005), pp. 175ff. Friedman suggests that Oakeshott's last words on Hobbes differ from previous interpretations by assimilating Hobbes to himself. For our purposes here, the correct interpretation of how Oakeshott reads Hobbes is not particularly important, since the version expressed here highlights our issue most directly. It should be noted that Shirley Letwin also offers a similar suggestion of Oakeshott's conception of the rule of law when she claims that for Oakeshott 'the rule of law is a moral practice' (Letwin, 2005, p. 313) and when she distinguishes rules from order and instrumental from non-instrumental (Letwin 2005, p. 334).

[14] Nardin, T., *The Philosophy of Michael Oakeshott* (Pennsylvania: Penn State UP, 2001), p. 209.

principles that define a political order are at least somewhere in the background. That *sui generis* character of the principles is what gives law and morality, as well as other human practices their authority precisely because those principles are not in themselves expressions of anyone particular pursuits. These conceptions answer to nothing but themselves. As a particular form of human practice involving the generation of principles for living together, politics may incorporate other authoritative practices in various ways, but in the end it carries its own special authority.

Again by contrast, 'authority' for Spinoza would consist entirely in the possession of power—the more power the more authority. Obligations, symbols, practices and rules are the tools of power for Spinoza, not constraints upon it as would seem to be the case with Oakeshott's sovereign. This conception of authority means that Spinoza's politics is akin to an Oakeshottean enterprise association, whereas the Hobbes's conception of authority creates the possibility of a civil association. In Spinoza's case all the dimensions of authority are instrumentalized to power and authority is maintained by the exercise of power alone.

Our problematic is now simple enough to consider: can we keep Oakeshott from being collapsed into Spinoza? Can we, in other words, come up with some basis for claiming that the political order cannot be reduced to an explanation such as Spinoza's where all is but modalities of power? Can we put our finger on what is missing or irreducible in any endeavour to account for politics in a Spinozistic fashion? It is not enough to state the differences between the two thinkers and let that be sufficient in itself in claiming that Spinoza's views need not be accepted. Because power incontrovertibly exists in politics, as in all human endeavours, Spinoza's challenge is to answer why all does not reduce to it, especially if a plausible story can be told about how power is actually wielded in every aspect of political reality.[15] Oakeshott may wish to claim, for example, that law has its own authority, but legal positivists or realists might respond that there is finally nothing, even in law, beyond the exercise of power. What dimension of political life, then, cannot be reduced to the exercise of power such that one might

---

[15] It should be noted that just because one can give an account of something in terms of X it does not follow that therefore X is the correct explanation. Hence it does not follow that because one can account for a political activity in terms of power that therefore power exhausts the explanation of that activity. Similarly, because one has an alternative account that is not reducible to power does not show that there is more to the matter than the pursuit of power. To defeat the reductionist thesis on power, one needs a candidate that is inherently distinct from power, or at least plausibly so. That is what we hope to provide below.

use that dimension as the basis for suggesting a real distinction between authority and power, whereby the artifice that claims the former is not a function of the latter? Our answer will be that at least one important element missing from an account where authority is reduced to power is the poetic, and the poetic in politics is expressed through myth.

The Poetics of Politics

Given the title, it may seem necessary that we begin this section by saying something about poetics as Oakeshott conceives it. It is actually more helpful, however, to say something more about politics first. I shall not recount the already familiar distinction between enterprise and civil associations wherein only the latter form counts as true politics for Oakeshott. But I do want to mention that in merely stating the distinction the tendency is immediately to become vulnerable to a power thesis like Spinoza's. Once stated, the strong temptation is to make 'civil association' into a normative concept and then to measure our distance from it as a failing to be truly political. However valuable that may be, the quick move to the normative can be troublesome. As we have seen repeatedly over the last couple centuries, any normative doctrine can be recast instrumentally as the tool of some race, class, gender, special interest or ideological orientation.[16] And in the end, these recastings are themselves easily regarded as expressions of forms of power. To avoid this pitfall, we must treat 'civil association' first in descriptive terms and then move to the normative once we have found something that can, so to speak, stand on its own. This is what Spinoza demands[17] and what will keep us focused on finding that dimension of the political that is not so easily recast as being merely an aspect of power. For if we can find the element that prevents us from reducing all to power, the normative will actually carry more authority when it is finally brought to bear.

So our problematic is to find a description of an irreducible dimension of politics or civil association.[18] We might begin by noting what has been at least implicit in all we have stated about Oakeshott to this point.

---

[16] I once attended an academic conference on Oakeshott's work where a number of those present saw 'civil association' as a tool of an aristocratic class.

[17] *Tractatus Politicus* 1.

[18] As Terry Nardin notes quite rightly, 'the prescriptions of civil association are not conclusions derived from any foundational set of natural conditions, propositions about human needs, moral truths, or principles of justice' (Nardin, 2001, p. 208).

> Power, then, is categorically distinguished from authority. To have power does not, itself, endow a man or an office with authority; to be acknowledged to have authority does not, itself, endow a man or an office with power; and to recognise the power behind a demand, although it may be a good reason for complying with what is demanded, cannot be a reason for acknowledging an obligation to do so.[19]

Authority, then, seems to derive from elsewhere than from power for Oakeshott, but from whence does it come? The foregoing suggests that authority is connected to obligation whereas power is connected to obedience. For its part, 'obligation' seems strongly associated to something like morality, though as we noted above, civil associations are not merely instantiations of the moral. So if there can be something inherently connected to obligation as it might subsequently manifest itself in the political — however connected to other forms such as the moral — our quest would be to determine what that might be. And whatever it might be, it would need to be of such a nature that it both separates itself off from obedience, while at the same time not being simply a form of moral conduct or prescription. Should we find such a thing, we could then proceed to see how the genesis of obligation might manifest itself in a political order.

A term that Oakeshott uses that can help us here is 'moral imagination'. Although the word 'moral' appears in the term, 'moral imagination' is broader than the strictly moral. It is a form of imagination utilized by the moral but not used exclusively by, or limited to, the moral. This term refers to a type of imagination that generates within us a sense of commitment or obligation, moral or otherwise. It generates this sense because we find it compelling in itself. We can see the connection between moral imagination and civil association in the following from Oakeshott:

> A rule of civil association is desirable in respect to the accuracy with which it reflects, or does not affront, the moral imagination of the associates when it is directed to what they have learned to distinguish as a relationship not of moral perfection but of civility or justice. There are, in this matter, no absolute standards; this moral imagination, concerned with civil obligations, is all there is. Nevertheless, the political engagement to deliberate the rules that spell out an acceptable image of civility is the most difficult of all human engagements simply because it has no

---

[19] Oakeshott, M., 'Talking politics', in *Rationalism in Politics and Other Essays* (Indianapolis: Liberty Press, 1991), p. 445.

place for the consideration of what is most readily considered, namely, interests.[20]

Notice that the moral imagination connected to civil obligations is not about developing norms for directing behaviour so much as it is in fashioning an 'mage of civility' that will thereby distinguish the acceptable from the unacceptable. Obligation, then, will be tied to the 'image' we develop about appropriate conduct, which stands quite apart from any interest or purpose or goal we might have. Such an image has its own integrity as an image and as such we find it compelling. Since for Oakeshott such images develop out of practice,[21] it might be said that simply to have the image is to be committed or attached to it. It has this obliging effect upon us because it is the way through which we come to *understand* our conduct. The compelling character of the image is not a function of any desire that might otherwise have motivated someone's conduct, because that compelling character does not come from the desire, but rather any related desire is a function of the compelling quality of the image. Nor is this form of imagination an interest pursued with respect to a larger interest such as one's group, or class, or ideology. Rather, such 'larger interests' would be understood in light of the moral imagination they might otherwise invoke. In short, these 'images' — expressive of practice — stand on their own, are essentially pre-reflective, and oblige by their very independence of anyone's particular interests, desires or modes of conduct.[22] The sort of 'compulsion' exhibited by this sort of image is of the type one would associate with contemplation or aesthetic appreciation.

Our moral imaginings inevitably invoke senses of approval and disapproval. These senses can be seen as attitudes expressed in practice that 'fill our world with images both desired and approved'.[23] The images are the basis from which we will come to evaluate the conduct

---

[20] Oakeshott, M., 'Talking politics', in *Rationalism in Politics and Other Essays* (Indianapolis: Liberty Press, 1991), p. 455. Also cited in this connection in Nardin (2001, p. 210).

[21] Oakeshott, M., 'The Voice of Poetry in the conversation of mankind' (henceforth 'Voice of Poetry'), in *Rationalism in Politics and Other Essays* (Indianapolis: Liberty Press, 1991), p. 496.

[22] Oakeshott notes that 'moral ideals are not, in the first place, the products of reflective thought, the verbal expressions of unrealised ideas, which are then translated (with varying degrees of accuracy) into human behaviour; they are the products of human behaviour, of human practical activity, to which reflective thought gives subsequent, partial and abstract expression in words' ('Tower of Babel', in *Rationalism in Politics and Other Essays*, 1991, pp. 479-80). I am eliding somewhat all pre-reflective moral notions such as 'images', 'ideal', and 'attitudes'.

[23] 'Voice of Poetry', p. 502.

of ourselves and others. Because they make no reference to anyone in particular, but seem to apply to all, they are attitudes formulated independently of interests. Oakeshott puts this in an interesting way.

> [A]s Hobbes observed, a man achieves this moral attitude 'if when weighing the actions of other men with his own, they seem too heavy, to put them in the other part of the balance, and his own in their place, that his own passions and self-love, may add nothing to the weight.' In other words, selves in moral activity are equal members of a community of selves: and approval and disapproval are activities which belong to them as members of this community. The moral skill in practical activity, the *ars bene beatique vivendi*, is knowing how to behave in relations to selves ingenuously recognised as such.[24]

Notice that what goes on here is a recognition, not a reflection, and thus connects to our moral imagination rather than to any particular form of moral conduct or prescription. There is no denial of the existence of passions, interests and self-love in these moral attitudes, but these propensities are essentially irrelevant to the attitudes themselves. Instead, these attitudes are derived from the moral imagination that accompanies actual practice when diverse selves endeavour to live well with each other. As the passage above indicates, there is something aesthetic about the recognition of our intersubjective context and thus the attitudes that recognition generates. However, it is important to realize that what we have been describing is not moral activity itself but the conditions for its exercise.

We have suggested that at the root of political obligation we will find moral imagination and that its aesthetic and disinterested character gives us a sense of obligation to it. One final touch needs to be added: how do we come to recognize the moral imagination that underlies political obligation? We do so through political education. Here is what Oakeshott says about political education:

> [P]olitical education is not merely a matter of coming to understand a tradition, it is learning how to participate in a conversation: it is at once initiation into an inheritance in which we have a life interest, and the exploration of its intimations. There will always remain something of a mystery about how a tradition of political behavior is learned, and perhaps the only certainty is that there is no point at which learning it can properly be said to begin.[25]

We have here Oakeshott's well-known propensity to think in terms of 'conversations' when thinking about human interaction. The practical

---

[24] 'Voice of Poetry', p. 502.
[25] Oakeshott, M., 'Political education', in Fuller, T., ed., *The Voice of Liberal Learning* (Indianapolis: Liberty Fund Inc., 2001), pp. 179-80.

and the scientific are the two most common conversations and the ones that come to mind for most people at first. But there is another conversation, the poetic. In this regard Oakeshott suggests that there is a 'poetic character of all human activity'.[26] Indeed, the 'conversation of mankind' is a 'meeting place of various modes of imagining'[27] which includes the poetic form.

Oakeshott defines poetry as 'the activity of making images of a certain kind and moving about among them in a manner appropriate to their character.'[28] As Oakeshott notes immediately afterwards, the form of imagining appropriate to the poetic experience is contemplating or delighting. And as Oakeshott notes further, 'images in contemplation are merely present; they provoke neither speculation nor inquiry about the occasions or conditions of their appearing but only delight in their having appeared.'[29] Furthermore, 'contemplation does not use or use-up or wear-out its images, or induce change in them: it rests in them, looking neither backwards or forwards.'[30] Oakeshott concludes by saying that 'contemplating, then, is an activity of making and entertaining mere images.'[31] Consequently, 'poetic imagining is contemplative activity. Poetry appears when ... images are not recognized either as "fact" or as "not-fact".'[32] They are, in a significant way, self-sufficient.

Given that there is a poetic character to all human activity, we need to look for it in the political context now that we have a basic sense of what poetic experience is about. But what are the chief characteristics of poetic experience generally? Wendell Coats summarizes a number of these characteristics in an essay devoted to exploring Oakeshott's understanding of the poetic.[33] First of all Coats reiterates that the poetic is to be found in 'all settled forms of human activity', and even more importantly notes that the poetic presence is found 'even in moments of practical experience'.[34] In this connection, Coats cites Oakeshott saying that some activities (love and friendship, for example) 'intimate contemplation and may be said to constitute a connection between voices

---

26 'Tower of Babel', p. 479.
27 'The Voice of Poetry', p. 497.
28 'The Voice of Poetry', p. 509.
29 'The Voice of Poetry', p. 509.
30 'The Voice of Poetry', p. 510.
31 'The Voice of Poetry', p. 513.
32 'The Voice of Poetry', p. 516; see also ibid., note 23, p. 525.
33 Coats, Jr., W.J., 'Michael Oakeshott and the poetic character of human activity', in Abel, C. and Fuller, T., eds., *The Intellectual Legacy of Michael Oakeshott* (Exeter: Imprint Academic, 2005), pp. 311-15.
34 Coats, Jr. (2005, p. 315). He also states that 'all mediated human experience has affinities to poetic mediations', ibid., p. 311.

of poetry and practice'.³⁵ It seems plausible, then, to conclude that some dimension of the political would also include the poetic. If so, we would need to look for an 'experience of contemplative imagining'³⁶ that can be associated with the political.

Coats also notes that the poetic experience presents itself in the 'absence of any pre-meditated design'³⁷ and 'creates the experience of contemplative delight for its own sake'.³⁸ Indeed, such delight is 'devoid of any concern about the truth of assertions, or moral responsibility, or the accuracy of its depictions'.³⁹ Such descriptions of poetic experience suggest an aesthetic form of imagining that draws us to it because of its very self-sufficiency. Such self-sufficiency, as mentioned above, is also the source of the *compelling* character of the experience precisely because we delight in it for its own sake. But can we find such poetic experiences in politics, apart from inferring they must be there somewhere since the poetic is found throughout human experience? As it turns out, Oakeshott does point directly to this possibility.

The assimilation of 'politics' to practical activity is characteristic (though not exclusively so) of the history of modern Europe, and during the last four centuries it has become increasingly complete. But in ancient Greece (particularly in Athens) 'politics' was understood as a 'poetic' activity in which speaking (not merely to persuade but to compose memorable verbal images) was pre-eminent and in which action was for the achievement of 'glory' and 'greatness' — a view of things which is reflected in the pages of Machiavelli.⁴⁰

---

35 Coats, Jr. (2005, p. 315).
36 Coats, Jr. (2005, p. 311).
37 Coats, Jr. (2005, p. 311).
38 Coats, Jr. (2005, p. 312).
39 Coats, Jr. (2005, p. 312).
40 'The Voice of Poetry', pp. 493-4, note 2. The mention of 'memorable' here reminds one of Oakeshott's claim later that 'memories seem to be a fruitful spring of poetic images because in remembering ... we are already halfway released from the practical world of desire and emotion. But even here, what can be contemplated is not an actual and recognised memory, but an abstraction — a memory not identified as "fact" and one divorced from space and time' ('Voice of Poetry', p. 525, note 23). That myth may be a central feature of politics is hinted at elsewhere as well. Consider: 'Every society, but the underpinnings it makes in the book of its history, constructs a *legend* of its own fortunes which it keeps up to date and in which is hidden its own understanding of its politics' (emphasis added). The role of myth in the hermeneutics of politics does not thus seem limited to antiquity.

Setting aside for the moment the purging of the poetic from politics in modern Europe, it now becomes clear where we are headed with all this given that the poetic can indeed be merged with the political: our thesis is simply that the poetic in politics is myth—the subject with which we began this essay. With myth we have a plausible candidate for grounding the authority of an artifice whose structure is guided by myth and which thereby separates authority from power.

We might recall that we opened with Oakeshott's claim that Hobbes's *Leviathan* is a work of art that deploys some of the basic myths of Western civilization. The characteristics of myth included being 'an imaginative interpretation of human existence' which we 'perpetually recall' and 'recreate ... in each generation'. We find myth in the 'literature of civilization', and 'the gift of the greatest literature — of poetry — is a gift of imagination.' Myth, then, is one of the gifts of imagination, and it is reasonable to expect that it thereby shares the basic aspects of the poetic identified above. First of all, Oakeshott tells us that the general myths of Western civilization, utilized in *Leviathan*, were saved from formulaic degeneration by the 'true custodians' of the dream that defines Western civilization, namely by 'poets and artists'.[41] The poetic and the mythical are thus inherently linked. And furthermore when we reflect on the nature of myth, we are likely to realize that myth shares a number of the characteristics we associated above with poetry: myths are absent of any premeditated design; we delight in them for their own sake; they are objects of contemplation; they present neither facts or non-facts; they compel by their self-sufficiency; they are memorable; and our experience of them is separated off from interest and strategy. In this respect, myth is the poetry of politics.

When we reflect upon the idea of myth as the poetry of politics, we do recognize that Oakeshott is right that the history of the modern European state has been to increasingly move politics into the practical — in essence, making the state an enterprise association. Nevertheless, reflection might also lead us to the recognition that many, if not most, political orders do have their own myths, and that those myths do, from time to time at least, still insert themselves into political consciousness. In the United States, for example, myths about liberty, individualism and a classless social order can still carry weight.[42] They

---

[41] Oakeshott, M., *Hobbes on Civil Association* (Indianapolis: Liberty Fund Inc., 1975), p. 161.

[42] For an excellent crystallization of the myth of America, see for example *Letters from an American Farmer* (1784), Hector St. John de Crevecoeur, online at xroads.virginia.edu/~hyper/crev/home.html. See also Winthrop, J., *A Modell of Christian Charity* (1630), Hanover Historical Texts Project, online at http://history.hanover.edu/texts/winthmod.html.

certainly are objects of contemplation when presented in works of art such as literature, films and poetry itself. But, more importantly, they are often appealed to in actual political contexts where debates about policy are taking place. We might see the myth of American individualism being called upon by advocates of the Second Amendment of the United States Constitution or by advocates of free markets. That same individualism might be appealed to in anti-discrimination debates. The myth of classlessness is appealed to by both political parties in the United States when they seek to distance themselves from the rich and for being advocates for the 'middle class'. The point is that the myths, which are neither 'fact' nor 'not-fact', give authority to political proposals and programmes. Indeed, the authority of such proposals and programmes is enhanced to the degree they seem to incorporate the spirit of any myth they evoke.

The Myth of Politics

Our argument has been to link at least some aspects of myth to the poetic experience and then link that further to politics itself. Though I believe this argument is true to Oakeshott, it also extends his vision a bit beyond what is typically found in his writings. The extension comes from the suggestion that we might find myth in the background of virtually all political orders and that such myths separate power from authority in particular regimes and are not simply general with respect to Western civilization. If so, there might be some interesting implications if myth is forgotten or repressed or somehow not present at all. We shall mention some of these possible implications in a moment. Our point here is to reiterate what seems implied from the foregoing discussion, namely that political orders can and do partake in the poetic conversation through myth.

Recall, however, that the ostensible problem with which we began was the problem of power. Oakeshott rejects the 'Spinozistic'[43] notion that politics is completely and solely about power. Our task was thus to find something about politics that was not reducible to power and which lent authority to a political artifice. If we are correct that myth shares the characteristics of poetic experience and that it can be found in politics—however hidden it often may be today—then myth offers us something fundamentally different from power. Myth differs from power because it evokes contemplation, and we recall that contemplation is not an engagement of anyone's particular interests, strategies,

---

[43] Oakeshott does allow that Spinoza had a contemplative dimension in his *scientia intuitive* ('Voice of Poetry', p. 511). However, this contemplative dimension seems far removed from the practical and political.

purposes or projects. Rather the reverse is the case: interests, strategies, purposes and projects are often inspired by myth, which is independent of any of them. Because myth is self-sufficient in this way, it belongs to no one and can be possessed by no one. As such, it is not in itself reducible to, or an expression of, power. This is not to suggest that myth cannot generate things that are the tools of power. Oakeshott, for example, tells us that the deployment of symbols should not be confused with the poetic experience.[44] For him it is actually practical and scientific experience that manipulates symbols most regularly, and these conversations are distinguished from poetic activity.[45] Consequently, we could obviously find in politics the manipulation of symbols for the purposes of power—including symbols connected to myths. Moreover, people could certainly position themselves as guardians of myth in such a way as to serve their own purposes in gaining power. But even in such cases, the myth still stands beyond the services to which it may be put.

Earlier we noted that for Oakeshott there is a strong distinction between authority and power. In the modern state 'the relationship set up with its subjects is not a power relationship of compulsion and obedience but a relationship of authority and obligation. And its authority to enforce the fulfillment of obligations derives from its authority to prescribe them.'[46] Oakeshott typically thinks of authority in terms of rules that govern a *societas*. As he puts it,

> The idea *societas* is that of agents who, by choice or circumstance, are related to one another so as to compose an identifiable association of a certain sort. The tie which joins them, and in respect of which each recognises himself to be *socius*, is not that of an engagement in an enterprise to pursue a common substantive purpose or to promote a common interest, but that of loyalty to one another, the condition of which may achieve the formality denoted by the kindred word 'legality'. Juristically, *societas* was understood to be the product of a pact or an agreement, not to act in concert but to acknowledge the authority of certain conditions in acting ... [S]*ocii*, ... [are] related to one another in the continuous acknowledgement of the authority of rules of conduct indifferent to the pursuit or the achievement of any purpose.[47]

Notice that the rules, indifferent to particular purposes, have authority over the actors because of a certain mutual respect the *socii* have for one another. But this sort of authority, and the loyalty it requires, must itself derive from somewhere, and unless we want to adopt a kind of

---

[44] 'Voice of Poetry', p. 540.
[45] 'Voice of Poetry', pp. 503, 508.
[46] 'Talking Politics', p. 448.
[47] Oakeshott, M., *On Human Conduct* (Oxford: Clarendon Press, 1975), p. 201.

Kantian formalism where noumenal selves are inherently endowed with respect for each other, we need to look elsewhere for those sources of loyalty—presumably to some dimension of actual practice. The suggestion being advanced here is that a place to look is to the myth(s) that define(s) the political order. Those myths may not be the only sources of authority. Circumstances and habitual practices, not to mention the attitudes of the actors themselves, would come into play in giving any set of rules authority in the way Oakeshott defines them above. But fundamental myths of a political order bear all the characteristics needed to supply authority to rules governing appropriate conduct whether they be moral or political in nature.

It is not difficult to imagine how myth might give rules their authority, indeed their moral standing. If there is, for example, a myth of individualism in the American psyche, then those rules which preserve the separate pursuit of one's interests would seem authoritative because they both distinguish themselves from anyone's particular interests and are grounded in what seems prior to anyone's particular interests. Similarly, we can imagine pathologies connected to myth. If rules were constructed which seemed to run contrary to an extant myth of individualism, for example, one might expect political unrest or a disrespecting of those rules. Furthermore, myths could conceivably clash or be in tension. Tocqueville long ago noted the potential clash in the United States between liberty and equality.[48] And people who possess or seek power could certainly position themselves as advocates of the superiority of one myth over another. Finally, in situations where efforts are made to create political orders in the absence of any uniting myth, such as democracies where none previously existed before, we might expect less than stable or satisfying results.

The argument here has not been that myth removes power from politics or even necessarily moderates its pursuit. But myth does stand apart from power and can be a significant source of the type of authority Oakeshott argues is needed for civil authority. One of the great advantages of myth in this regard is that myths are lived and contemplated by acting agents and are not the product of abstract reasoning and philosophical speculation. If we are correct that a property of myth is to engender contemplation in acting agents, then there appears to be something permanent about myth:

> [T]he image which partners contemplation may be destroyed by inattention, may be lost, or may decompose. It is permanent merely

---

[48] de Tocqueville, A., *Democracy in America*, edited by Eduardo Nolla (Indianapolis: Liberty Fund, 2010), Second Part, Ch. 1.

because change and destruction are not potential in it; and it is unique because no other image can fill its place.[49]

Such comments indicate that myth as it would actually function in a political culture can be called upon again and again to lend authority to proposed rules and conceptions of appropriateness.

But the same passage points to something else that is important; namely, the possibility of the *loss* of myth through inattention, decomposition, forgetfulness or deliberate suppression. Without myth and its attendant benefits, politics would become precisely the pure exercise of power we have attributed to Spinoza and to which much of postmodernism seems attached. Since power is actually so much a part of actual politics, a rush to power would be a natural consequence of the absence of any irreducible factor that might lend alternative authority to a given political artifice. Yet because myth possesses us only through contemplation, it has no power once one's gaze is turned. Hence, one cannot but help thinking that myth is continually being averted today by the practical enterprise form of politics that promises outcomes rather than rules of association. It is a form of distraction away from myth that actually does exhibit a process of pure power. Spinoza may thus have been more prescient than Hobbes in seeing this as the final culmination of modern politics, but we might want to agree with Oakeshott that such a world is a 'dreadful insomnia' possessing the characteristics of a 'nightmare'.[50]

References

Coats, Jr., W.J. (2005) Michael Oakeshott and the poetic character of human activity, in Abel, C. & Fuller, T. (eds.) *The Intellectual Legacy of Michael Oakeshott*, Exeter: Imprint Academic.

Crevecoeur, H.St. John de (1784) *Letters from an American Farmer*, [Online], http://xroads.virginia.edu/~hyper/crev/home.html.

Den Uyl, D.J. (2005) Spinoza and Oakeshott, in Abel, C. & Fuller, T. (eds.) *The Intellectual Legacy of Michael Oakeshott*, Exeter: Imprint Academic.

---

[49] 'Voice of Poetry', p. 510. Noël O'Sullivan notes that there is an unresolved tension between idealism and power in liberal theory, and we might want to argue that myth could very well be a way to mitigate such tension. See O'Sullivan, N., 'Civil association and the quest for a political liberalism', translated into Spanish as 'La asociación civil y la búsqueda de un liberalism político', in *Cuadernos de Pensamentio Politico*, No. 34, April 2012, pp. 21–54.

[50] We use these terms in note 2 above. In that context Oakeshott was speaking of science, not politics, but it seems to me even more applicable to modern politics.

Friedman, R. (2005) Michael Oakeshott and the elusive identity of the rule of law, in Abel, C. & Fuller, T. (eds.) *The Intellectual Legacy of Michael Oakeshott*, Exeter: Imprint Academic.

Letwin, S.R. (ed.) (1993) *Michael Oakeshott: Morality and Politics in Modern Europe*, New Haven, CT, & London: Yale University Press.

Letwin, S.R. (2007) *On the History of the Idea of Law*, Cambridge: Cambridge University Press.

Nardin, T. (2001) *The Philosophy of Michael Oakeshott*, University Park, PA: Penn State University Press.

O'Sullivan, N. (2005) Philosophy, politics and conservatism in the thought of Elie Kedourie, *Middle Eastern Studies*, **41** (5), Sept.

O'Sullivan, N. (2012) Civil association and the quest for a political liberalism, translated into Spanish as 'La asociación civil y la búsqueda de un liberalism político', *Cuadernos de Pensamentio Politico*, **34** (April).

Oakeshott, M. (1975) *Hobbes on Civil Association*, Indianapolis, IN: Liberty Fund Inc.

Oakeshott, M. (1975) *On Human Conduct*, Oxford: Clarendon Press.

Oakeshott, M. (1991) Talking politics, in *Rationalism in Politics and Other Essays*, Indianapolis, IN: Liberty Press, inc.

Oakeshott, M. (1991) Tower of Babel, in *Rationalism in Politics and Other Essays*, Indianapolis, IN: Liberty Press, inc.

Oakeshott, M. (1991) The Voice of Poetry in the conversation of mankind, in *Rationalism in Politics and Other Essays*, Indianapolis, IN: Liberty Press, inc.

Oakeshott, M. (2001) Political education, in Fuller, T. (ed.) *The Voice of Liberal Learning*, Indianapolis, IN: Liberty Fund.

Tocqueville, A.de (2010) *Democracy in America*, Nolla, E. (ed.), Indianapolis, IN: Liberty Fund.

Spinoza, B. (1965) Tractatus Politicus, in *The Political Works*, Wernham, A.G. (ed. & trans.), Oxford: Clarendon Press.

Spinoza, B. (1985) Ethics, in *The Collected Works of Spinoza*, Curley, E. (ed. & trans.), Princeton, NJ: Princeton University Press.

Winthrop, J. (1630) *A Modell of Christian Charity*, Hanover Historical Texts Project, [Online], http://history.hanover.edu/texts/winthmod.html.

Natalie Riendeau

The Role of Legend in Oakeshott's Political Thought
The Practical and Historical Past

Introduction

'Civil association', Oakeshott writes in his *Notebooks*, is 'concerned with people whom we do not particularly like, with whom we do not agree, whom we may even despise or even hate, but with whom we must have a relationship because we live near them or have come to be concerned with them in common undertakings' (Oakeshott, 2014, p. 421). Put another way, civil association, following Oakeshott, is 'the art of living together' (Oakeshott, 2014, p. 444). But how precisely do we live together? How is solidarity amongst strangers ensured, according to Oakeshott? It is my contention that legend and the practical past have a fundamental role to play in the art of living together. This approach leads me to discuss Oakeshott's distinction between history and the practical past and to highlight a tension in Oakeshott's political thought. That is, although his model of civil association is very 'thin' when it is treated, as he treats it, entirely in terms of its postulates, at times, however, he seems to situate it in the broad context of a conception of order in which myth and legend play a vital constitutive part.

In terms of the civil association, the art of living together would appear to be the continued recognition of the authority of the rules of association as rules by civil associates (Oakeshott, 1975, p. 128). For Oakeshott, civil association is a rule-articulated association and the language of civil intercourse is a language of rules (Oakeshott, 1975, p. 124). However, this is only a partial view of Oakeshott's thought on the political and the art of living together, one that overlooks the fundamental question of identity, which is of central importance to his political thought. In this respect, Oakeshott holds that the political enterprise of legend-making, that is, of 'constructing and confirming a social identity and consciousness' is 'a perennial practical necessity' (Oakeshott, 2008, p. 194).This statement suggests that legend and myth play a foundational role in relation to a political society's identity and sense of self-consciousness. Indeed, Oakeshott declares that 'every people awakened to political self-consciousness constructs a myth, an imaginative interpretation of how this came about' (Oakeshott, 2006, p. 46). In the case of England, Oakeshott asserts that the myth of modern English politics 'began to be constructed in the seventeenth century' (Oakeshott, 2006, p. 46). Significantly, when addressing the English political legend, and with reference to Magna Carta, Oakeshott distinguishes between two different sorts of past. In this sense, he writes that 'the historical understanding of the Great Charter, like that of nearly every important event or occasion, has emerged gradually out of the quite different enterprise of assigning it a significant place in the legend of English life' (Oakeshott, 2008, p. 194). The distinction Oakeshott draws between the historical understanding of the Charter and the legend-making enterprise intimates that a different sort of past, a legendary past, is involved in legend-making and that it is indispensable for the political.

It is the character and function of this legendary past that I wish to explore in what follows. I begin by discussing Oakeshott's concept of legends of political life. I then examine the distinction Oakeshott establishes between the historical past and the practical or legendary past. I proceed to argue that the difficult emancipation of history from the authority of practice demonstrates the fundamental role played by the legendary past in relation to the political. In order to illustrate my argument that legends of political life and the practical past are indispensable to a political society, I examine the political legend of ancient Rome which, according to Oakeshott, has never been surpassed in its ability to endow a political society with an identity and sense of self-consciousness. Finally, I return briefly to the relationship between the historical and practical pasts in order to determine the political role of the legendary past. With reference to ancient Rome, I show that this relationship is complex and that in certain circumstances the assimilation of the past to the present may be necessary and serve an important political purpose. In this respect, historians such as Cicero and Livy had recourse to arguments founded in the practical past in order to defend the integrity of the Roman city. In sum, I wish to argue that the legendary past is not an illegitimate past for Oakeshott. Rather, it is a categorially different past with an important role to play in terms of ensuring the art of living together.

Legends of Political Life

As commentators have noted, despite the central role Oakeshott attributes to legend and myth, he never fully theorizes their political function (Nardin and O'Sullivan, 2006, p. 15). Whenever he introduces the concept, it is usually while discussing the modes of experience and philosophy. Briefly, following the idealist tradition, Oakeshott posits that experience is thought and as such constitutes a world of ideas (Oakeshott, 1995, p. 27). Modifications may be distinguished within experience. These are modes, and they may be thought of as the whole of experience perceived from a limited standpoint. Alternatively, Oakeshott also refers to modes of experience as arrests in experience. He contends that, at the point of the arrest, a separate world of ideas is constructed, thus constituting a mode of experience (Oakeshott, 1995, pp. 73-4). As for philosophy, it is 'experience without reservation or presupposition' (Oakeshott, 1995, p. 82). It is experience which is self-conscious, self-critical and is pursued for its own sake (Oakeshott, 1995, p. 82). Although Oakeshott asserts that the number of potential modes of experience is unlimited, he identifies four: practice (practical experience or activity including the modulation of politics), science, poetry and history. Because modes of experience are abstract, homogeneous worlds of ideas, it therefore follows for Oakeshott that each mode is 'wholly and absolutely independent of any other' (Oakeshott, 1995, p. 75). In other words, there is no direct relationship between the modes of experience, and consequently it is impossible to pass in argument from one mode of experience to another (Oakeshott, 1995, p. 76). This idea is key to understanding Oakeshott's concept of the legendary or practical past. History is modally irrelevant to practice.

Oakeshott mentions legend and myth when discussing history, poetry and philosophy in order to distinguish them from what they are not. I argue that a close study of the relationship of legends to history, poetry and philosophy reveals that Oakeshott's concept of legends of political life is composed of three constitutive elements: foundational reflection upon the political (as opposed to philosophy), the practical past (as opposed to history) and poetry. I posit that political legends are poetic constructs which tell the story of a past event, such as the foundation of Rome by Romulus, and which allow political societies to understand their political fortunes, whether actual or imaginary, in the idiom of general ideas. They do this in a manner which is not overly reflective. As to the content of legend and myth, they are prescriptive narratives in that they carry and transmit an explicit moral and message and, as such, serve as an authority for the political. In sum, legends of political life endow political societies with their identity and sense of self-consciousness, thereby ensuring solidarity amongst strangers.[1]

The Legendary Past and the Historical Past

For the purposes of the chapter, I focus on one of political legends' three constitutive elements, the legendary past. It is important to understand Oakeshott's differentiation between the historical and the legendary past. History is a mode, or a universe of discourse, which is logically different from practice. To this end, Oakeshott's concern in the essay 'Present, Future and Past' is to distinguish between the historical past and the practical past. He carries out a similar exercise in the essay 'The Activity of Being an Historian' where, in addition to the historical and the practical pasts, he also identifies the scientific and the contemplative pasts (Oakeshott, 1991). For Oakeshott, the category of the past is large and each mode of experience has a distinct past to which corresponds a distinct present. He holds that the historical past may be distinguished from the practical past in terms of 'the presents to which they are related and of the procedure in which they may be discovered or created' (Oakeshott, 1999, p. 37).

With respect to the historical past, Oakeshott argues that historical understanding is an engagement exclusively concerned with the past (Oakeshott, 1999, p. 11). Put another way, history represents an interest in the past for its own sake (Oakeshott, 1991, p. 170). It does not view the past in relation to the present (Oakeshott, 1991, p. 169). Its counterpart is a present, conceived of as a universe of discourse, which is composed of a subject exclusively concerned with past (an historian) related to objects recognized as survivals from past and which speak only of past (Oakeshott, 1999, pp. 29–31). Oakeshott emphasizes that the present in historical understanding is composed of objects which evoke past and are incapable invoking future (Oakeshott, 1999, p. 30). Put another way, these objects are recognized solely as survivals, vestiges, remains and fragments of a conserved past, and not merely to have survived (Oakeshott, 1999, p. 30). In this sense, the present in historical understanding is itself a past (Oakeshott, 1999, p. 32). Oakeshott refers to this past as a present-past and a recorded past (Oakeshott, 1999, pp. 30, 32).

---

[1] For the theorization of Oakeshott's legends of political life and an exposition of the argument that they serve as constructed foundations for the political, see Riendeau, N., *The Legendary Past: Michael Oakeshott on Imagination and Political Identity* (Exeter: Imprint Academic, 2014).

For Oakeshott, historical inquiry begins in the present-past as it is the historian's only entry into the past (Oakeshott, 1999, pp. 34-5). However, the present-past is not an historical past (Oakeshott, 1999, p. 35). What Oakeshott conceives of as an historically understood past is a past which cannot have survived as it was never a present (Oakeshott, 1999, p. 36). Thus, it cannot be found, discovered or dug up (Oakeshott, 1999, p. 36). Rather, the historically understood past is the conclusion of a critical inquiry and can only be inferred (Oakeshott, 1999, p. 36). This critical inquiry constitutes the procedure in which it may be pursued. It is an inquiry in which, following Oakeshott, 'authenticated survivals from the past are dissolved into their component features in order to be used for what they are worth as circumstantial evidence from which to infer a past which has not survived' (Oakeshott, 1999, p. 36). This inferred, or historical, past is composed of related historical events which are assembled as answers to questions formulated by an historian and it is to be 'found nowhere but in a history book' (Oakeshott, 1999, p. 36). Oakeshott asserts that everything that the evidence reveals is recognized to have its place. For this reason, nothing is excluded and nothing is considered to be 'non-contributory' (Oakeshott, 1991, p. 169). Moreover, these historical events have no message since their meanings lie in their unrepeatable conditions. That is, they cannot be detached from their circumstantial conditions without losing their meanings (Oakeshott, 1999, pp. 41-2). The meanings of historical events are neither universal nor timeless, but rather contingent and circumstantial.

The very opposite is true of events and objects that have survived from a near or distant past and which comprise legends of political life, such as the story of the foundation of Rome. In this respect, Oakeshott defines the legendary past as 'what is "read" and what may be read with advantage to ourselves in our current engagements' (Oakeshott, 1999, p. 19). That is, the purpose of the practical past is to be of worth to the current practical engagements of the practical present. Thus, objects and events which are valued for their usefulness in current practical engagements are divorced from their circumstantial conditions (Oakeshott, 1999, p. 42). From authentic and circumstantial historical meanings, survivals are transformed into emblematic characters and episodes, symbolic and stereotypic *personae*, actions, exploits and situations (Oakeshott, 1999, p. 42).

Oakeshott posits that the past is assimilated to the present in a procedure of recollection. By this he means that objects or events of worth which have survived from the past become available to agents in a procedure of recall (Oakeshott, 1999, p. 18). The procedure of recollection, as it is understood by Oakeshott, involves 'joining a puzzling or intractable present with a known and unproblematic past to compose a less puzzling or more manageable present' (Oakeshott, 1999, p. 18). This is a significant assertion. Oakeshott claims that the practical past's usefulness is derived from the fact that it contributes to composing a less mystifying and unwieldy present. That is, the practical past offers stability and sense to the present-future of practical engagement. Oakeshott contends that the practical present contains an 'ever-increasing deposit' of fragments of past that have survived and which are available to be listened to and consulted (Oakeshott, 1999, p. 18). These fragments are relevant to present circumstances and, as such, may be related to current conduct (Oakeshott, 1999, p. 18). The recalled fragments consist of artefacts, recorded anecdotes and episodes of bygone human fortune used to elaborate stories of past human circumstance, exemplars of human character and images of human conduct (Oakeshott, 1999, p. 18). The virtue of the fragments lies in their familiarity and usefulness to the practical present. They are useful in that they communicate useful information or advice, and in that they may be listened to, consulted and used. In this sense, authority may be attributed to these fragments which have survived from the past (Oakeshott, 1999, pp. 18–19). It is important to note, however, that Oakeshott ultimately finds that the legendary past is not a past at all. Rather, the legendary past is part of the present-future of practical engagement in which survived objects are stored (Oakeshott, 1999, p. 41).

Oakeshott asserts that every society has an inheritance of such survived objects. Whether these are actual or imaginary is irrelevant since what is important is what they can teach a society and tell its members about themselves (Oakeshott, 1999, p. 19). Part of the living past is an actual or imaginary ancestral past in which members of a society locate the society to which they belong. As regards the self-understanding of a society, Oakeshott argues that when considerable passages of the practical past are assembled by putting together fragmented survivals they 'yield important conclusions about ourselves and our current circumstances' (Oakeshott, 1999, p. 21). In this sense, the constructed living past recalled by the political may take the form of a legend or saga, a kind of past which Oakeshott qualifies as poetic and defines as a 'drama from which all that is casual, secondary and unresolved has been excluded: it has a clear outline, a unity of feeling and in it everything is exact except place and time' (Oakeshott, 1991, p. 182). Oakeshott's point is that humans, because of their primordial, practical attitude, assimilate the past to the present in order to build a world of sense for themselves and for generations to come. Therefore, the identity of a society and the knowledge its members have of it are directly related to the practical past. The legendary past, through the process of recollection to mind, endows political societies with 'unequivocal lineage and character' (Oakeshott, 1991, p. 182). In sum, the legendary past's virtue is to make persons and association of persons 'at home in an otherwise mysterious and menacing universe' (Oakeshott, 1991, p. 182).

So far as the knowledge members have of their society and its political tradition is concerned—a 'tricky thing to get to know', as he puts it—Oakeshott argues that every society has recourse to legends as a means of political education (Oakeshott, 1991, p. 61). He asserts that a society 'by the underlinings it makes in the book of its history, constructs a legend of its own fortunes which it keeps up to date and in which is hidden its own understanding of its politics' (Oakeshott, 1991, p. 63). Legends, as Oakeshott understands them, are essentially representations of the manner of a society's political thinking (Oakeshott, 1991, p. 63). Rather than abridging a political tradition and translating it into a system of foundational abstract principles, a legend represents the tradition and reflects it back to society. By familiarizing oneself with a society's political legend it is possible to acquire the requisite political knowledge. Legends thus constitute stabilizing constructs for society and the political. They ensure a society's self-knowledge and self-understanding.

The Difficult Emancipation of History from the Authority of Practice

Thus, the assimilation of the past to the present by recalling the past for use in the present constitutes a different sort of past, *viz.* the practical past. In the practical past, history is subordinated to practice. The practical manner of understanding the past is 'as old as the human race', Oakeshott argues (Oakeshott, 1991, p. 165). For this reason, a categorially distinct historical past only emerged hesitatingly (Oakeshott, 1999, p. 127). However, such a past was eventually achieved in a process of emancipation from 'the primordial and once almost exclusive practical attitude of mankind' (Oakeshott, 1991, p. 171). Put another way, historical inquiry emerged in a redirection of practical activity (Oakeshott, 1999, p. 127). Oakeshott emphasizes that the emancipation of history from the practical attitude is an immensely difficult achievement given that the past is 'so important a component in practical activity' (Oakeshott, 1991, p. 171). History emerged gradually and progressively acquired its specific character in a process in which new techniques for the critical treatment of sources of information were developed and in which general organizing concepts were generated, criticized, experimented with and rejected or reformulated (Oakeshott, 1991, p. 167). Oakeshott asserts that the effect of these technical achievements of historiography over the last two hundred years has been to insulate the historical understanding of the past from the practical past (Oakeshott, 1991, p. 175).

In spite of these technical achievements, which have permitted the emergence of historical inquiry, Oakeshott holds that history remains a 'somewhat uncertain and confused engagement' (Oakeshott, 1999, p. 127). By this he means that the engagement to understand the past historically is prone to relapse into the practical engagement of assimilating the past to subsequent or present events. In this sense, Oakeshott writes of 'the insinuating voice of practical understanding, recalling us to a present ... of objects recognized in terms of their practical use' (Oakeshott, 1999, p. 31). The emancipation of history from the authority of practice is made all the more difficult by the fact that the past always comes to us, first, in the idiom of practice and, second, has subsequently to be translated into the idiom of history (Oakeshott, 1991, p. 176). For these reasons, Oakeshott asserts that history 'did not and could not supersede or destroy this older and more compelling practical awareness of the past' (Oakeshott, 1999, p. 127). Thus, the historical understanding of the past has not been achieved once and for all.

Thus, due to the primordial human need to make ourselves at home in the world, it has proved particularly difficult for history to emancipate itself from the authority of practice: that is, for history to emerge from myth and legend. That being said, Oakeshott does not for this reason deem the legendary past to be illegitimate. On the contrary, he states that it is an 'indispensable ingredient of an articulate civilized life' since it is this past that constructs and confirms a society's identity (Oakeshott, 1999, p. 48). Oakeshott argues the point vigorously throughout his extensive writings on the philosophy of history. In this regard, he maintains that speaking about the past in the practical idiom cannot be dismissed as merely illegitimate nor can it be forbidden as this would amount to proscribing the 'primordial activity of making ourselves at home in the world by assimilating *our* past to *our* present' (Oakeshott, 1991, p. 180). For Oakeshott, the practical past is 'not the enemy of mankind, but only the enemy of "the historian"' (Oakeshott, 1991, p. 180).

The Roman Legend of Political Life

Perhaps the best known legend of political life, and the most successful in Oakeshott's opinion, is the one created by the poets of ancient Rome which tells the story of the foundation of Rome. No other legend of political life, Oakeshott contends, has transcended the Roman legend in its ability to endow a people with an identity, a sense of self-consciousness and self-understanding (Oakeshott, 2006, pp. 176-8). The story of the foundation of Rome by Romulus is an event recalled to mind from the practical past, the story of which, constructed or created by Roman poets, endowed Roman political society with its identity and heightened sense of political self-consciousness. As the case of Rome highlights, the practical past is emblematic and not historical. Its usefulness lies in its capacity to stabilize the practical present. Romans, Oakeshott contends, astutely secured their identity by recalling the emblematic action of the foundation of Rome by Romulus (Oakeshott, 2006, pp. 43-5).

Oakeshott holds that the political experience of ancient Rome was expressed in a story which mixed fact and legend in a way in which legend was more important than fact (Oakeshott, 2006, p. 177). That is, the legendary past was more important than the historical past in order for the Romans to understand their political experience in the idiom of general ideas. As for the story, Oakeshott identifies both the Aeneas version and the Romulus version of the legend. Although his object of study is the Romulus version of the legend, which for him is the definitive representation of the foundation of the *civitas Romana* by means of a treaty (*foedus*), he nevertheless acknowledges that in Livy, as well as in legend, the idea of a community emerging from a treaty is pushed back further into the legendary past in that *Alba Longa* is said to have emerged from a 'treaty' between Trojans led by Aeneas and the 'Latin' people of the locality which created a single 'polity' (Oakeshott, 2006, p. 181). Thus, for Oakeshott, the idea that the *civitas Romana* was based upon a treaty was very ancient and is of central importance to the Roman political legend.

While Oakeshott refers to the Aeneas version of the legend, it is the story which centres on the foundation of Rome by Romulus which, according to him, is understood by the Romans as 'the most momentous "free act" in their history' (Oakeshott, 2006, p. 248). For Oakeshott, in the Roman legend this 'was, and remained, the most momentous event' of Roman history (Oakeshott, 2006, p. 181) as it represents the foundation of Roman freedom. According to the legend, Rome, the *civitas Romana*, was founded by Romulus, the son of Mars and of a vestal virgin, a niece of a king of the Latin settlement of *Alba Longa*. The act of foundation is the origin of the *populus Romanus*, the Roman people. The momentousness of the event, that is, the impact the legendary foundation had on the Roman psyche, is reflected in part in the fact that every subsequent event of Roman history was dated from the year of the foundation. Traditionally, the foundation of Rome is said to have taken place in 753 BC. The Romans called that year the year of the foundation of the *civitas Romana,* or *anno urbis constitution,* year 1 (Oakeshott, 2006, pp. 180–1, 225). Thus, every event and action in Roman history is directly tied to the act of foundation. Oakeshott stresses the importance of the original foundation, and therefore of the past, for Roman political experience and thought when he asserts that 'the Romans might, at some period in their history, look forward, but they never failed to look back with wonder and pride to the foundation of their *civitas*' (Oakeshott, 2006, p. 181). The magnitude of the importance of the story of the foundation of Rome by Romulus for Roman politics should not be underestimated.

Following Oakeshott's understanding of the practical past, I argue that the free act of foundation is best understood as a survived artefact recalled from the practical past in order to stabilize the present-future of Roman society and to found its identity. For Oakeshott, the Romans had as their mission the exploration of the intimations of the foundation in order to elaborate it (Oakeshott, 2006, pp. 248–9). It is for this reason that the Romans developed an understanding of religion conceived of as being 'bound' to the original act of foundation and a conception of authority viewed as the preservation and augmentation of the foundation (Oakeshott, 2006, pp. 214–18 and 224–9). The Roman legend, then, is the story of the foundation of Rome and of the freedom of the Roman people, the exploration of the intimations of that foundation as well as its preservation and augmentation such as it is represented by symbolic persons and events.

Oakeshott greatly admires the genius the ancient Romans showed for politics. He holds that 'it is hardly an exaggeration to say that the Romans are the only people to show a genuine genius for government and politics' (Oakeshott, 2006, p. 176). It is important to understand that, for Oakeshott, the Roman genius for politics relates specifically to a political society's sense of self-consciousness and identity. For this reason, when Oakeshott writes that 'no people of modern times has exceeded the Romans in their self-consciousness', he is in fact highlighting their most important political achievement (Oakeshott, 2006, p. 178). In this sense, the Romans, Oakeshott posits, identified human genius with man's 'procreative spirit' as well as with the 'human ability to act' (Oakeshott, 2006, p. 248). Consequently, when referring to the Roman genius for politics, Oakeshott means the Roman people's ability to act and create politically. They acted and created politically by means of an 'imaginative construction', a legend of Roman politics which 'constitutes the political self-consciousness of the Romans' (Oakeshott, 2006, pp. 176 and 177). This political legend, which enabled the Roman people to understand the manner of their political thinking and thus endowed Roman political society with a heightened self-consciousness, has never been exceeded in modernity (Oakeshott, 2006, pp. 176-8). Roman historians, poets and lawyers—notably Livy, Tacitus, Polybius, Cicero and Virgil—constructed this legend in which 'the events and the fortunes of this remarkable people was endowed with a universal significance by being made to compose a work of art— a drama, or a story, whose moral was always being made explicit in events' (Oakeshott, 2006, p. 208).

No other people in European history, either before or since the Romans, Oakeshott claims, has constructed a legend of its politics which surpasses the Roman political legend in its ability to endow a political society with a sense of identity and self-consciousness and, consequently, stability. In other words, the ancient Romans, Oakeshott contends, were the first people to create a viable political legend. However, as Oakeshott acknowledges, theirs was not the first legend of political life to be constructed. The Greeks, a people undeniably awakened to political self-consciousness, also constructed a legend of their political fortunes (Oakeshott, 2006, p. 46). And while the legend they created to represent their own awareness of their politics was one of the most notable achievements of their political thought, it nevertheless did not match the Roman legend (Oakeshott, 2006, pp. 45-6). Oakeshott claims that the Greek legend of politics is 'remarkably thin and unelaborate' (Oakeshott, 2006, p. 46). This is due to the fact that the Greeks gave 'remarkably little thought to their past' and were unimpressed by precedent (Oakeshott, 2006, p. 46). Oakeshott contends that 'they rarely looked to the past for the authority for current conduct' (Oakeshott, 2006, p. 46). In other words, the principle difficulty with the Greek legend of politics is that it fails to recognize the past. Key, then, to the Roman genius for politics is the fact that the Romans recognized the function the practical past serves in stabilizing political conduct. While the Roman political experience did undergo considerable change over the course of its history, all change was bound back to the foundation of Rome and its freedom, thus lending Roman political life greater stability and continuity. In sum, the Romans grasped the importance of looking to the past as a source of authority for political conduct.

The Political Role of the Legendary Past

The legendary or practical past, then, plays a fundamental role in securing a political society's identity and sense of self-consciousness. Moreover, the assimilation of the past to the present by recalling the past for use in the present also plays an important role in stabilizing a society's political, social and economic present. For this reason, the emancipation of history from the authority of practice has been a gradual and difficult process, and it has never fully been achieved. In what follows, I wish to explore in more detail the difficult emancipation of history from practice with reference, once again, to ancient Rome. For this purpose, I will contrast Oakeshott's understanding of the relationship between the historical and practical pasts with that of Henry Tudor. Tudor was a contemporary of Oakeshott's who wrote on political myth and, like him, distinguished between myth and history. Tudor posits that myths provide 'a practical understanding' in that 'they make sense of men's present experience' (Tudor, 1972, pp. 123 and 124). History is 'an attempt to achieve a critical understanding of past events' (Tudor, 1972, p. 137). My aim is to show that Oakeshott's distinction between the historical and practical pasts does not imply that the practical past is an illegitimate past. Rather, it is merely a logically or categorially different past. It is my position that it is a past which, for Oakeshott, is indispensable for the political.

Oakeshott argues that the historical understanding of the past is not 'a gift bestowed suddenly upon the human race'; rather, it is an achievement (Oakeshott, 1991, p. 174). At what point in time Oakeshott believes an historical understanding of the past was achieved is somewhat difficult to ascertain. However, he does note that Cicero distinguished between the 'historical' past, concerned with 'truth', from the 'imagined' past, concerned with 'pleasure', thereby suggesting that the historical past, such as he understands it, had emerged in ancient Rome (Oakeshott, 1991, p. 154, note 2). Nevertheless, this does not mean that Roman historians such as Cicero and Livy only exhibit an historical attitude to the past. In this sense, Oakeshott states that 'I do not contend that an historical past is ... the only past to be found in alleged pieces of historical writing' (Oakeshott, 1999, p. 37). In this respect, while Oakeshott identifies Cicero and Livy as historians, nevertheless, he underlines that their attitude to the past was not always historical. For instance, the Roman political legend appears in the writings of Livy and Cicero (Oakeshott, 2006, p. 177). As concerns Livy more specifically, Oakeshott does denote an historical attitude to the past when he writes that he is 'cautious about the founding of Rome' (Oakeshott, 1999, p. 43, note 12). This does not prevent him, however, from qualifying 'Livy' as a 'well-known collection of *legenda*' (Oakeshott, 1999, p. 42). In this sense, Livy's *History* is 'an expression of pride in the civil and martial exploits of the *populus Romanus*' (Oakeshott, 2004, p. 352). Clearly, for him, it is one of the 'stories of past deeds and sufferings, epics of doings and happenings, which were unfolded by those who have endowed their fellows with an understanding of themselves; Herodotus and Livy ...' (Oakeshott, 2004, p. 348).

We find, then, the historical past intertwined with the practical past. Roman historians made both historical and legendary statements about the past. As Tudor observes, this raises the question of truth in regards to statements about the past. He gives as an example the statement of fact that Romulus was the son of Mars. It is either true or false, Tudor maintains (Tudor, 1972, p. 135). While he supposes that older Roman historians, such as Naevius, took this as a statement of fact, clearly Cicero and Livy, he argues, believed that the statement was false, but were 'less than candid' and 'refuse[d] to say so in plain terms' (Tudor, 1972, p. 135). As to why this may be the case, Tudor argues that Cicero and Livy held the view that ancient traditions often contain useful fictions that should be preserved (Tudor, 1972, p. 135). In other words, the legendary past is useful to the practical present. To this end, Tudor maintains that popular traditions cannot simply be dismissed as the 'follies' of the superstitious because they are not confirmed by historical research (Tudor, 1972, pp. 135–6). Rather, Tudor asserts that an account of the past which confirms the necessity of the action persons may have in mind is deemed to be a true account (Tudor, 1972, p. 137). That is, it is 'the validity of men's present purposes that validates their view of the past' (Tudor, 1972, p. 137). Put another way, popular traditions find their justification in the moral and political truths they imply (Tudor, 1972, p. 136). To illustrate his point, Tudor refers to the speech Cicero made to the Senate when the Roman republic's existence was threatened by Cataline's bid for power. In his speech, Cicero recalled that Romulus, in the context of battle with the Sabines, had vowed a temple to Jupiter if he would stay the flight of the army. Jupiter intervened and a temple to Jupiter the Stayer was built (Tudor, 1972, p. 136). Cicero, addressing the Senate in the temple of Jupiter at a time of crisis, appealed to Jupiter and called upon the god to save the city as he had saved it before (Tudor, 1972, p. 136). Therefore, although historically false, Cicero nevertheless invoked the episode in his defence of Rome's mixed constitution. Following Tudor, his political purpose validated his view of the past. Tudor notes that Cicero also defended Rome's constitution by recalling that it was originally established by the founder-heroes of the republic and that the Roman people, to maintain their position, had to remain faithful to the principles that had inspired the foundation (Tudor, 1972, p. 126).

Oakeshott's position with respect to truth and the invocation of the legendary past in the context of particular political circumstances is perhaps more straightforward than Tudor's. As regards the question of truth, Oakeshott holds that statements in the practical idiom about the past must be recognized, not as 'untrue', but as 'non-historical' statements about the past (Oakeshott, 1991, p. 170). He maintains that there is nothing that excludes practical statements about the past from being true in their own universe of discourse (Oakeshott, 1991, p. 170). Oakeshott never goes so far as to state that a legendary statement about the past implies a moral or political truth and, although he argues that past events are recalled for political ends, this does not necessarily mean that he believes that present political purposes validate views of the past. For Oakeshott, legendary statements about the past are true in and of themselves in their universe of discourse. His point is simply that events may be recalled from the practical past in order to stabilize the practical present. In this sense, following Oakeshott, Cicero's purpose in defending Rome's established constitution does not necessarily validate his view of the past. Rather, he recalled the legend of Jupiter the Stayer simply because to do so in a political crisis might bring political and social stability. Moreover, there is nothing that excludes the legend from being true in the practical universe of discourse. Thus, legendary statements play a fundamental political role in and of themselves by assimilating the past to the present.

In sum, although Cicero and Livy, as historians, distinguished between the historical past and practical past, this did not prevent them from assimilating the past to the present or from invoking the legendary past for political purposes. The Roman experience illustrates not only that history emerges with difficulty from the authority of practice, but that this is so because the practical past and political legend play a vital role in that they allow a political society to understand itself and to act politically in a manner that is coherent with its identity and self-consciousness.

Conclusion

I conclude with another quote from the *Notebooks*: 'The past is the past only for history; elsewhere it is present. The event has gone; but it lives on in fable, in gesture, in turns of speech, in habit, and above all in myth' (Oakeshott, 2014, p. 422). By stating that the past is past only for history, Oakeshott establishes a sharp distinction between history and the legendary past. However, it is important to emphasize that this distinction is philosophical and has no hierarchical implications. That is, the legendary past is not an inferior or illegitimate type of past. Only, in so far as it assimilates the past to the present in a procedure of recollection, it has a political function. The legendary past plays an essential political role in that it endows a political society with its identity and sense of self-consciousness, thereby ensuring solidarity amongst strangers. Moreover, the difficult emancipation of history from the authority of practice makes plain the indispensable nature of the legendary past for stabilizing politics and the practical present.

Thus, with respect to the civil association and the art of living together, although Oakeshott's model is very 'thin' when it is treated entirely in terms of its postulates, his writings on identity suggest that he wishes to situate it in a broader conception of order in which myth and legend plays a vital constitutive part. In this respect, the continued recognition of the authority of rules as rules does bind the associates of civil association to one another. However, this is only one part of his thought on the art of living together. For Oakeshott, as the example of ancient Rome shows, fundamental to human living-together is a political society's identity and self-consciousness, which are intimately linked to, and ultimately ensured by, political legends and the legendary past.

References

Nardin, T. & O'Sullivan, L. (2006) Introduction, in Oakeshott, M., *Lectures in the History of Political Thought*, Exeter: Imprint Academic.

Oakeshott, M. (1975) *On Human Conduct*, Oxford: Oxford University Press.

Oakeshott, M. (1991) *Rationalism in Politics and Other Essays: New and Expanded Edition*, Indianapolis, IN: Liberty Fund.

Oakeshott, M. (1995) *Experience and Its Modes*, Cambridge: Cambridge University Press.

Oakeshott, M. (1999) *On History and Other Essays*, Indianapolis, IN: Liberty Fund.

Oakeshott, M. (2004) *What is History? And Other Essays*, O'Sullivan, L. (ed.), Exeter: Imprint Academic.

Oakeshott, M. (2006) *Lectures in the History of Political Thought*, Nardin, T. & O'Sullivan, L. (eds.), Exeter: Imprint Academic.

Oakeshott, M. (2008) *The Vocabulary of a Modern European State: Essays and Reviews 1952-88*, O'Sullivan, L. (ed.), Exeter: Imprint Academic.

Oakeshott, M. (2014) *Notebooks, 1922-86*, O'Sullivan, L. (ed.), Exeter: Imprint Academic.

Tudor, H. (1972) *Political Myth*, New York: Praeger Publishers, Inc.

Terry Nardin[1]

Oakeshott as a Moralist

To interpret Oakeshott as a moralist might seem strange for someone who has long argued that he should be read not as a conservative thinker or a liberal one but as a philosopher. Oakeshott distinguished theorizing from practical engagement and was careful to observe that distinction even when he seems to flout it. When commentators criticize his moral or political views it is sometimes to expose what they see as prejudice or hypocrisy. As someone interested in his contribution to philosophy, I've paid more attention to his arguments than to their political implications. I've not used the tools of critical theory or Cambridge School historicism to uncover political intentions or ideological biases in his writings. The effect of reading a thinker in that way is often to foreground the ordinary or conventional in his thought, which undercuts an important reason for studying him. But even if we avoid doing that, the question is how much we learn by treating Oakeshott as a practical moralist rather than as a theorist of morality.

Oakeshott did not think that that it was the philosopher's business to make moral judgements, and the judgements he does make are not especially astute. They are, I think, consistent with the broad outlines of his Christian moral heritage and with an understanding of morality and its relationship to law that he found in Hobbes, Kant, Hegel and other theorists of the modern state. To read Oakeshott as a theorist of morality is not to deny that he sometimes judges people or policies, trading the role of a spectator for that of an actor. Nor is it to ignore the interplay between these different roles. As he once observed, 'what one needs to explain in trying to understand a writer is the *tensions* in his thought' (Oakeshott, 2014, p. 539). We should, then, consider his judgements in relation to his efforts to understand the distinctive character of moral judgement. By doing that, we can focus on what is most interesting in his contribution to understanding morality and moral conduct.

---

[1] This paper was presented as the Inaugural Michael Oakeshott Lecture at the University of Hull on 17 September 2015, in connection with the 2015 conference of the Michael Oakeshott Association.

What is a Moralist?

If we start not with Oakeshott but with the English language, we cannot treat moralizing and theorizing as entirely distinct. A 'moralist', as the word is often used, is one who offers moral insight and guidance — a Confucius or Michel de Montaigne — but can also be one who systematizes a body of moral ideas. To say that someone is a teacher or a student of morals leaves open the question of what is taught or studied under that label and in what manner. If you ask moral philosophers what their business is, most will tell you that it is not only to look at moral ideas from the outside (they might even deny that such objectivity is possible) but also to reach conclusions about what is and is not morally justified. That response already acknowledges a distinction between moralizing and theorizing. Theoretical reflection might begin with moral precepts but soon moves beyond them, problematizing rather than making moral judgements. The moralist takes a further step towards theorizing when he articulates the principle on which a judgement rests. And the moralist who begins to examine such principles is well on the road to being a theorist of morality: an historian of moral beliefs or a philosopher concerned with the structure and foundations of a moral system. The would-be theorist must break free from his activity as a performer in a moral practice whose morals are on display in his performance.

In many contexts the words 'moralist', 'moralize' and 'moralism' are pejorative, and it is worth considering why. One reason may be that we suspect the moralist of misrepresentation. The verb 'to moralize' can be transitive: it is to assign a moral quality *to* something as well as to engage *in* moral activity. 'Why do we always attempt to make our passions appear other than they are?', Oakeshott rhetorically asks in an early notebook entry. 'Why do we attempt to moralise them and to make them consistent?' (Oakeshott, 2014, p. 229). The implication is that to moralize is to rationalize and therefore to distort.

Another reason these words have negative connotations is that, where people disagree, they dislike being told not only that they are mistaken but also that they are *bad*. Or maybe it's that they think the moralist is making an unwarranted claim to authority. To moralize is to teach and sometimes to preach. When we say 'teach' the judgement is neutral unless the context suggests otherwise. A moral teacher is someone who expounds a moral doctrine or whose conduct illustrates a way of life — a sage. But to say 'preach' is often to imply disapproval; it is to pontificate. 'The good man', Oakeshott wrote in a 1944 notebook entry, does not regard himself as 'called upon to tell others what they should do' (Oakeshott, 2014, p. 326). And commenting on the word 'moralist' in 1931, he wrote:

> misleading; the abstract meaning attached to it—the preacher and evangelist. Get away from this; something less noisy than a gospel, something more complete than a creed. Not aiming to convince and persuade, but to see clearly and to speak unambiguously. (Oakeshott, 2014, p. 241)

What is objectionable is imposing one's views on those who ought to be free to make up their own minds. 'Moralism', for those who disapprove of it, means meddling in other people's business and doing so on the basis of questionable assumptions. The moralist might even be accused of improperly failing to resist an impulse. The *OED* captures this negative subtext when it defines moralizing as 'indulging' in moral reflection or talk, and a moralizer as one who indulges in moralizing. Moralizing itself, then, can be immoral.

Whether the context is religious or not, the moralist claims authority. This authority might be bolstered by his occupying a position that requires appointment or ordination, or because others recognize him as someone learned in a moral tradition. In either case, the moralist is a person who thinks he should be listened to. If his claim is that he possesses knowledge, the implication is that there is an independent standpoint from which moral beliefs can be judged and that this standpoint can be identified. This is how moralists in the past often saw the matter. 'Morality' for them was not merely a system of beliefs or practices. It was a standard for judging such systems and one by which everyone should aspire to live, even in the face of censure or oppression. A moralist, on this view, is someone who thinks that moral principles are universal and that moral considerations trump other considerations in judging conduct. But there are moralists who don't believe this. Moral cynics like Marx or Nietzsche think that moralities express not truths but desires. Those we call 'social critics' admonish a community by drawing on its shared traditions and values.

What kind of moralist was Oakeshott? This is not an easy question to answer. He went though phases—on the evidence of his notebooks, for example, he was obsessed with death in his early years but resigned later on to enduring 'the rot of time'. His postwar worries about the political condition of Britain appear to have given way to a darker brooding about Europe's moral trajectory. Mostly, however, he saw himself as a theorist of morality, not a practical moralist, and though he did not object to moralizing he did disparage the kind of moralizing that comes from applying abstract rules or ideals to practical life and even more to governing, and above all to passing this kind of thing off as philosophy. He claimed that he was not especially interested in current affairs and challenged the claim that politics is more important than other aspects of life. His self-conception as a theorist of politics required distance from everyday politics, and what applies to politics applies also to morality. He thought that the philosopher, *qua* philosopher, cannot be a practical moralist; he cannot use and question a principle at the same time. He says:

> The philosopher's attitude to 'practice' is, really, ironical — his 'practical' attitude. He can recognise the moral world only with a kind of irony. (Oakeshott, 2014, p. 477)

This remark (from a notebook dated 1964) echoes words Oakeshott wrote forty years before: 'Moral philosophy is not morality and can never make us moral: our knowledge about a thing in no way renders more probable our spiritual possession of it' (Oakeshott, 2004, p. 103). We need not take these remarks at face value, but neither can they be dismissed. I'd like, then, to examine Oakeshott's arguments about the character of moral conduct before considering his performance as a moral practitioner.

Oakeshott as a Theorist of Morality

Oakeshott made theorizing moral conduct and its relationship to other aspects of life — religion, law and government in particular — a project. Although his discussion of the 'forms of moral life' in his 1948 essay 'The Tower of Babel' is the first place one might think to look for a theory of morals, I'd like to begin when the project had matured: the discussion of morality and moral conduct in *On Human Conduct* (1975) and the essay 'The Rule of Law' which, though published only in 1983, was probably written in the early 1970s. Moralities, here, are practices, each an historical product of past changes and subject to continuing change. A moral practice is distinguished from other practices in being concerned with the intrinsic qualities of acts, not their consequences. A practice is moral in relation to the considerations it prescribes, not the purposes it may serve to promote: 'it is concerned', he says,' with good and bad conduct, and not with performances in respect of their outcomes' (Oakeshott, 1975, p. 62). These outcome-independent conditions to be considered in pursuing any desired outcome Oakeshott calls 'moral' conditions. This is not a statement about how the word 'moral' is used (though it is often used in that way); it is the product of his effort to clarify that usage by distinguishing moral from prudential considerations and moral relationships from relationships based on interests.

This view of the distinctive character of moral conduct rests on three assumptions. First, it assumes agents seeking desired outcomes in their transactions with one another or in enterprises to promote a common purpose. Second, it assumes practices that agents see as expedient for achieving these outcomes: prudential practices, or, as we might say, skills or techniques. But, third, it also assumes agents participating in practices that are not prudential: moral practices. The usages or rules of a moral practice are not 'devices for procuring satisfactions'. They are, Oakeshott says, 'considerations specifying conditions to be subscribed to in choosing performances, indifferent to the wished-for outcome of any performance' (Oakeshott, 1975, p. 182). A moral practice 'is not a prudential art' and, though it may be advantageous to observe its strictures, it 'does not stand condemned if no such advantages were to accrue' (Oakeshott, 1975, p. 60). Oakeshott is here distinguishing different views of how human beings can be related to one another, and his suggestion that their relationships can be either prudential or moral is intended to capture these views. In making it, he is not asserting the superior value of the moral; he is identifying an aspect of agency itself in a world in which there is more than one agent.

If this is Oakeshott's mature view of morality, let us consider how he arrived at it. 'The Voice of Poetry in the Conversation of Mankind', an essay first published in 1959, provides evidence of its Hegelian origins. All practices presuppose agency on the part of their performers; those we call 'moral' also presuppose recognition of agency in others. Prudential practices are instrumental: the skills they teach are devices for producing desired results. They are the skills required to gain pleasure and avoid pain (Oakeshott, 1991, p. 499), to satisfy wants and avoid deprivations (Oakeshott, 1975, p. 60), and may involve using other people as resources in pursuing those ends. A moral practice, in contrast, is one that emerges when human beings recognize one another as agents and, importantly, as entitled to have their agency respected. A moral practice is in this sense non-instrumental, though it may permit agents to use each other appropriately and provide ideas, such as 'consent', for judging what is appropriate. But so tight for Oakeshott is the link between the moral and the non-instrumental that he often treats the words as synonyms.

Tracing the emergence of moral understanding, Oakeshott suggests that the idea of morality appears when agents go beyond acknowledging the mere fact that other agents exist to recognizing that those agents are, like themselves, entitled to choose ends of their own: they have rights. This recognition presupposes a standard according to which rights and their correlative duties are determined. Such a standard enables agents to judge their own conduct and the conduct of others. It implies criteria for approval and disapproval as distinct from desire and aversion. An action can 'be wrong' when it is judged by such criteria as well as 'go wrong' when it fails to get a desired result. A morality, in these terms, is a practice composed of considerations that pertain to the manner in which an act is performed, not to the interests its performance serves (Oakeshott, 2004, pp. 424–5). There is a distinction between moral considerations, which are based on such criteria ('principles'), and considerations of prudence, which are based on achieving desired satisfactions and therefore on outcomes or consequences.

Because they emerge from shared practices, moral standards are communal. 'Selves in moral activity are equal members of a community of selves: and approval and disapproval are activities which belong to them as members of this community' (Oakeshott, 1991, p. 502). This does not mean that moral agents must respond only to the claims of other agents, but the claim to be a self presupposes an identity shaped by communal practices and therefore by the roles or personas they enable. Oakeshott's notebooks contain many entries that sound this theme:

> Who is to be satisfied in moral conduct? ... 'the self.' This is what Kant was saying as much as Hobbes. It is the morality of 'honour' ... One's own good opinion of oneself. Self-respect. (Oakeshott, 2014, p. 467)

> To be 'immoral' is, in the first place, to commit offences against our own affections, our own identity. (Oakeshott, 2014, p. 479)

> The old-fashioned reproof to children: 'You forget yourself'. A relic of the morality of honour: a utilitarian could never forget (or remember) himself. (Oakeshott, 2014, p. 497)

These remarks anticipate the discussion of motives in *On Human Conduct*. When we act in ways that depend on the responses of others we are hostages to contingency. But 'where the consideration in doing is not what is intended to be achieved but the sentiment in which it is done' (Oakeshott, 1975, p. 73), our conduct is freed from the compromises needed in dealing with others. Agents in respect to the sentiments in which they act—their motives—are bound only by the integrity of their characters. To be virtuous is to cultivate sentiments that are appropriate to one's character. But though the choice is self-regarding, it is not subjective. Choosing a motive is no more subjective than choosing an action; both choices are performances in a moral practice and are affected by considerations of conduct (doing the right thing) or virtue (doing it for the right reason), accordingly.

The moral element in this concern with persons, whether in one's treatment of others or in honouring one's own character, lies in the idea of limit. This is a recurrent theme in the notebooks:

> The supreme word, 'No'; the essence of morality. (Oakeshott, 2014, p. 467)

> The implication of 'consideration for others' — avoidance of interference with others or using them for our own ends. (Oakeshott, 2014, p. 326)

> The daemon of Socrates, according to the *Apology*, would sometimes hold him back, but it never urged him forward. (Oakeshott, 2014, p. 448)

And on the Socratic argument that it is better to suffer injustice than to perpetrate it: 'This is the heart of a morality' (Oakeshott, 2014, p. 534). To say that a morality is 'a practice without any extrinsic purpose', that it is 'concerned with good and bad conduct and not with performances in respect of their outcomes' (Oakeshott, 1975, p. 62), is to say that moral principles are not standards of good and bad in the sense of helping or harming the satisfaction of wants, needs or desires. Moral conduct is not in itself a good but a limit on the pursuit of goods.

Morality is plural because there are different moral communities. There are different 'languages' of moral conduct, each with a distinctive character that has been shaped by the history of its use and changes as it is used. These languages give speakers their identities as moral agents. What we ought to do depends on who we are and who we are depends on the communities to which we belong, though we should bear in mind that belonging can be qualified and can even involve rejecting a community or being rejected by it, as in Spinoza's relationship to the Jewish community in Amsterdam. Our identities depend on beliefs and values embedded in the practices of our communities. And like other languages, moral languages are learned in being used and can be used skilfully or not. Knowing how to behave morally is a kind of literacy (Oakeshott, 1975, p. 133), an ability to judge moral propriety. One could say that Oakeshott is moralizing as well as theorizing when he writes that, in a moral language, expressions

> harden into clichés and are released again; the ill-educated speak it vulgarly, the purists inflexibly ... The conduct of some is no better than an adventure in verbiage; clutching at imperfectly recollected and vaguely understood expressions, their conversation is thick with pretension and littered with moral malapropisms. They are aware only of the fashionable indignations. (Oakeshott, 1975, p. 65)

Oakeshott's moralizing here, if that is what it is, is deployed to make a theoretical point and does not corrupt it.

A moral practice can be codified in a body of rules but rules are abstractions — truncated expressions of the practices from which they are abstracted. Rules are 'abridgments', moral ideas 'metaphors'. Commenting on Confucius, Oakeshott writes:

> Out of a vast variety of customs and behaviour he chose a few; out of concrete morality he made one abstract, universal morality ... For example, *jen*, consideration for others, is a universal abstraction from filial piety and respect for elders: these were the primitive virtues of the Chinese, the roots of their moral conduct. What Confucius did was to universalise them ... But in doing so, much was lost. (Oakeshott, 2014, pp. 419-20)

And he adds: 'But neither can we forget all rules or precepts. "To make up one's life as one goes along." This requires not a *less* firm hold upon principle than a life lived according to rule, but a *more* firm hold' (Oakeshott, 2014, p. 282). '*Fay ce que vouldras*. This, in Rabelais, was a maxim, not an axiom ... A plea for a little more play between the working part of a society, not a gospel of anarchy' (Oakeshott, 2014, p. 447).

We approach here the view of morality one finds in Oakeshott's criticism of 'Rationalism', a view that reduces moral understanding to abstractions. In practical affairs people do not usually begin with a rule which they then apply or an ideal which they then try to achieve. Rather, they act in a certain manner, engage in an activity, and in due course may come to formulate rules or ideals to clarify and codify what they have been doing. These are shorthand for the practices they represent but it is a mistake to think that they refer to objects. The idea of tolerance, for example,

> emerged from a disposition to put up with other people and to think it right to do so; but there is no such 'thing' as 'toleration'. And if we are disposed to put up with other people we never imagine that we ought to put up with *everything* they do: that's the sort of thing we begin to imagine when we begin to speak of 'toleration'. (Oakeshott, 2004, p. 251)

Nor can a moral practice be reduced to a logically tight system: 'The only moral life we have ever known, if we would only admit it, is one in which "principles" are continuously bouncing off one another' (Oakeshott, 2014, p. 476). In the end, no amount of juggling principles can substitute for judgement. This is the meaning of the saying 'casuistry is the grave of moral judgement' (Oaleshott, 2001, p. 52).

Oakeshott's view of the non-prudential character of morality carries over into his understanding of law. To have an instrumental relationship with the world around us is to view its resources as things to be used, on which we can impose our purposes. But, says Oakeshott, 'what we call "morality" is, in part, a refusal to take this attitude to other human beings, a refusal to regard them ... simply as materials to be merely used' (Oakeshott, 2004, p. 304). His theory of civil association rests upon this understanding of morality. To be a person is to be an individual, and this, morally speaking, means that one has a right to set one's own goals. A system of public law is necessary to define those rights. So non-instrumentality goes to the heart not only of morality but also of the rule of law. Like Kant in *The Doctrine of Right*, Oakeshott in *On Human Conduct* is concerned with the question of how being governed by laws in a non-voluntary association, a state, can be made compatible with individual freedom. Like Kant, Oakeshott understands that people can use one another if there is consent and can impose their choices on one another if the imposition does not constitute arbitrary interference. Like Kant, he is concerned with 'the *jus* of *lex*' — the 'rightness' of law (Oakeshott, 1983, pp. 140–4) — by which he means the obligations that positive law can prescribe without encroaching on individuality. And like Kant he thinks this raises questions about the proper ground, use and limits of coercion. A theory of 'rightness' is a theory of justifiable coercion, and one of its conclusions is that right or justice requires a system of authoritative laws. A just state is one whose laws enable those governed to pursue ends of their own choosing by protecting them against arbitrary coercive interference. For a state to govern otherwise is to violate their rightful independence and therefore to dominate or tyrannize them.

Oakeshott as a Practical Moralist

In Oakeshott's writings we find a theory of morality as a mode of human conduct. But we do not find a body of precepts or rules. We learn what a moral rule is — that it is an abstraction, that it is a standard of propriety rather than utility, and that its relationship to other rules is discursive rather than demonstrative. And we get a sense of the principles that underlie conventionally recognized rules: that in pursuing our ends we should exercise restraint in imposing them on others and that such restraint is especially important in governing because the state is a non-voluntary association. We might identify these as principles of 'respect' or 'non-domination', though Oakeshott does not often use these words. But there is no moral system, no universal moral grammar uniting the diversity of moral languages. Oakeshott dismissed normative ethics in his first book, *Experience and Its Modes* (1933), and afterwards seldom wavered. 'To avoid ambiguity and inconsequence', he wrote then, ethics must put aside 'this attempt to organise, integrate and complete our world of values and to apply its conclusions to our conduct of life'. If ethics pursues this end it must abandon 'what is strong and disciplined in the ethical tradition for what is merely popular and pedantic' (Oakeshott, 1933, p. 340), and this, he later explains, would mean foregoing philosophy as the activity of examining presuppositions (Oakeshott, 1975, pp. 1–27). Ethics can be practical and prescriptive, or it can be conceptual and philosophical, and Oakeshott is clear about which path he has chosen even if he occasionally wanders from it.

This is not, let me emphasize, a rejection of moralizing. Practical moralizing is often 'disfigured by pedantry and … vitiated by lack of practical knowledge' (Oakeshott, 1933, p. 340), but it can avoid these defects. The moralist must be skilled in a moral practice and, if inclined to reflect on that practice, aware that in judging he draws on the resources of a tradition that can be interpreted in different ways and that moral discourse is a matter of persuasion rather than proof. The competent moralist is not a systematic theorist but a sage: a maker of judgements, not guidebooks, a 'connected critic' (to borrow an expression from Michael Walzer) who holds the members of a community to the sometimes inconsistent principles they share. Is Oakeshott a practical moralist in the style of Confucius or Montaigne? Not really—that's not his genre, even in the notebooks, where his remarks are in any case more miscellaneous and less polished than those of the *Analects* or the *Essais* and were not intended for anyone's use but his own. The notebooks are, however, a good place to look for unguarded judgements, like this gloves-off entry:

> Karl Marx is a remarkable writer. No other can turn possible truths into superstitions so rapidly and so conclusively. Every truth that came to him he turned into a falsehood. He is, possibly, the most *corrupt* writer who ever lived. (Oakeshott, 2014, p. 510)

Such pronouncements are rare in his published writings. We do find aphorisms and also fables, most notably in the second (1983) 'Tower of Babel' essay, along with essays and reviews that veer towards the engaged. But on the whole Oakeshott succeeds in keeping his distance, 'objectifying' his judgements by taking an observer's perspective and reporting on beliefs instead of asserting them. His judgements are sometimes practical in the sense that they are judgements of conduct, but it is not clear how far they are practical in aiming to alter it.

It is interesting that Oakeshott uses strongly emotive words in discussing the vocation of the theorist. Should the theorist, he writes, 'confuse … theorising formal conduct with knowing how to subscribe to a moral practice' he would 'commit the enormity of deserting his own character as a theorist' for that of a moral tutor (Oakeshott, 1975, p. 26). This has led some readers of *On Human Conduct* to accuse him of committing an enormity of his own by claiming theoretical purity for the idea of civil association while covertly advocating it as a political programme. But Oakeshott need not be read as engaging in advocacy when he asserts, for example, that 'no European alive to his [moral] inheritance ... has ever found it possible to deny the superior desirability of civil association without a profound feeling of guilt' (Oakeshott, 1975, p. 321). This might imply a 'preference', as if it mattered what a theorist's preferences were, but what it mainly does is call attention to a contradiction between the enterprise state and individual liberty that leads those who defend such a state to qualify their defence in ways that suggest discomfort with their own position. Oakeshott's assertion is not a policy prescription or even a piece of moral judgement or advocacy. It is a statement about the implications of a moral tradition.

Driving much of the criticism that Oakeshott has attracted over the years is disapproval of his much misunderstood 'conservatism' and disbelief that his stance of philosophical disengagement is either possible or sincere. This has contributed not only to the indignation with which his writings have sometimes been greeted but also to his marginal status in Anglo-American political and legal philosophy. Since the question of whether Oakeshott's thought is or is not conservative has been exhaustively discussed, there is little to be gained by treating it here. Nor is there much point in discussing reactions to his moral ideas that combine anger with incomprehension.

More recent criticism, often coming from those who understand Oakeshott well and who share many of his views, has focused less on his politics than on what the critics identify as more fundamental difficulties in his thought. These include his inclination towards conceptual compartmentalization — in particular, putting theory and practice into separate boxes — and, related to this, a formalism that manifests itself in an unwarranted rejection of useful theories or concerns. Such objections get expressed in various ways: as criticism of his romanticism, his aestheticism, his hostility to work and career, his view of the university years as an 'interval' between the rigours of school and work, and his focus in politics on justice at the expense of order. Some of these complaints might be characterized as moralizing and the outlook that underlies them as realist or pragmatic. Romanticism and aestheticism are judged unrealistic and impractical, as is hostility to the so-called 'real' world of work, effort, career and service. His vision of the university as a place for intellectual discovery rather than vocational training seems quaint. But the criticism that is most clearly 'realist' (as that expression is now used by political theorists) is that Oakeshott's political thought is all philosophy and no politics because he ignores the conditions for political order, including the kind of order whose principles he theorizes and also values.

There are, I think, several things wrong with these objections and, underlying them, the suggestion that Oakeshott is unacceptably detached from the business of life and, by implication, fundamentally lacking in seriousness. I do not identify particular sources for these objections, which are recurrent, simply to keep the focus on Oakeshott and to avoid polemics. But they capture judgements one can find in the secondary literature and that might occur to anyone encountering arguments that Oakeshott often provocatively asserts in opposition to what seem to him to be the prevailing views.

First, the objections amount to a charge, if not of quite of frivolity, at least of an ivory-tower purism that makes Oakeshott's thought less interesting than it might otherwise be. But would his thoughts on, say, education have been more interesting if he had not defended liberal education against vocationalism? He did not say that the university experience must be limited to that of enjoying an interval between school and work. He thought a liberal education could be transformative because the relative freedom from doing other people's bidding that it provides allows the young to discover interests and abilities that shape their characters as individuals, and that the experience was in danger of vanishing before the onslaught of instrumental visions of the university. As the critics rightly observe, Oakeshott never dealt with the problem of scale in higher education: only a tiny proportion of people went to university in the era that defined his experience of undergraduate life. Mass post-secondary education must provide vocational or professional training but even so probably a larger number and proportion of students are liberally educated today than in the early twentieth century.

Second, the objections reassert conventional beliefs and attitudes that as a philosopher Oakeshott was led to question. Why would one wish a philosopher to embrace the sovereignty of practical experience, and in particular of instrumentalism? His explication of the non-instrumental character of morality and his use of it to illuminate the idea of the rule of law are signature contributions. One can disagree with his arguments, but this more general impulse to reject what makes him important as a thinker in favour of an incoherent eclecticism is depressing. Should Mill have been less utilitarian and Kant less deontological? Should Socrates have embraced sophism and Hobbes scholasticism? We enjoy Boswell's anecdote in which Samuel Johnson refutes Berkeley's philosophical idealism by striking his foot against a stone, but the gesture is of course no refutation. In his version of the cave allegory, Oakeshott challenges the naïve assumption that philosophical conclusions should conform to appearances (Oakeshott, 1975, pp. 27–31). There is no point in being a philosopher, a critic of received beliefs and their presuppositions, if the criterion of truth is conformity with those beliefs. Hobbes and Nietzsche are interesting because they resisted the pull of the ordinary, Locke and Rawls boring because they did not. Oakeshott is worth reading for the passion, flair and cogency with which he challenges our unreflective pragmatism.

Third, the objections confuse things that are better kept separate. It's a mistake, for example, to equate formalism and aestheticism. To distinguish between form and substance and to appreciate the purpose and importance of forms — of procedures, habits, rituals — is not necessarily to be an aesthete. This charge of aestheticism reminds one of the realist canard that the principled moralist values his own integrity more than other people's well-being. It is an accusation of narcissism. Aestheticism — which, as a term of reproach, as in 'Bloomsbury aestheticism', means valuing beauty excessively or substituting artistic values for moral ones — suggests frivolity, irresponsibility, a lamentable lack of seriousness. This has no more purchase against Oakeshott than it does against, say, Virginia and Leonard Woolf or John Maynard Keynes. Running through the condemnations of Oakeshott's formalism is an implied deprecation of conceptual distinctions and an unreflective pragmatism.

Linked to this charge of aestheticism is the suggestion that Oakeshott's attitude towards life was 'romantic' in important ways. The romantic and the aesthetic are not the same, however. Romanticism can be many things and in sorting these out one might keep in mind its origins in the romance as a medieval literary genre, an imaginative narrative of chivalric adventure or legendary heroism, and its later identification with any kind of extraordinary, sentimental or idealized love, including love for adventure. There is little doubt that Oakeshott had a romantic streak of this kind:

> In the flush of youth I believed in socialism, because I thought it would be thrilling. I did not hate injustice, I merely wanted to escape from an existence without a purpose. Now I believe in love — and for the same reason. (Oakeshott, 2014, p. 158)

It is harder to find traces of the kind of romanticism we find in that late eighteenth- and early nineteenth-century movement in the arts in which passion and the picturesque replaced classical ideals of proportion and balance. For if Oakeshott valued romantic individuality, he also valued order and form. The charge of aestheticism embraces the contradictory ideas of 'romanticism' and 'formalism', leaving us to wonder which is supposed to bother us more. It also distracts us from noticing that Oakeshott rather cleverly brings the two together in the idea of civil association as a form that enables individuality, including that of the adventurer, Bohemian or saint.

The idea of romantic love is well captured by Oakeshott himself when he writes: 'To enjoy and to glory in the conflicts, the fire, the passions of love for their own sake. To be in love with love' (Oakeshott, 2014, p. 237). His notes can be eyebrow raising—'In pretty girls moral qualities are not so awfully relevant' (Oakeshott, 2014, p. 350)—or mordantly funny—'*Marriage*: Two stags with their antlers locked together dying in a knowledge of one another they never wanted, dying of starvation' (Oakeshott, 2014, p. 272). But none of this has much to do with his arguments about morality or civil association.

Still another manifestation of Oakeshott's romanticism is his Wordsworthian embrace of the pastoral:

> [T]he best environment for the young child: country, gardens, orchards, meadows … hills, flowers, trees. The town, its pavements, over-stimulate children … As proof: an intelligent countryman can quickly grasp the life of a town, its complexity; no townsman can *ever* fill the gap caused by the failure to know the country and grow up in it. (Oakeshott, 2014, p. 345)

In this notebook entry, Oakeshott gives us a cliché rather than a genuine insight. In an earlier entry he had commented on the absurdity of this sort of romanticism:

> To fly the world … and find a life of simple contentment in some distant spot of earth, cultivating one's own garden and living upon what one can produce for oneself … How? Are we to pass an existence four fifths of which is the mere securing of the leisure to live? (Oakeshott, 2014, p. 145)

Oakeshott had his romantic impulses, moods and moments but as a thinker he is not a romantic in the ordinary sense of that word. The rule of law is only an idea: it 'bakes no bread' (Oakeshott, 1983, p. 164), and to be more than 'a logician's dream' (Oakeshott, 1983, p. 149) it must be realized in circumstances that conspire periodically to destroy it. In his published works on the civil condition we find a most realistic concern with tyranny and barbarism—one, incidentally, that he shares with those eighteenth-century Romantics who first cheered the revolution in France and were then appalled by its excesses. This concern is echoed in the notebooks, which contain entries on domination as the meaning of injustice.

> Like everyone else, I find myself full of contradictions. For example: how much I desire to dominate those with whom I come into contact … and on the other hand, how little can I justify to myself this desire, how foreign it is to some of my moods and all my principles. (Oakeshott, 2014, p. 196)

And: 'All the troubles of the world come from men wanting what they can only get with violence' (Oakeshott, 2014, p. 296). And again: 'The horror of all compulsion, of getting or keeping anything by force or subterfuge or importunity' (Oakeshott, 2014, p. 408). The civil condition can only mitigate this horror, not erase it.

In a state understood to be a civil association, coercion is used to resist coercion. It is thwarting wrongful coercion that makes coercion right. But in an enterprise state, coercion is indifferent to right. In such a state, subjects are 'property', items in its store of 'capital resources'. In such a state, whether a subject 'remains or whether he is permitted to go must be a management decision' and 'it is not easy to rebut the view that the logic of a state thus constituted assigns to the office of its government the authority to exterminate associates whose continued existence is judged to be irredeemably prejudicial to the pursuit of its purpose'. At best, Oakeshott continues, 'the member of such a state enjoys the composure of the conscript assured of his dinner. His "freedom" is warm, compensated servility' (which is not always such a bad thing: Oakeshott seems rather to have enjoyed his army days). And he concludes: 'This, it might be thought, reveals a state understood in the terms of enterprise association to be a somewhat rickety moral construction, but that is a matter which I have refrained from exploring in order not to prejudice the investigation' (Oakeshott, 1975, p. 317).

In his replies to critics of *On Human Conduct*, Oakeshott's language becomes even less guarded, more passionate. The desire for substantive satisfactions becomes a 'slavish concern for benefits' and the effort to impose a substantive purpose on the subjects of a state, which is a non-voluntary association from which subjects cannot easily withdraw, is 'a moral enormity' regardless of whether it is the effort of one, few or many (Oakeshott, 2008, p. 279). There is no mistaking the judgement that, as a trait of human character, the disposition to be an individual, to prefer adventures in self-determination to the satisfaction of desires, is superior to the wish to submerge oneself in some enterprise hostile to individuality. Each disposition is even assigned a god in its own image, the first a god who announces formal rules, the second a provider of substantive benefits (Oakeshott, 1975, pp. 324–5). We need not, of course, agree with the judgement. But if the morality is non-consequential, it is not inconsequential; it expresses an understanding of the terms on which human beings can justly coexist while respecting one another's character as free individuals. And if Oakeshott neglects to explore the conditions of its realization in the ever-changing circumstances of human existence, one answer might be that this is a question not for philosophy but for politics.

Conclusion

If I am right, the common objections to Oakeshott's performance as a moralist, whether as a maker of moral judgements or as a theorist of moral conduct, are mostly beside the point. The recurrent charge that his concern with the non-instrumental was not only mistaken but frivolous would have struck him as ungenerous, narrow-minded and, as he used the term, barbaric. It seems to miss the point of morality, which is to make room for conversation by silencing boors, to enable individuality by resisting domination, and to make coexistence possible by resisting enslavement and extermination.

If Oakeshott is more interesting as a theorist of morality than as a practical moralist it is because his morality is conventional. He recognizes the distinction between mores and morality but in the end does not want to make too much of it. He leans towards *Sittlichkeit* but is never free of *Moralität*, as can be seen in his definition of a moral practice as 'the *ars artium* of agency' – 'agents related to one another in terms of conditional proprieties which are expressly or tacitly recognised in the conditions of all other special prudential relationships and manners of being associated in conduct' (Oakeshott, 1975, p. 88). On a suitably broad definition of the term he can be read as a moralist but he does not betray his character as a theorist in making moral judgements: there is no reason not to do both provided one does not confuse theorizing a moral practice with making judgements according to the practice one is theorizing. His contribution lies not in judging or prescribing conduct but in clarifying the presuppositions of the judgements and precepts we call moral. It is a philosophical contribution which we can also read, if we wish, as a moral one.

References

Oakeshott, M. (1933) *Experience and Its Modes*, Cambridge: Cambridge University Press.
Oakeshott, M. (1975) *On Human Conduct*, Oxford: Oxford University Press.
Oakeshott, M. (1983) *On History and Other Essays*, Oxford: Basil Blackwell.
Oakeshott, M. (1991) *Rationalism in Politics and Other Essays*, new and expanded edition, Fuller, T. (ed.), Indianapolis, IN: Liberty Fund.
Oakeshott, M. (2001) *The Voice of Liberal Learning: Michael Oakeshott on Education*, Fuller, T. (ed.), Indianapolis, IN: Liberty Fund.
Oakeshott, M. (2004) *What is History? and Other Essays*, O'Sullivan, L. (ed.), Exeter: Imprint Academic.
Oakeshott, M. (2008) *The Vocabulary of a Modern European State*, O'Sullivan, L. (ed.), Exeter: Imprint Academic.

Oakeshott, M. (2014) *Notebooks, 1922–86*, O'Sullivan, L. (ed.), Exeter: Imprint Academic.

Timothy Fuller

Historicism and Political Philosophy
Reflections on Oakeshott, Collingwood, Gadamer and Strauss

The voice of practical activity may be the commonest to be heard, but it is partnered by others whose utterance is in a different idiom ...'history' also has acquired, or has begun to acquire, an authentic voice and idiom of its own. — Michael Oakeshott, 'The Voice of Poetry in the Conversation of Mankind'

History is a predicament for man who must live in it. In order to act in history, he must seek to rise above it. He needs perspectives in terms of which to understand his situation, and timeless truths and values in terms of which to act in it. Yet the perspectives which he finds often merely reflect his age; and what he accepts as timelessly true and valid is apt to be merely the opinion that is in fashion. Thus while man must always try to rise above his historical situation he succeeds at best only precariously. — Emil Fackenheim, *Metaphysics and Historicity*

Preface

What follows reflects on the issue of historicism and the status of political philosophy as illustrated in the thought of Michael Oakeshott, R.G. Collingwood, Hans-Georg Gadamer and Leo Strauss. All four take seriously that we live in an age of heightened historical consciousness, and they all reflect on the status of past thought in the present. Modern historical research makes us aware that the more detailed historical knowledge we gain of the past, the more the past can seem distant and strange. Accumulating historical knowledge questions the prospect of an agreed upon historical narrative, and casts doubt on access to perennial questions and timeless truths. In the Introduction to Hegel's *Philosophy of History*, one already encounters a typology of different approaches to understanding the past, coupled with Hegel's attempt to find meaning in history through a philosophic narrative of history's rational progress toward its end, seeking to mediate the tension between the quest for meaning in history and the historian's detailed account of history. Since Hegel's time the question of the relationship of historical and philosophical thought has become unavoidable, especially when we turn to the question of political philosophy which inevitably involves both. This question was raised in the twentieth century in a particularly trenchant way by these four thinkers who struggled to make sense of the philosophical relevance of history and the historical relevance of philosophy in the face of the political catastrophe that engulfed European civilization. In addressing such matters, the four thinkers discussed here offer varied responses ranging from Collingwood's embrace of historicism to Strauss's critique of historicism. Oakeshott and Gadamer occupy a middle ground seeking to mediate this opposition in ways discussed below.

Oakeshott on Political Philosophy

In his original Introduction (1946) to Hobbes's *Leviathan*, Oakeshott remarks that 'Every masterpiece of political philosophy springs from a new vision of the predicament; each is the glimpse of a deliverance or the suggestion of a remedy.'[1] And he identifies three great traditions of philosophic reflection on politics. The first involves the 'master conceptions of Reason and Nature', associated pre-eminently with Plato's *Republic*, of which tradition he says:

> It is coeval with our civilization; it has an unbroken history into the modern world; and it has survived by a matchless power of adaptability all the changes of the European consciousness.[2]

Oakeshott also identifies the tradition of 'will and artifice' with Hobbes and the tradition of 'rational will' with Hegel. He does not treat them as superseding the Platonic tradition in a linear progression. They are persisting ways of thinking about politics which are available to us through changing historical circumstances: 'I cannot detect a history of political thought which reveals a gradual accumulation of political wisdom and understanding ... anything which could properly correspond to the expression *the* history of political thought.'[3] Implicit is a

---

[1] Oakeshott, M., Introduction to *Leviathan*, by Thomas Hobbes (Oxford: Blackwell Political Texts, 1946), p. xi.
[2] Oakeshott, M., Introduction to *Leviathan*, by Thomas Hobbes (Oxford: Blackwell Political Texts, 1946), p. xii.
[3] Oakeshott, M., *Lectures in the History of Political Thought*, edited by Terry Nardin and Luke O'Sullivan (Exeter: Imprint Academic, 2006), p. 32; italics in original.

vital conversation among the great voices of political philosophy. Here, for example, is his summary of the achievement of Saint Thomas Aquinas:

> [His is] the enterprise of *explaining* political activity and the activity of governing. It is a subtle union of Christian theology and the Aristotelian philosophy of 'nature', in which these two components were brought together, and made to modify one another and generate an explanation, not only remarkably new in the thirteenth century, but one that has had a profound influence upon all subsequent explanatory enterprises in this field.[4]

And having described the various dimensions of Aristotle's analysis of polis-life in which Aristotle 'finds a place for *politike* on the map of human activity', Oakeshott remarks that there is a 'mode of activity in which human beings employ an aptitude which Aristotle understands to be the supreme aptitude of their "nature", an aptitude even more fundamental than that of a life governed by rational choice of what to do and not to do ... another aptitude which he calls "theoretical reason" ... the ability to understand and explain what they are doing ... human beings are not only *praktikos*, but also *theoretikos* ... This Aristotelian map, with a few amendments scribbled on it by later thinkers, was the context of all European political thought for 2,000 years.'[5] In short, human beings know that they are historically situated and thus are drawn to wonder about the greater context of their situatedness. This would not be possible if their situatedness entirely determined and confined their thinking. The historical perspective is a particular response to situatedness which is universal to human existence; in principle, historicism cannot foreclose philosophic argument about its own premises.

Political philosophy for Oakeshott, then, while it may acknowledge both, is confined neither to the historian's past (the mere history of thought which is neither *praktikos* nor *theoretikos*), nor to serving the practical life which exploits the past in its concern for present and future political purposes. Oakeshott identifies 'masterpieces' which rise above their contexts to become permanent contributions to our thinking. Philosophers of politics, situated in their own time and place, under the philosophic impulse look beyond, even to 'eternity'. 'There has been', Oakeshott remarks, 'no fully considered politics that has not

---

[4] Oakeshott, M., *Lectures in the History of Political Thought*, edited by Terry Nardin and Luke O'Sullivan (Exeter: Imprint Academic, 2006), p. 358; italics in original.

[5] Oakeshott, M., *Lectures in the History of Political Thought*, edited by Terry Nardin and Luke O'Sullivan (Exeter: Imprint Academic, 2006), pp. 128-9.

looked for its reflection in eternity. The history of political philosophy is, then, the context of the masterpiece.'⁶ Moreover, a philosophy of politics is 'an explanation or view of political life and activity from the standpoint of the totality of experience...'⁷ This meant for Oakeshott to embrace a conversational exchange where the initial context of time and place does not confine the masterpiece of political thought. Speaking of Hobbes's *Leviathan*, he says, 'in reading the *Leviathan* I seem to find, not only a book the significance of which lies in the seventeenth century, not only a book which offers an explanation of the origin and character of political life constructed to meet particular circumstances, but to find also something which, because it can relevantly be separated from time and place and for other reasons, I should call a philosophy of politics.'⁸

Oakeshott on the Nature and Limits of the Historical Mode of Experience

The historical point of view is not an inevitable acquisition imposing itself upon us as the practical task of survival does; it is not an obvious view of the past; it is an acquisition motivated by our critical faculty in developing methods that are to be learned in learning to become not just a receptor but a critical analyst of the past. The historical point of view does not replace the practical life, but nor is the practical life the key to understanding the historical point of view. These are 'categorially distinct modes of understanding'.⁹ Nonetheless, they are prone to tension: the historian's present 'is perhaps the most sophisticated of all presents, difficult to achieve and difficult to sustain ... historical understanding is especially prone to relapse into some other engagement'.¹⁰

In the historical mode of explanation events cannot be understood apart from the particular manner in which the historian considers them. 'The historian's business is not to discover, recapture, or even to interpret; it is to create and construct ... discovery without judgment is impossible; and a course of events independent of experience,

---

[6] Hobbes's *Leviathan*, p. xi.
[7] Oakeshott, M., 'The Concept of a Philosophy of Politics', in *Religion, Politics and the Moral Life* (Newhaven: Yale UP, 1993), pp. 126-7.
[8] Oakeshott, M., 'The Concept of a Philosophy of Politics', in *Religion, Politics and the Moral Life* (Newhaven: Yale UP, 1993), p. 119.
[9] Oakeshott, M., 'Present, Past and Future', in *On History and Other Essays*, (Indianapolis: Liberty Fund edition, 1999).
[10] Oakeshott, M., 'Present, Past and Future', in *On History and Other Essays*, (Indianapolis: Liberty Fund edition, 1999), p. 31.

untouched by thought and judgment, is a contradiction.'[11] Historical 'facts' are conclusions historians may eventually reach, not the raw material from which the historian begins. To achieve this requires training in the historian's task in order to master the presuppositions of historical inquiry.

What are these presuppositions? First, experience is understood as past. Separating from the practical/political past is the most significant development of the historical consciousness: 'In practical experience, the past is designed to justify, to make valid practical beliefs about the present and the future, about the world in general ... the language is that of history, while its thought is that of practice.'[12] By contrast the historical past 'is the past for its own sake'. The historian's is a 'dead past'.[13]

On the other hand, the persistence of the Platonic, the Aristotelian, the Thomistic, the Hobbesian and the Hegelian voices shows that, in responding to them, we are not merely locating them in the flow of events. They speak to us through all the contingent changes of temporal existence. Oakeshott does not foreclose a dialogue with past thinkers and thus distinguishes political philosophy both from the past 'for its own sake', and also from political ideology.

What the historian accounts for is not what 'really happened', but rather for 'what the evidence obliges us to believe' happened.[14] 'The present in historical understanding, then, is itself a past ... a past which itself survived and is present. It is composed of actual utterances and artefacts which have survived, which are understood as survivals, and are now present exactly as they were uttered or made except for any damage they may have suffered on the way.'[15] 'There are not two worlds—the world of past happenings and the world of our present knowledge of those past events—there is only one world, and it is a world of present experience...' full of survivals which are evidence. 'The past in history is, then, always an inference; it is the product of judgment and consequently always belongs to the historian's present world of experience. All he has is his present world of ideas, and the

---

[11] Oakeshott, M., *Experience and its Modes* (Cambridge: Cambridge UP, 1933), pp. 93-4.
[12] Oakeshott, M., *Experience and its Modes* (Cambridge: Cambridge UP, 1933), p. 105.
[13] Oakeshott, M., *Experience and its Modes* (Cambridge: Cambridge UP, 1933), p. 106
[14] Oakeshott, M., *Experience and its Modes* (Cambridge: Cambridge UP, 1933), p. 107.
[15] Oakeshott, M., 'Present, Past and Future', in *On History and Other Essays*, (Indianapolis: Liberty Fund edition, 1999), pp. 32-3.

historical past is a constituent of that world or nothing at all.'[16] In contrast, to engage with the masterpieces of political thought is to consider arguments about what is true about politics independent of what political actors may claim to be doing, and in terms that speak beyond mere time and place. Oakeshott does not think that the study of history for its own sake will elicit practical wisdom or philosophic argument. We see also why, for Oakeshott, this is an abstract account of the whole of experience since the whole of experience is never solely past experience. To assess the argument of a masterpiece as merely reflective of the time and place of its author may be the task of the historian *qua* historian, but it cannot be the sole task of human understanding: 'whenever history invades any other world of experience, the result is always the disintegration of experience.'[17] Oakeshott did not adopt historicism. He saw that, in the great thinkers, while there are of course historical elements, there is also a capacity to express something surmounting those elements, inviting our response: 'Wherever there is genuinely philosophical reflection something is being said, such that if true, things will be as they permanently are—that is, as they are *not* in the world of practical politics.'[18]

Collingwood on Re-enacting Past Thought

Is historical understanding for Collingwood basic? Oakeshott thought so. In his review of *The Idea of History*, Oakeshott says, 'it must be observed that, almost imperceptibly, Collingwood's philosophy of history turned into a philosophy in which all knowledge is assimilated to historical knowledge, and consequently into a radically sceptical philosophy.'[19] To explore this further, consider Collingwood's *Essay on Metaphysics*:[20]

In that essay, Collingwood asserts that metaphysical questions are historical questions: 'Metaphysics has always been an historical science; but metaphysicians have not always been fully aware of that fact.'[21]

---

[16] Oakeshott, M., *Experience and its Modes* (Cambridge: Cambridge UP, 1933), p. 109.
[17] Oakeshott, M., *Experience and its Modes* (Cambridge: Cambridge UP, 1933), p. 156.
[18] Oakeshott, M., 'Political Philosophy', in *Religion, Politics and the Moral Life* (Newhaven: Yale UP, 1993), p. 155.
[19] Oakeshott, M., Review of *The Idea of History* by R.G. Collingwood, in *English Historical Review*, 1947.
[20] Collingwood, R.G., *An Essay on Metaphysics* (Oxford: Clarendon Press, 1940).
[21] Collingwood, R.G., *An Essay on Metaphysics* (Oxford: Clarendon Press, 1940), p. 58.

Metaphysics identifies 'absolute presuppositions', assumptions a thinker or set of thinkers take to be indispensable. Metaphysical analysis identifies what for a given thinker or group those absolute presuppositions are. This is not a matter of whether they are 'true' or 'false', but a matter of identifying what grounds for disciplined inquiries their practitioners take to be indispensable to do their work.

The historian studies the context in which questions arise to which answers, grounded on metaphysical assumptions, are given. These absolute presuppositions can be identified and described. Collingwood dismisses the idea that we could judge among absolute presuppositions in terms of which are 'true' or not because the 'efficacy of a supposition does not depend on its being true, nor even on its being thought true, but only on its being supposed...'[22]

How, on Collingwood's terms, could there be a conversational relationship with or among these thinkers? He argued that, once identified, absolute presuppositions are shown to be grounded in particular historical contexts; they are not universal or eternal. It is a mistake, he argues, to think that 'the characteristics of a certain historical milieu' are 'characteristics of mankind at large'.[23] This conclusion is Collingwood's absolute presupposition: 'The problems of metaphysics are historical problems; its methods are historical methods. We must have no more nonsense about its being meritorious to inhabit a fog. A metaphysician is a man who has to get at facts ... We live in the twentieth century; there is no excuse for us if we do not know what the methods of history are.'[24]

If absolute presuppositions are to be treated as historical facts, philosophers must become historians, accounting for what have at different times been taken to be absolute presuppositions. One can gain a history of presuppositions, but metaphysics reveals no transcendent questions: comparative study will show that 'there are no "eternal" or "crucial" or "central" problems in metaphysics.'[25] In short, metaphysicians properly understood are intellectual historians.

Thus, when Collingwood proposes that we can re-enact past thought in the present, he means only that we can describe the absolute presuppositions as evidence of past circumstances in the stream of

---

[22] Collingwood, R.G., *An Essay on Metaphysics* (Oxford: Clarendon Press, 1940), p. 52.
[23] Collingwood, R.G., *An Essay on Metaphysics* (Oxford: Clarendon Press, 1940), p. 57.
[24] Collingwood, R.G., *An Essay on Metaphysics* (Oxford: Clarendon Press, 1940), pp. 62-3.
[25] Collingwood, R.G., *An Essay on Metaphysics* (Oxford: Clarendon Press, 1940), p. 72.

historical becoming. We may be able to understand absolute presuppositions, and some might even convince themselves to believe in such presuppositions though living in a different historical context from the original; but we cannot forget that we are choosing without an independent standard of judgement. In 'A Philosophy of Progress', he said: 'Whether you think the course of events is an upward or downward course depends not on *it* but on *you*.'[26] And, 'we have developed social and political institutions that suit *our* psychological structure...'[27]

Collingwood had also said that 'the historian must re-enact the past in his own mind.'[28] The strong meaning of the re-enactment of past thought is that the historian re-enacts 'in his own mind the experience' as it occurred to those he studies.[29] What does the word 'experience' mean in this context? The historian must re-think 'for himself the thought of his author, and nothing short of that will make him the historian of that author's philosophy'.[30] This seems to mean that one must try to understand an ancient thinker as he understood himself. But this does not mean one identifies with that thinker or reaffirms his thought. Rather, one describes the thinker's response to his historical situation, while one's own historical situation distances one from the thinker whose thought one is re-enacting. In re-enacting the thought, one is responding to the recorded expression of an experience, but one is not thereby re-enacting (or undergoing) the experience which gave rise to the expressed thought. The 'allegory of the cave' is an image intended to express an encounter with transcendent reality. But does Collingwood re-enact the encounter itself? To identify Plato's 'absolute presupposition' does not mean Collingwood experiences an encounter with transcendent reality; it only means he is describing an experience Plato claimed to have had and recorded.

Collingwood distinguishes the thought he is re-enacting from the situation of those whose thought he is re-enacting; but their situation included the experience of transcendence. Collingwood asserted that there can be no 'science of being', distancing himself from classical expressions of transcendence which classical thinkers understood to go beyond science in responding to the mystery of existence, not as final

---

[26] Collingwood, R.G., 'A Philosophy of Progress' (1929), in *Essays in the Philosophy of History*, edited by William Debbins (Austin: Unniversity of Texas Press, 1965), p. 109; italics in original.
[27] Collingwood, R.G., 'A Philosophy of Progress' (1929), in *Essays in the Philosophy of History*, edited by William Debbins (Austin: University of Texas PRess, 1965), p. 119; italics in original.
[28] Collingwood, R.G., *The Idea of History* (Oxford: Oxford UP, 1946), p. 282.
[29] Collingwood, R.G., *The Idea of History* (Oxford: Oxford UP, 1946), pp. 282-3.
[30] Collingwood, R.G., *The Idea of History* (Oxford: Oxford UP, 1946), p. 283.

explanations of that experience. If we take their situation to include attempts to find adequate expression of their encounter with transcendent truth, Collingwood is not re-enacting past thought even if he is reporting its recorded expressions accurately. In short, the meaning of experiencing past thought in his usage is equivocal. Collingwood says that if we are to bridge the gap of time we must bridge it 'at both ends'.[31] To rethink past thoughts, one 'must be the right man to study that object'. The 'historian's mind must be such as to offer home for that revival'.[32] But metaphysicians, *qua* intellectual historians, have already distanced themselves from the past thought's significance for the one who expressed it. I may see that a past thought is really a past thought present to me now, but is the experience which gave rise to the thought present to me? Collingwood does not provide a convincing answer to this question. This led Strauss, as we shall see shortly, to doubt that Collingwood was really rethinking past thought, and Oakeshott to conclude that Collingwood ended in scepticism.

Historicism and Political Philosophy:
Strauss and Gadamer

Living in our age of heightened historical consciousness has imposed the question whether traditional philosophy, and hence traditional political philosophy — examining permanent questions, seeking timeless truth or permanent standards of right and wrong — are shown to be impossible. Here I introduce the argument between Leo Strauss and Hans-Georg Gadamer alongside Oakeshott and Collingwood on the presentness of past thought, noting Strauss's critique of Collingwood, and Gadamer's critical engagement with Strauss in *Truth and Method*.

Strauss is well known for his critique of historicism. He insisted that the task of the modern reader of ancient texts is to understand authors as they understood themselves before one could seek to understand better than they did. For Strauss, this meant, among other questions, whether the inquiry into the best regime for human beings is meaningful or an illusion. Such an inquiry involves taking seriously the classic view that the search for truth beyond one's situation is not fruitless. In 'Natural Right and the Historical Approach', Strauss says,

> The modern opponents of natural right reject precisely this idea. According to them, all human thought is historical and hence unable ever to grasp anything eternal. Whereas, according to the ancients, philosophizing means to leave the cave, according to our contemporaries all philosophizing essentially belongs to a 'historical world,'

---

[31] Collingwood, R.G., *The Idea of History* (Oxford: Oxford UP, 1946), p. 304.
[32] Collingwood, R.G., *The Idea of History* (Oxford: Oxford UP, 1946), p. 304.

'culture,' 'civilization,' 'Weltanschauung,' that is, to what Plato had called the cave. We shall call this view 'historicism.'[33]

From this perspective, we can only approach old texts from within the spirit of our own age and hence reinterpret them in ways that make sense to us from our perspective. Strauss did not accept that all thinking is conditioned by present and future concerns of practical life. Denial of transcendent reality means that the metaphysical claim of ancient writers to encounter such reality cannot be taken seriously. We have, so it is said, become wiser than the ancients and thus we can understand better than they understood. Here is Collingwood's assertion of that: 'Was it really true that different philosophies were, even in the loosest sense of that word, eternal? I soon discovered that it was not true; it was merely a vulgar error, consequent on a kind of historical myopia which, deceived by superficial resemblances, failed to detect profound differences.'[34] It seems to me that he confuses the experience of the eternal with varying efforts to describe in words that experience.

Gadamer's response to Strauss sheds further light on the issues discussed above. He recognizes that we live in a global age wherein we experience the pressures of different ways of life on each other, questioning that there is a single historical narrative, grounded in the Western experience, which reveals a unique standard. The question of understanding past thought in our own tradition is paralleled by the question of understanding other civilizational experiences. It seems to me that Strauss's argument for natural right, albeit facing this further complexity, is relevant in calling for an investigation of universality without presupposing in advance an answer one way or the other.

In *Truth and Method*, Gadamer takes up Strauss's critique of historicism in the section on 'Hermeneutics and Historicism', where he enters a dialogue with Strauss, both on the ground of historicism and on the question of how we understand the thought of past thinkers. The premise of *Truth and Method* is that, despite the importance we now attribute to the methods of modern science, methods cannot capture truth in its fullness: Gadamer is 'concerned to seek that experience of truth that transcends the sphere of the control of scientific method ... Hence the human sciences are joined with modes of experience which lie outside science: with the experience of philosophy, of art, and of history itself. These are all modes of experience in which a truth is

---

[33] Strauss, L., 'Natural Right and the Historical Approach', in *An Introduction to Political Philosophy, Ten Essays by Leo Strauss*, edited by Hilail Gildin (Detroit: Wayne State UP, 1989), p. 102.

[34] Collingwood, R.G., *An Autobiography* (Oxford: Oxford UP, 1939), pp. 60-1.

communicated that cannot be verified by the methodological means proper to science.'[35] Gadamer adds,

> The philosophical endeavor of our day differs from the classical tradition of philosophy in that it is not a direct and unbroken continuation of it. In spite of all its connections with its historical origin, philosophy today is well aware of the historical distance between it and its classical models ... the emergence of historical consciousness over the last few centuries is a much more radical development. Since then, the continuity of the Western philosophical tradition has been effective only in a fragmentary way. We have lost that naïve innocence with which traditional concepts were made to support one's own thinking.[36]

But we have not lost the 'natural inclination' to philosophy:

> It is evident that what we call philosophy is not science in the same way as the so-called positive sciences are. It is not the case that philosophy has a positive datum alongside the standard research areas of the other sciences to be investigated by it alone, for philosophy has to do with the whole ... As the whole, it is an idea that transcends every finite possibility of knowledge, and so it is nothing we could know in a scientific way.[37]

The similarity of this to Oakeshott's statement of philosophy is obvious though Gadamer does not mention him. But Gadamer does say that the way Collingwood presents the idea of rethinking past thoughts involves him in tension between past thoughts and the 'psychological particularity' of a past thinker who had the thoughts being rethought. Collingwood seeks access to the thought freed from the contingent conditions (including the encounter with the divine that many ancient thinkers report) in which the thought appeared. In order to achieve this, Gadamer thinks that Collingwood relied on the 'spirit of the age' (what Collingwood called 'constellations of presuppositions') in which the thought occurred in order to depersonalize the thought which is being rethought, a task for the intellectual historian. Can a thought detached from its original context be a rethinking of the past thought (re-enacting the experience which gives rise to the thought) or is it a rethinking that inevitably is a reinterpreting of thought (as an 'absolute presupposition' but not as an encounter with transcendence)? In re-enacting past thought are we not reinterpreting what the original

---

[35] Gadamer, H.-G., *Truth and Method* (New York: Crossroad Publishing, 1985; English translation, 1975), p. xii.
[36] Gadamer, H.-G., *Truth and Method* (New York: Crossroad Publishing, 1985; English translation, 1975), pp. xiv–xv.
[37] Gadamer, H.-G., 'On the Philosophic Element in the Sciences and the Scientific Character of Philosophy', in *Reason in the Age of Science* (English translation, Cambridge: MIT Press, 1981), p. 1.

thought meant to the one thinking it in accord with a modern criterion? This is the logic of Collingwood's position: the re-enactment of past thought as here understood precludes encounter with permanent truths or questions.

Strauss was a radical critic of this historical point of view. Gadamer sympathetically approaches Strauss's view in terms of Strauss's commitment to reopening the famous quarrel of the ancients and the moderns which, for modern thinkers, is taken to have ended with a decisive victory for the moderns and their view that the insights of the ancients have been superseded, or that philosophy has been revealed to be historical, which is to say that philosophy as such has been superseded, since we have radically altered the meaning of the term 'philosophy'. For such moderns, the fundamental questions now cannot be what they were in antiquity. Strauss's aim is to 'set against the modern historical self-confidence the clear rightness of classical philosophy ... Such an elementary human concern as the distinction between right and wrong assumes that man is able to raise himself above his historical conditionedness.'[38] Strauss put it this way in commenting on Collingwood's *The Idea of History*:

> The largest part of his book is devoted to a history of historical knowledge. That history is on the whole conventional. In studying earlier thinkers, Collingwood never considered the possibility that the point of view from which the present day reader approaches them, or the questions which he addresses to them, might be in need of a fundamental change. He set out to praise or blame the earlier thinkers according to whether they helped or hindered the emergence of scientific history. He did not attempt to look at scientific history, for once, from the point of view of earlier thinkers ... Collingwood writes the history of history in almost the same way in which the eighteenth century historians, whom he censored so severely, are said to have written history in general. The latter condemned the thought of the past as deficient in full reasonableness; Collingwood condemned it as deficient in the true sense of history ... Collingwood therefore rejected the thought of the past in the decisive respect. Hence he could not take that thought seriously, for to take a thought seriously means to regard it as possible that the thought in question is true. He therefore lacked the incentive for re-enacting the thought of the past; he did not re-enact the thought of the past ... For, if to understand the thought of the past necessarily means to understand it differently from the way the thinkers of the past understood it, one will never be able to compare the thought of the present with the thought of the past: one would merely compare one's own thought with the reflection of one's own thought in ancient

---

[38] Gadamer, H.-G., *Truth and Method* (New York: Crossroad Publishing, 1985; English translation, 1975), pp. 482–3.

materials or with a hybrid begotten by the intercourse of one's own thought with earlier thought.[39]

Granted that human beings are historically situated, it remains to be shown that one cannot think outside, or rise above, the constraints of the dominant views of one's time. Collingwood denies access to timeless truths. Strauss calls for openness to the possibility of timeless truths. The questioning of historicism requires such openness, otherwise the resolution of the argument (on both sides) is assumed from the start: 'that there are N types of absolute presuppositions, as Collingwood called them, none of which can be said to be rationally superior to any other ... means the abandonment of the very idea of the truth as rational philosophy has always understood it ... the choice of any of these presuppositions is groundless and leads us again into the abyss of freedom.'[40]

For Collingwood, there is a conspectus of presuppositions that have been asserted. Classical philosophy, as the 'science of being', he rejects on historicist assumptions. But historicism is itself subject to criticism since the advent of historicism (for Collingwood, the advent of our intellectual maturity) was a matter of argument, and classical arguments against it remain known to us (as of course Collingwood knows even as he dismisses them). This is what Gadamer called our fragmentary connection to the classics; the now alien ancient orientation hauntingly reminds us of limits to what we can settle once and for all. One response is to conceal these issues in the name of 'progress'.

The question is not only whether we are precisely describing Plato's thought; rather, it is a matter of whether we take seriously the fundamental questions posed by Plato and other classical thinkers as questions for us as well. It is not a matter of 'going back' to the classics; rather, it is a matter of discovering in our own situation the presence of fundamental questions whose continual presence has been covered over by the dominance of the historical point of view. Strauss thought that the crisis of meaning in our time has alerted us to the possibility of the continuing presence of those questions against the 'spirit of the age', where 'spirit of the age' is a device, an assertion, inhibiting the questioning of historicism. Strauss is thus criticizing the claim of intellectual progress for refusing to acknowledge the questioning of its assumptions.

---

[39] Strauss, L., 'Review of *The Idea of History* by R.G. Collingwood', in *Review of Metaphysics* (1952), pp. 566, 574, 575, 578–9.

[40] Strauss, L., 'An Introduction to Heideggerian Existentialism', in *The Rebirth of Classical Political Rationalism, and Introduction to the Thought of Leo Strauss*, edited by Thomas Pangle (Chicago: Chicago UP, 1989), p. 34.

Collingwood thought we had for centuries in our 'immaturity' thought unhistorically, and he questioned whether one who does think that way is to be taken seriously. Collingwood could only take such thought seriously as an artefact of a bygone historical situation, but not seriously in its own terms. Logically, the absolute presuppositions of historicism cannot command the future any more than previous absolute presuppositions could. This led Strauss to the view that Collingwood necessarily must judge in terms of his own assumptions. We must ask the question whether we necessarily understand past thought better than it understood itself given the advance claimed for our historical perspective. Not to question the historicist insight is to neglect an essential element in responding to past thought as it presented itself. In posing such questions Strauss identifies the dogmatism of historicism which denies the dialogue or what Gadamer refers to as the quarrel of the ancients with the moderns. Gadamer agrees with Strauss in part:

> What he [Strauss] criticises is that the 'historical' understanding of traditional thought claims to be able to understand the thought of the past better than it understood itself. Whoever thinks like this excludes from the outset the possibility that the thoughts that are handed down to us could simply be true. This is the practically universal dogmatism of this way of thought ... The application of the superior perspective of the present to the whole of the past does not appear to me at all to be the true nature of historical thinking, but characterises the obstinate positivity of a naïve historicism.[41]

But Gadamer also questions Strauss:

> But when Strauss argues that in order to understand better it is necessary first to understand an author as he understood himself, he under-estimates, I think, the difficulties of understanding, because he ignores what might be called the dialectic of the statement.[42]

Gadamer thinks that, given that we must live in an ever-changing 'present', it is not possible for there to be a final, superior view of past thought. Hence the claim of superior understanding is always subject to counter claims. Claims to understand better tempt us and arise because we see the works of the past in changing historical contexts. We have to establish the pertinence of an ancient work in our historical context—to see the ancient expression of an experience in terms of an equivalence in our experience. The desire to understand a past author

---

[41] Gadamer, H.-G., *Truth and Method* (New York: Crossroad Publishing, 1985; English translation, 1975), p. 484.

[42] Gadamer, H.-G., *Truth and Method* (New York: Crossroad Publishing, 1985; English translation, 1975), p. 484.

as he understood himself is not mistaken, but we must see this task as dialectical, as a response to past thought, not mere repetition of it: 'I would define hermeneutics as the skill to let things speak which come to us in a fixed, petrified form, that of the text.'[43] In this respect, Gadamer seeks a middle ground between the classical and the historical, and proposes something resembling what Oakeshott meant by 'the conversation of mankind'. Finding relevance in a new historical context is not just thinking the same thought even if it preserves the significance of that thought. 'The interpreter of what is written, like the interpreter of divine or human utterance, has the task of overcoming and removing the strangeness and making its assimilation possible.'[44] Gadamer likens this to the task of the translator who must make a foreign language accessible to us while preserving the thought thus expressed. Interpretation in this sense is not the overcoming or supersession of past thought.

In discussing Plato, Gadamer points out the dialectical character of the dialogues which has stimulated many extraordinary interpretations of Plato's thought, not least those of Strauss himself. Plato understood this in addressing the problem of writing down philosophy. The dialogues are a way of writing down which eludes the fixity of writing down. Gadamer says, 'Everything that is set down in writing is to some extent foreign and strange, and hence it poses the same task of understanding as what is spoken in a foreign language.'[45] It is clear that for Gadamer there is a fundamental starting point in the Socratic/Platonic experience which is valid for us: 'I believe there is continuity, for example, in the sense that the famous Socratic inquiry into the good, his claim that no one in society had the expertise to give a satisfactory answer to this question, remains significant for our times, for we face the danger of becoming too dependent on experts.'[46]

Plato, in other words, was aware of the issue of interpretation and the unavoidable necessity for argument about how to understand what has been thought and said, which does not preclude entering into past thought. For Gadamer, 'the Platonic dialogue is a model of writing that

---

[43] Gadamer, H.-G., 'Interview: Writing and the Living Voice', in *Hans-Georg Gadamer on Education, Poetry and History, Applied Hermeneutics* (New York: State University of New York Press, 1992), p. 65.

[44] Gadamer, H.-G., *Truth and Method* (New York: Crossroad Publishing, 1985; English translation, 1975), p. 487.

[45] Gadamer, H.-G., *Truth and Method* (New York: Crossroad Publishing, 1985; English translation, 1975), p. 487.

[46] Gadamer, H.-G., 'Interview: Writing and the Living Voice', in *Hans-Georg Gadamer on Education, Poetry and History, Applied Hermeneutics* (New York: State University of New York Press, 1992), p. 67.

embraces many meanings and inner relationships.' Does an author know exactly what he means to say in every sentence he utters or writes down? Part of the Platonic argument against writing down philosophy was to preserve the exchange through which interlocutors could attempt to clarify to each other what they really wanted to say. The fixity of written words constrains such exchange. In other words, we can resist historicism without denying the necessity of interpreting past thought in light of current circumstances. In rejecting 'naïve historicism', Gadamer does not simply endorse Strauss's position. Rather, he engages to mediate the quarrel of the ancients and the moderns. His thinking eludes easy categorization.

So far as I know, Strauss never claimed to have reached final, definitive understanding of past thinkers even though he argued vigorously for his readings of them, and for the importance of their questions. The search for wisdom in these matters requires a combination of tenacious argument and of reserve, even if one has strong inclinations in one direction or another, about claiming to have acquired final knowledge. We recall Heidegger's remark that for all our mental effort we are still not thinking.

We encounter these issues on at least two different levels: one is the conviction that political philosophy in the classical sense is now impossible and therefore we must reinterpret political philosophy as the history of political thought, that is as responses to contingent and limiting historical conditions — analysis as intellectual history; the other considers political philosophy as engagement in current politics, providing intellectual support either for or against such practical political goals as currently capture the interests of politicians by adjudicating among past authors as to whether they advance or hinder present and future practical goals. This intellectual impasse demands thinking further. The authors considered here are catalysts for reinvigorating the philosophical conversation in order, as Oakeshott said, to listen to the conversation in which human beings forever seek to understand themselves.

References

Collingwood, R.G. (1939) *An Autobiography*, Oxford: Oxford University Press.

Collingwood, R.G. (1940) *An Essay on Metaphysics*, Oxford: Clarendon Press.

Collingwood, R.G. (1942) *The New Leviathan or Man, Society Civilization and Barbarism*, Oxford: Oxford University Press.

Collingwood, R.G. (1946) *The Idea of History*, Oxford: Oxford University Press.

Collingwood, R.G. (1965) 'A Philosophy of Progress' (1929) and 'The Philosophy of History' (1930), in Debbins, W. (ed.) *Essays in the Philosophy of History*, Austin, TX: University of Texas Press.

Gadamer, H.-G. (1985) *Truth and Method*, New York: Crossroad Publishing; English translation, 1975.

Gadamer, H.-G. (1981) 'On the Philosophic Element in the Sciences and the Scientific Character of Philosophy' and 'On the Natural Inclination of Human Beings Toward Philosophy', in *Reason in the Age of Science* English translation, Cambridge, MA: MIT Press.

Gadamer, H.-G. (1992) 'Interview: Writing and the Living Voice', in *Hans-Georg Gadamer on Education, Poetry and History, Applied Hermeneutics*, New York: State University of New York Press.

Oakeshott, M. (1933) *Experience and its Modes*, Cambridge: Cambridge University Press.

Oakeshott, M. (1946) Introduction to Hobbes's *Leviathan*, Oxford: Blackwell Political Texts.

Oakeshott, M. (1947) Review of Collingwood's *The Idea of History*, *English Historical Review*.

Oakeshott, M. (1991) 'The Activity of Being an Historian', 'The Voice of Poetry in the Conversation of Mankind', and 'The Study of Politics in a University', in *Rationalism in Politics and Other Essays*, Indianapolis, IN: Liberty Fund, new expanded edition.

Oakeshott, M. (1993) 'The Concept of a Philosophy of Politics' and 'Political Philosophy', in *Religion, Politics and the Moral Life*, Newhaven, CT: Yale University Press.

Oakeshott, M. (1999) 'Present, Past and Future', in *On History and Other Essays*, Indianapolis, IN: Liberty Fund Edition.

Oakeshott, M. (2001) 'A Place of Learning', in *The Voice of Liberal Learning*, Indianapolis, IN: Liberty Fund Edition.

Oakeshott, M. (2006) *Lectures in the History of Political Thought*, Nardin, T. & O'Sullivan, L. (eds.), Exeter: Imprint Academic.

Strauss, L. (1952) Review of Collingwood's *The Idea of History*, *Review of Metaphysics*.

Strauss, L. (1989) 'Natural Right and the Historical Approach', in *An Introduction to Political Philosophy, Ten Essays by Leo Strauss*, Gildin, H. (ed.), Detroit, MI: Wayne State University Press.

Strauss, L. (1989) 'An Introduction to Heideggerian Existentialism', in *The Rebirth of Classical Political Rationalism, an Introduction to the Thought of Leo Strauss*, Pangle, T. (ed.) Chicago, IL: University of Chicago Press.

Edmund Neill

The Nature of Oakeshott's Conservatism

This chapter seeks to investigate the nature of Michael Oakeshott's conservatism. At first sight, this might appear to be a relatively straightforward task, since Oakeshott has often been viewed as Britain's preeminent twentieth-century conservative theorist—in the sense of being an uncritical upholder of traditional social and political norms against the pernicious influence of rationalism, or even as a trenchant critic of the Enlightenment. Thus in the 1950s and 1960s in particular, when Oakeshott was best known for the essays published in *Rationalism in Politics and Other Essays*, commentators tended to latch on to his argument in the essay 'Political Education' that the only way one could successfully pursue political activity was through 'the pursuit of intimations' rather than by using self-consciously produced moral rules and ideals, and often linked this traditionalist position to the critique of the more rationalist aspects of the Enlightenment that Oakeshott gave in 'Rationalism in Politics' (Benn and Peters, 1959, pp. 312–28; Tseng, 2004). On such a reading Oakeshott, by definition, must be regarded as some kind of conservative. However, I seek to argue here that Oakeshott's relationship with 'conservatism' is far more complex than this, and for three main reasons. First, Oakeshott's position arguably developed after writing 'Rationalism in Politics' and 'Political Education', so that he did not merely stick to upholding the importance of tradition in politics, but instead developed a normative position that advocated a certain conception of pluralist individualism, which Oakeshott associated with modernity. Indeed, in his most detailed late work in particular, *On Human Conduct*, Oakeshott set out to delineate the kind of state (which he called 'civil association') that could guarantee such pluralist individualism, using a newly created vocabulary. Thus to understand in what sense Oakeshott might be labelled as a 'conservative', we need, first, to delineate his mature position accurately. Second, following on from this, since it is a key part of Oakeshott's project to try and clarify our philosophical and political vocabulary by reformulating the terms we use to make them more precise, we need to address the objection that it is pointless to try and identify Oakeshott as a 'conservative' at all, given that such ideological terminology is so contested, and so loaded with different historical and philosophical meanings. This case has been forcefully argued by Terry Nardin in particular (Nardin, 2015), but although it raises important questions, I argue here that terms such as 'conservative' and 'liberal' cannot be easily dispensed with. In particular, the abstract nature of Oakeshott's ideal-types means that they are, almost by definition, incapable of fully capturing the more dynamic aspects of political ideologies. Finally, since I argue that is worth describing Oakeshott in ideological terms, there remains the important (and much discussed) question of whether it is more legitimate to categorize Oakeshott as a 'conservative' or as a 'liberal', given that his strong commitment to individual freedom. Ultimately, I argue, Oakeshott is best identified as a moderate, modernist conservative, since although he is in favour of modern pluralist individualism, and wary of criticizing the Enlightenment excessively, he is nevertheless cautious about historical change, and the degree to which reason can help us formulate normative goals in politics. To make my case, I will explore these three areas in turn.

First, then, let us examine how Oakeshott's arguments about politics develop from writing 'Rationalism in Politics' in 1947, to his *magnum opus*, *On Human Conduct*, in 1975. In 'Rationalism in Politics', and other essays from the late 1940s and early 1950s, Oakeshott was largely committed to a traditionalist position, in that his main point was to mount an epistemological critique of the way in which practical activities have often come to be conceptualized in modernity, criticizing the doctrine of 'rationalism' in particular. Oakeshott associated rationalism with certain tendencies that he detected in the Enlightenment, namely the desire to have certain knowledge without prior experience, and blamed these particularly on the followers of Bacon and Descartes (Oakeshott, 1991, pp. 17–22). And the fundamental problem with such a rationalistic desire for certain knowledge, Oakeshott argued, was that it tended to lead to the claim that practical activities could be performed without reference to what he calls 'practical knowledge' – namely a form of knowledge that cannot be precisely formulated, that resists reduction to 'rules, principles, directions [and] maxims', cannot be 'learned from a book ... repeated by rote, and applied mechanically', and instead 'exists only in use, is not reflective' and 'can neither be taught nor learned, but only imparted and acquired' (Oakeshott, 1991, p. 12). (This is in contrast to 'technical knowledge', which can be explicitly and precisely formulated.) However, in fact, Oakeshott argues, such knowledge is always necessary for the successful performance of any kind of human activity, and hence practical activities, including politics, must always be performed with reference to a tradition of prior behaviour. This does not simply imply submitting to a changeless tradition, but rather to embrace the resources offered by a complex and sophisticated set of past practices, so that there is some possibility of innovation, as well as of maintaining the status quo.

However, although provocative and stimulating, since they effectively criticize an influential modern method of conceptualizing practices in general, and of understanding modern politics in particular, 'Rationalism in Politics' and the other essays written around the same time — such as 'Political Education' and 'The Tower of Babel' — do not really provide an answer to the question of how human agents *should* behave. Rather, all they do is to point out that political actors are necessarily conditioned by the tradition within which they are performing, rather than to judge particular types of political behaviour as good or bad. Thus from the mid-1950s at the latest, Oakeshott begins to reformulate his position. Instead of conceptualizing tradition purely philosophically, as an inescapable background condition that inevitably affects the way in which agents act in practice, Oakeshott shifts to analysing tradition in more genuinely historical terms. So in such works as 'The Masses in Representative Democracy' (1957), the Harvard lectures *Morality and Politics in Modern Europe* (Oakeshott 1958) and ultimately the third essay in *On Human Conduct*, Oakeshott seeks to identify the most important trend in the Western European tradition, arguing that this consists of the gradual emergence of individualism in theory and practice from the twelfth and thirteenth centuries onwards, and the concomitant loosening of the communal ties and self-identifications of the medieval period. For, due to the advent of the phenomenon of privacy above all, he argues, modern individuals are presented with an unprecedented opportunity to develop and explore their own differing tastes and inclinations, and — with some exceptions — gradually come to value this opportunity as 'the main ingredient of "happiness"' (Oakeshott, 1991, pp. 365-7). Crucially, Oakeshott maintains, such a development as a whole is not something that should be regarded as something negative, or at best ambivalent, but rather as highly positive, as the most crucial practical development in the modern era. As such, this not only gives Oakeshott a more genuinely normative, practical reason to object to rationalism in politics — namely that rationalistic principles and ideologies will necessarily fail to respect such a diverse set of individuals—but also offers him the opportunity to recommend the form of state which he believes can best respect such a pluralistic diversity, and he begins to attempt this in 'On Being Conservative' (1956) (Oakeshott, 1991, pp. 407-37). To do this, he believes, one must have a government which is genuinely 'sovereign'— in other words one powerful enough to be able to overcome 'the communal pressures of family and guild, of church and local community' (Oakeshott, 1991, p. 368)—and hence be able to enforce its laws successfully. But it must also be a government which not only accepts that individuals must not be artificially dragooned together in pursuit of a single predetermined end, but also one which operates according to 'the rule of law', whereby individuals are all equally subject to the same known laws (Oakeshott, 1991, p. 369). Oakeshott did not proceed beyond these points in the 1960s, however, and only gave a more detailed account of what such a state would look like in the second essay of *On Human Conduct*, entitled 'The Civil Condition'.

To understand precisely how Oakeshott thought that the high degree of diversity amongst modern individuals could best be respected in the context of the modern state, therefore, we need to examine this essay, since this is where Oakeshott seeks to delineate how such a state, which he labels 'civil association', can best be organized. For if it is clear that he regards such a state as an ideal-type, as something that can never be fully realized in practice—since it will always have to be partially organized around certain common goals— nevertheless it is equally clear that Oakeshott wants the state to conform to this model, as far as is practically possible. Vital to such a form of association is, as he established in his earlier work, that it is not organized around the pursuance of any one particular end, unlike its analytical opposite, namely 'enterprise association', but beyond this, Oakeshott also seeks to specify various important features which are key to its constitution.

To do this, Oakeshott first seeks to argue that a crucial *part* of understanding the way in which individual agents should be related to one another in a 'civil association' is that they are related purely practically, as heirs to a tradition which qualifies the ways in which they act, but does not specify how they should do so. In contrast to an 'enterprise association' therefore, citizens' courses of action are not specified by the government, in order to achieve a particular end, but are the result of previous (and diverse) traditions of behaviour. He is thus true to his earlier contention that tradition is an inescapable part of how human agents act freely. But he also goes beyond this argument in explicitly delineating what the nature of rules in a civil association should be, both formally and substantively. Essentially he thinks they have three key features. First, he argues that rules must be distinguished from pieces of advice, since they are not to be evaluated in terms of their desirability, but rather are intrinsically authoritative in nature. To be so, Oakeshott specifies, they must not be arbitrary, secret, retroactive or in hock to special interests—and more widely that judicial proceedings must be independent and that there must be no penalties without specific offences (Oakeshott, 1975, p. 153 n.1). Second, specifically to distinguish rules from commands, which demand the performance of a particular action from an assignable agent on an individual basis, Oakeshott stresses that rules must be general and abstract in nature. Thus a rule cannot be 'used up' in any one case, Oakeshott maintains, but instead must not only exist in advance of any particular situation, but also 'remains "standing" for unknown future occasions' (Oakeshott, 1975, p. 127). Third, however, it is also important that rules do not prescribe particular courses of action in detail (Oakeshott, 1975, p. 129). Rather, Oakeshott maintains, what rules do is to qualify citizens' actions 'adverbially'—so that, for example, it is not illegal to light a fire, but it *is* illegal to light one 'arsonically' (see Oakeshott, 1975, p. 58 n.1). And thus to obey a rule is necessarily to engage in an act of interpretation, not to perform a particular action, Oakeshott insists—so that, if properly constituted, a system of rules can never be a threat to individual freedom, since it neither requires individuals to perform particular actions, nor forbids them from doing so, but merely qualifies adverbially the actions that citizens choose to perform.

Rather than simply advocating an adherence to tradition, therefore, Oakeshott's mature political philosophy in fact recommends a certain type of pluralist individualism, and provides details of the kind of state that he believes can best safeguard this. And in an effort to making his argument as clear as possible, Oakeshott devoted considerable effort to the task of developing a new and precise analytic vocabulary to describe social and political arrangements and activities, including not only 'civil' and 'enterprise' association, but also terms such as 'lex', 'respublica' and 'self-disclosure' and 'self-enactment'. Given Oakeshott's efforts, however, this raises the obvious question of whether it is worth using complex and contested terms, such as 'conservative' and 'liberal' to describe Oakeshott's work at all. This argument has been most effectively made by Terry Nardin, who has been at the forefront of arguing that Oakeshott should be treated seriously as a philosopher, rather than simply an ideologue, and it is obviously an important one in this context, since, if accepted, it would render the description of Oakeshott as a 'conservative' analytically superfluous. For Nardin, the key to understanding Oakeshott's work is to appreciate that it rests, above all, on the idea of *modality* — in other words upon the argument that Oakeshott makes from *Experience and its Modes* onwards that when one attempts to understand human activities and their intellectual products, the most advanced ways of doing so (short of philosophizing) are not only distinct, but also irreducible to one another (Nardin, 2015, pp. 24-6). (For Oakeshott, in other words, each of the genuinely developed modes is a self-subsistent world of ideas which provides its own criteria of factuality, truth and reality.) And in a political context, Nardin argues, Oakeshott uses this method to develop his two modal ideal-types, namely 'civil association' and 'enterprise association', which, as we have already seen, Oakeshott believes are the best means to understand the nature of the modern state. Being ideal-types, neither is found in its pure form in reality, but nevertheless the closer a state is to 'civil association', the freer the citizens of that state will be.

Nardin argues that such an analysis of the state, of 'civil' and 'enterprise' association, is more penetrating than those that persist in using such contested terms as 'liberal' and 'conservative', and as such, we should take seriously Oakeshott's desire to replace these older terms with the terminology that he painstakingly developed during his career (Nardin, 2015, pp. 23-4). For although 'civil' and 'enterprise' associations are ideal-types, they are nevertheless derived from a careful reading of modern Western European history, and, he argues, following Oakeshott, they represent the most revealing way of viewing the development of the modern nation state. Such an analysis clearly has considerable force, not least because it takes seriously Oakeshott's own intentions in developing such a vocabulary. Furthermore, it must certainly be conceded, as Nardin argues, that some attempts at diagnosing Oakeshott's political thought as being either 'conservative' or 'liberal' end up being far too reductive, since they end up attempting trying to explain Oakeshott's arguments purely with reference to the Cold War context in which Oakeshott was writing, rather than accepting that Oakeshott's political philosophy might have any separate validity (Villa, 2012, pp. 320-30). Nevertheless, there are several reasons to suggest that there may still be considerable mileage in trying to diagnose whether Oakeshott is a 'conservative' or not. First, even Oakeshott himself maintains that tracing the development, historically, of a complex and contested practice is a legitimate historical engagement, even though he has a preference for understanding past human conduct as the result of contingent, but intelligent, responses by individual agents to one another (see Oakeshott, 1975, p. 100 n.1). So even for Oakeshott himself the historical investigation of a political ideology appears to be a possible engagement, so that the labelling of past thinkers as 'conservative' or 'liberal' cannot be rejected out of hand, even if he believes that the use of his own ideal-types offers greater precision; indeed Oakeshott himself discussed the history of liberalism at various points in his work, and wrote an essay 'On Being Conservative'.

Second, more concretely, whilst it is true that the ideal-types of 'civil' and 'enterprise' association that Oakeshott created have considerable explanatory power, it is worth querying whether they are so uniquely penetrating that they render more traditional concepts such as 'conservative' and 'liberal' redundant even when analysing the development of the Western European nation-state, let alone the nature of Western political thought more generally. Certainly it can be argued that Oakeshott's analysis of the modern Western European state represents an improvement on a number of other influential postwar thinkers, such as Isaiah Berlin and Karl Popper, since his conception of 'civil' and 'enterprise' association allows for an analysis of freedom that goes beyond simply thinking of every intervention of the state as impinging on citizens' freedom. Rather than simply separating modern states in terms of their degree of intervention, in other words, as arguably Berlin and Popper do, Oakeshott's distinction between 'civil' and 'enterprise' association provides a more sophisticated method of distinguishing between those states which allow citizens a genuine and sustainable ability to pursue their own life-plans, and those which do not (see O'Sullivan, 1999).

However, the abstract nature of Oakeshott's concepts also means that they have their limitations. At the very least it seems plausible to maintain that historians and political theorists might need alternative 'ideal-types' if they are seeking to analyse certain political phenomena successfully — so that if attempting to examine the rise of Hitler or contemporary right-wing populists, such as Nigel Farage or Marine Le Pen, they might well need to have recourse to Max Weber's famous concept of 'charismatic authority', rather than 'civil' and 'enterprise' association, or reach for Hannah Arendt's famous concept of spontaneous political 'action' when seeking insights into the 'Velvet Revolution' in 1989 or the 2011 'Arab Spring' (Weber, 2009, pp. 245–53; Arendt, 1958, pp. 175–247). Even if the political theorist or historian of political thought confines their field of investigation to the question of the history of the state, or the different types of legitimate rule, in other words, it may well be that they need more concepts other than simply 'civil' and 'enterprise' association to analyse these successfully. But more fundamentally, too, the use of ideal-types in general arguably fails to capture the more historical and diachronic aspects of political phenomena, since they are, almost by definition, abstractions from concrete historical reality. Even if they are constructed so as to be empirically corrigible and adaptable, in other words, as certainly one of their main advocates Max Weber intended them to be, nevertheless the abstract nature of such concepts mean that they struggle to capture the more dynamic and adaptable aspects of political life. So although Oakeshott devotes considerable time, particularly in the third part of *On Human Conduct*, to constructing histories of *societas* and *universitas*, of civil and enterprise association, these remain, ultimately, somewhat abstract in nature—a legitimate but limited historical inquiry which seeks to identify how particular features of the ideal-types came to prominence. By contrast, using terms such as 'conservative' and 'liberal' allows the theorist to chart and diagnose the more historically mutable and dynamic aspects of a theorist's thought, so that, for example, they can examine a theorist's attitude to historical change. The aim here is not so much the pure conceptual analysis facilitated by ideal-types, but rather an *ideological* analysis—in other words one that embraces the interrelationship of theory and practice within an ideology as something to be investigated, rather than necessarily an analytic weakness, and one that pays due weight to the importance of context without, however, reducing all arguments to it. To quote Michael Freeden, probably the pre-eminent theorist in favour of taking political ideologies seriously, as opposed to viewing them as merely inferior versions of more analytically precise political philosophies, such an analysis 'entails superimposing diachronic on synchronic analysis and multiple synchrony on the examination of a single system, as well as appreciating that political concepts combine the contingent and the quasi-contingent' (Freeden, 1996, p. 5). Whilst there may well be a case, in some cases, for arguing that Oakeshott's own ideal-types provide a degree of clarity that more traditional terms cannot, particularly when one is undertaking a purely synchronic, conceptual analysis, therefore, it is much less clear that such ideal-types render terms such as 'conservative' and 'liberal' more redundant, particularly when one seeks to undertake an analysis that seeks to examine the ideological position of a theorist (in a full scale, non-pejorative sense of the word).

Third, then, if it is indeed reasonable to ask about the nature of Oakeshott's ideological position, rather than confining ourselves to using his own ideal-typical terminology, the next major question concerns how Oakeshott should be described, in ideological terms— namely, as 'conservative' or 'liberal'. This question has caused considerable controversy amongst Oakeshott commentators, with influential scholars such as Efraim Podoksik and Paul Franco arguing that Oakeshott is best viewed as a liberal, while others, such as Roy Tseng and Michael Freeden, claim he is much better labelled as a conservative

(Podoksik, 2003, pp. 158–80; Franco, 2004, pp. 172–82; Tseng, 2003; Freeden, 1996, pp. 320–8). Resolving the issue is not easy, since it requires us to provide definitions of each of these ideologies, and both 'liberalism' and 'conservatism' not only have multiple variants but also have significantly altered over time. We will therefore briefly consider the nature of liberalism and conservatism as they have evolved since the nineteenth century, before examining how best to classify Oakeshott's position.

Taking liberalism first, then, it seems reasonably uncontroversial to claim that, despite some important precursors, the ideology arose due to significant new demands for individual freedom in the late eighteenth century, partly due to important philosophical innovations connected with the Enlightenment, and partly stimulated by significant social and political changes that took their most dramatic form in the French Revolution. And more specifically, it seems reasonable to claim that liberals have tended to advocate five fundamental normative goals to increase such freedom, particularly in the nineteenth century. First, they have tended to favour greater political liberty, on the basis that mankind in general has a broadly equal potential to reason, rather than being naturally hierarchical. Second, they have also tended to stress the beneficial effects that the free use of this reason would lead to, arguing that greater liberty would lead to greater progress. Third, this claim about progress has often (if not exclusively) been linked to the contention that only government by a nation-state could ensure prosperity and freedom, thus providing liberals with a specific normative goal in the political sphere. Fourth, liberals have tended to stress the importance of individuals having economic freedom, instead of labouring under 'artificial' constraints of governmental regulation and monopolies, on the basis that this would aid the prosperity of society as a whole, while finally they have also tended to have great respect for property rights and property laws, since these are not only necessary to maintain basic order and security with a given state, but also to ensure that individuals are able to have the means to express their personalities on a concrete basis within the state. It is true that, in the twentieth century, the nature of liberalism tended to alter somewhat, in response to fighting two world wars, and to the growth of an increased moral pluralism, with the result that arguably three new types of the ideology appeared.

In the first place, thinkers such as L.T. Hobhouse and J.A. Hobson responded to an increasingly industrialized and commercial society by arguing that the liberals' traditional suspicion of state intervention in the economy should be revised, since socio-economic pressures posed more of a threat to liberty than had previously been admitted. And in view of this, they argued, the state should provide a far greater level of public services as well as intervening in the economy in order to ensure an individual's right to work (Hobhouse, 1911, p. 163). Second, however, less positively, other liberals, such as Isaiah Berlin, Karl Popper and Raymond Aron, argued that the key fact about modern life in Western Europe was not simply the new socio-economic challenges associated with industrialization, but the advent of the phenomenon of unbridgeable moral pluralism—in other words the appearance of what Max Weber famously called 'irreducibly competing ideals' (Weber, 1949, p. 57). As such, for such thinkers, often labelled the 'Cold War liberals', the way to maximize individual citizens' liberty could not be to use the state to increase the freedom of individuals in society—since their moral perspectives were far too diverse for the state to accomplish this with any certainty, and in any case they generally tended to be suspicious of the state's bureaucratic tendencies. At best, they maintained, in the absence of one indubitable set of values, one could aim, on a negative utilitarian basis, to reduce pain within society by respecting and upholding the rights of individual citizens, which (they argued) could best be served by having a responsible and well-educated civil service, and a moderate and open political culture—although they tended to be wary of providing detailed institutional prescriptions for how to do this (see Muller, 2008, pp. 53-5). Third, finally, more recently other thinkers have sought to overcome the moral pluralism associated with modernity far more ambitiously, using various philosophical devices to try and derive a normative commitment to prioritize the value of individual liberty—not as a 'least worst' option, but rather as a positive good (Rawls, 1971, p. 5). The most famous thinker to do this was John Rawls, who argued in his early work that by inviting human beings to imagine themselves behind a 'veil of ignorance', before they knew their position in society, one could deduce that they would favour both individual liberty and an important measure of equality—but there have been many other examples of such 'philosophical liberals' (as they have been dubbed) who have been committed to finding some universalist position, however modest, that is able to conquer the problem of modern pluralism (see Raz, 1986). In all cases, however, what unites all these thinkers as 'liberals' is that they believe strongly in a commitment to maximize individual liberty, and believe that this belief can be effectively justified by reason.

If liberalism, despite all of its variations, has always represented a relatively coherent ideology, by contrast conservatism has always been a much looser construction that has included a wider range of positions within it—especially after the middle of the nineteenth century. Like liberalism, conservatism arguably also arose in reaction to the social and political changes that had taken place in the eighteenth century, most notably industrialization, and the French Revolution—although there were, again, some important precursors. Initially, conservatives took aim at a variety of Enlightenment assumptions—including, variously, its claim that all men had more or less equal powers of reasoning, its scepticism about religious belief and its demands for greater political and economic freedom from the state. Whilst it was true that, even in the nineteenth century, virtually no conservative thinkers thought it was feasible to dispense with the whole of the Enlightenment heritage entirely (either intellectually or in practice), they nevertheless rejected enough to stake out a position that was distinctively different from liberalism. Thus, just to give one example, Edmund Burke, arguably the first distinctive conservative theorist, emphasized the extent to which societies were composed organically and were reliant on tradition so that any attempt to redesign them consciously was likely to fail; he argued that modern commercial freedoms were dependent on pre-modern traditions, rather than being independent of them, as liberals maintained (Burke, 1826, p. 155). Thus the pursuit of individual freedom was to be rejected (or at least subordinated) in favour of other goals, namely, promoting religious belief, traditional, social and political hierarchies—or more generally the nation-state in general, which it was essential (they believed) to conceptualize in organic rather than individualistic terms.

This, then, was the initial form that conservatism took. Again, like liberalism, although it did not alter completely in response to industrialization and the growth of the state in the nineteenth century, it was nevertheless forced to adapt in response to these pressures. Some conservative thinkers reacted very radically, taking such developments as a sign that not merely should one reject liberal arguments, but modernity as a whole. Thus, just to take one example, Thomas Carlyle argued romantically against industrialization and representative government, instead seeking—in such works as *Heroes and Hero-Worship* and the *Latter-Day Pamphlets*—to uphold the virtues of religion and heroic despotism (Carlyle, 1993; 1983). In general, however, the reactions were more moderate, and centred on upholding two commitments in particular. In the first place, conservatives continued to stress that the nation-state had conceptual priority over the individual, arguing that this should be the fundamental unit to which citizens should have allegiance—and often, in the late nineteenth century, buttressed this argument with support from social Darwinism, in, just to name two examples, the work of Benjamin Kidd and Heinrich von Treitschke (Kidd, 1894; Treitschke, 1915–19). Secondly, however, other conservatives sought to colonize territory vacated by the type of liberal thinkers who were becoming more willing to countenance state intervention, upholding the importance of freedom from the state, defending commerce from government intervention and (more often than not) advocating *laissez-faire*. Thus a number of former liberal thinkers such as Herbert Spencer became increasingly difficult to distinguish from conservatives like Lord Hugh Cecil by the end of the nineteenth century, despite some residual differences over issues like imperialism and franchise reform (Spencer, 1909, p. 87). And most of these forms of conservatism can also be found after 1945, although inevitably the impact of two world wars and the growth of the state inevitably had an impact. Thus, first, some postwar conservative thinkers continued to be critical of the Enlightenment, or even of the entire Western tradition. Most notably, Leo Strauss, in *Natural Right and History* and elsewhere, argued that Western political thinking since the Greek *polis* had been a story of decline, since political thinkers had increasingly rejected natural law, and, particularly since the Enlightenment, had tended to advocate an instrumental value-free political science instead (Strauss, 1953). Second, more moderately, others, such as Hans-Georg Gadamer, tended to uphold the continuing dialogue with the norms of an unbroken Western tradition, despite the trauma of totalitarianism, even if he was critical of the more instrumentalizing effects of the Enlightenment (Gadamer, 1989, pp. 360-1; Neill, 2014, pp. 433-5). Third, in response to the horrors of the Holocaust, and the perceived failures of legal positivism in the Weimar Republic to protect fundamental human rights, a number of conservative thinkers, including some as varied as Quintin Hogg and Jacques Maritain argued in favour of natural rights, linking the legitimacy of laws passed by the state to how closely they conformed to such rights (Hogg, 1947, pp. 70-5; Maritain, 1944). Finally, some conservatives, following the path established by Spencer and Cecil, sought to colonize territory vacated by liberals, arguing against any further interventions by the state—although they often combined this with a strong commitment to nationalism, as in the case of Margaret Thatcher (Gamble, 1994). Despite its many variations, therefore, conservatives have tended to lay more weight than liberalism on allegiances that go beyond the individual, whether these were to tradition, to the nation, to religion—and conversely have tended to be more sceptical about the possibility of rational progress.

How should Oakeshott's position be classified, then, according to this scheme? At first sight, there seems to be a good case to classify Oakeshott as a liberal, since he is highly committed to individual freedom. Clearly Oakeshott cannot be identified as a philosophical liberal like Rawls, because he does not believe that the problem of modern pluralism can be overcome philosophically, on a universal moral basis. (Because Oakeshott does not believe that moral norms can be self-consciously harmonized with one another, in other words, it would be fruitless to try and establish any kind of philosophical consensus on the moral ends of the state.) But given his acceptance of such pluralism, and his concern about the state imposing one particular vision upon a highly disparate set of individual citizens, Oakeshott certainly exhibits some similarities with the Cold War liberals such as Berlin, Aron and Popper—even if he laid a stronger emphasis than they did on the importance of political institutions in protecting their liberties. Beyond this, more substantively, some Oakeshott commentators, and notably Paul Franco, have argued that what Oakeshott does in his work is to 'purge' liberalism of its foreign elements, bestowing a new coherence upon the ideology by refocusing it on individual liberty (Franco, 1990, pp. 9, 159–60, 231). Thus, rather than muddling up liberalism with the possibility of progress (like most nineteenth-century liberals) or with the pursuance of socio-economic equality (like the New Liberals) or with the aim of economic productivity (as even a libertarian thinker such as F.A. Hayek is wont to do), Franco argues that what Oakeshott does is to concentrate on the core of liberalism, at least as it has evolved in the twentieth century—namely accepting that individuals are genuinely different from one another, providing a state with laws that cater for this and mechanisms for upholding individuals' private property and the free market so that they can express their individuality properly. And his case has been reinforced by Efraim Podoksik, who stresses the degree to which Oakeshott thinks individual citizens can *enjoy* their freedom—at least if they are capable of adapting to the demands of modernity (Podoksik, 2003, pp. 166–8). For if Oakeshott has no belief in human progress in the way that, for example, J.S. Mill had, then nevertheless, Podoksik argues, it is vital to realize that Oakeshott's arguments for 'civil association' are not simply based upon epistemological scepticism, but are also, more positively, based upon the demand by individuals for a state in which they can truly express themselves. If there is no room in Oakeshott's vision for Mill's argument that wide latitude for eccentricity is necessary for social development, in other words, then such eccentricity and individuality is still valuable in itself—only in such a way can the plurality of individual experience be respected.

However, there are several problems with these arguments, which suggest that Oakeshott's position is, on balance, better described as 'conservative', rather than as 'liberal'. Certainly it is difficult to associate him with some of the more radical forms of conservatism. Thus, except in a few of his middle-period essays, such as 'Rationalism in Politics', he appears to have few queries about the worth of the Enlightenment, and is instead a strong supporter of modernity, both philosophically and in practice. Furthermore, despite a brief flirtation with rejecting the Western tradition as a whole in 'The Tower of Babel' (Oakeshott, 1991, pp. 465–87), still less can Oakeshott be identified as a conservative like Leo Strauss, since he is adamant that upholding the best aspects of the Western tradition is vital if we are to achieve genuine freedom. And unlike many postwar European conservatives, such as Quintin Hogg and Jacques Maritain, who reacted to the horrors of Nazi Germany and totalitarianism more generally by developing arguments which claimed that legitimacy had to be based upon natural law, Oakeshott rejected this proposition, arguing that natural laws can only ever be regarded as abstract norms, ultimately derived from tradition. What, then, marks Oakeshott's work out as that of a moderate 'conservative' rather than of a 'liberal'?

Essentially, there are four reasons. First, Oakeshott's attitude to historical change is highly cautious, even agoraphobic. This is not merely a question of personal preference, but based upon a highly sceptical attitude about the degree to which we can know the nature of the actions of other human agents—both in the past and the present. Thus not only does he write approvingly in 'On Being Conservative' of an attitude which favours 'present laughter over utopian bliss' (Oakeshott, 1991, p. 408) but also, in *On History* and *On Human Conduct*, stresses the difficulty of understanding the actions of historical actors, since the evidence they leave is as complex and enigmatic as 'footprints left behind by agents responding to their emergent situations', and emphasizes the difficulty of understanding others' conduct, given how tricky it is to interpret the motives and sentiments in which they perform their actions (Oakeshott, 1975, pp. 100, 77). As such, although Oakeshott does not think we are reliant on pre-Enlightenment norms in the same way that Burke does, nevertheless the difficulty of knowing the nature of others' conduct should incline us, he believes, to have considerable respect for the traditional norms that we have inherited — an attitude that is typical of a conservative, rather than of a progressive liberal. Second, on a related point, although just like a liberal thinker Oakeshott constantly upholds the importance of individual liberty, ultimately this is something that he does on the basis that it is an important value that has been bequeathed to us by tradition. Rather than claiming that liberty should be valued because we have a fundamental right to it as human beings, or because it enables us to develop our abilities to the full, its value ultimately remains related to the tradition into which we have been socialized. Although Podoksik is undoubtedly right to suggest that Oakeshott intends us to enjoy the individualism that has fortunately developed in modernity, therefore, ultimately this is something that must be put down to good fortune — unlike most liberal thinkers, Oakeshott has no rational justification for the individualism that has appeared in modernity. And such a position is conservative and not merely 'sceptical' or 'anti-foundational', since Oakeshott does not merely claim that his commitment to liberty is based upon a simple scepticism of the powers of reason, but rather that we are the fortunate heirs of generations of gradually gained liberties, which we should seek to maintain.

Third, following on from this, although Oakeshott is in general highly supportive of pluralism, the way he sets the limits to it are much more typical of a conservative than a liberal. Thus rather than claiming, like Mill, that the state should interfere with individuals' conduct if and only if they are doing harm to others, or, like Hayek, to prevent intentionally designed infractions to a citizen's liberty — so that, for example, a citizen should be protected against the activities of thieves, but not against those of extreme imbalances in the market (Hayek, 1978, p. 19) — Oakeshott's position is different. Instead, Oakeshott argues that the limits of pluralism are ultimately established by tradition, and, as such, that there must always be some link, although a loose one, between the legitimacy of laws and the moral norms of a society. And finally, although he is rarely explicit about it, there is a much stronger sense in Oakeshott's work than one would expect from a late twentieth-century liberal of the value of the nation-state, and beyond this of the importance of patriotism. Thus the 'tradition' Oakeshott values is primarily a national, rather than an international, one. This strongly contrasts with the anti-nationalist views of most of the Cold War liberals, due to the experiences of World War Two, and indeed of Hayek, who was a strong supporter of some form of European Union.

If Oakeshott is hardly an uncritical traditionalist in the way that used to be claimed, therefore, there is nevertheless still ample reason to label him a conservative. As we saw, simply eschewing ideological terminology altogether, and attempting to use Oakeshott's own ideal-typical vocabulary as a replacement, fails to capture the more diachronic aspects of his thought properly. And attempts at identifying him as a liberal, on the basis of his commitment to individual liberty, underplay Oakeshott's cautious approach to historical change, the traditionalist way in which he justifies individual freedom, the traditionalist way in which he sets the limits to pluralism, and his cautious commitment to patriotism. So Oakeshott should not be identified as a liberal thinker; rather, he is a moderate conservative one.

References

Arendt, H. (1958) *The Human Condition*, Chicago, IL: University of Chicago Press.

Benn, S.I. & Peters, R.S. (1959) *Social Principles and the Democratic State*, London: Allen and Unwin.

Burke, E. (1826) *The Works of the Rt. Hon. Edmund Burke*, London: Printed for C. and J. Rivington, St Paul's Church-Yard and Waterloo-Place, Pall-Mall.

Carlyle, T. (1983) *Latter-Day Pamphlets*, Goldberg, M.K. & Seigel, J.P. (eds.), Port Credit, Ontario: Canadian Federation for the Humanities.

Carlyle, T. (1993) *Heroes and Hero Worship*, Goldberg, M.K., Brattin, J.J. & Engel, M. (eds.), Berkeley, CA: University of California Press.

Franco, P. (1990) *The Political Philosophy of Michael Oakeshott*, New Haven, CT: Yale University Press.

Franco, P. (2004) *Michael Oakeshott: An Introduction*, New Haven, CT: Yale University Press.

Freeden, M. (1996) *Ideologies and Political Theory: A Conceptual Approach*, Oxford: Clarendon Press.

Gadamer, H.-G.(1989) *Truth and Method*, Weinsheimer, J. & Marshall, D.G. (eds. & trans.), London: Sheed and Ward.

Gamble, A. (1994) *The Free Economy and the Strong State*, 2nd ed., Basingstoke: Macmillan.

Hayek, F.A. (1978) *New Studies in Philosophy, Politics, Economics and the History of Ideas*, London: Routledge and Keegan Paul.

Hobhouse, L.T. (1911) *Liberalism*, London: Williams and Norgate.

Hogg, Q. (1947) *The Case for Conservatism*, West Drayton: Penguin.

Kidd, B. (1894) *Social Evolution*, London: Macmillan and Company.

Maritain, J. (1944) *The Rights of Man and Natural Law*, London: Bles.

Muller, J.-W. (2008) Fear and freedom: On 'Cold War Liberalism', *European Journal of Political Theory*, **7** (1), pp. 45–64.

Nardin, T. (2015) Michael Oakeshott: Neither liberal nor conservative, in Nardin, T. (ed.) *Michael Oakeshott's Cold War Liberalism*, New York: Palgrave Macmillan.

Neill, E. (2014) Michael Oakeshott and Hans-Georg Gadamer on practices, social science, and modernity, *History of European Ideas*, **40** (3), pp. 406–436.

Oakeshott, M. (1975) *On Human Conduct*, Oxford: Clarendon Press.

Oakeshott, M. (1991) *Rationalism in Politics and Other Essays*, 2nd rev. ed. Fuller, T. (ed.), Indianapolis, IN: Liberty Fund.

Oakeshott, M. (1993) *Morality and Politics in Modern Europe*, Letwin, S.R. (ed.), New Haven, CT: Yale University Press.

O'Sullivan, N. (1999) Visions of freedom: The response to totalitarianism, in Hayward, J., Barry, B. & Brown, A. (eds.) *The British Study of Politics in the Twentieth Century*, Oxford: British Academy.

Podoksik, E. (2003) *In Defence of Modernity: Vision and Philosophy in Michael Oakeshott*, Exeter: Imprint Academic.

Rawls, J. (1971) *A Theory of Justice*, Oxford: Oxford University Press.

Raz, J. (1986) *The Morality of Freedom*, Oxford: Clarendon Press.

Spencer, H. (1909) *The Man Versus the State*, London: Watts.

Strauss, L. (1953) *Natural Right and History*, Chicago, IL: University of Chicago Press.

Treitschke, H. (1915-19) *Treitschke's History of Germany in the Nineteenth Century*, Paul, E., Paul, C. & Dawson, W.H. (eds. & trans.), London: Allen and Unwin.

Tseng, R. (2003) *The Sceptical Idealist: Michael Oakeshott as a Critic of Enlightenment*, Exeter: Imprint Academic.

Villa, D. (2012) Oakeshott and the Cold War critique of political rationalism, in Podoksik, E. (ed.) *The Cambridge Companion to Oakeshott*, Cambridge: Cambridge University Press.

Weber, M. (1949) *The Methodology of the Social Sciences*, Shils, E. & Finch, H.A. (eds. & trans.), Glencoe, IL: Free Press.

Weber, M. (2009) *From Max Weber: Essays in Sociology*, Gerth, H., Wright Mills, C. & Turner, B.S. (eds.), New York: Routledge.

David Boucher

The Depoliticization of Politics
Crisis and Critique in Oakeshott, Schmitt and Koselleck

Introduction

This chapter compares the ideas of Michael Oakeshott with those of Carl Schmitt and his disciple Reinhart Koselleck on the neutralization and depoliticization of contemporary politics. By which they referred to the deliberate subversion of the political by the social, cultural and moral, curtailing the ability of the sovereign to act decisively (Schmitt, 2007, pp. 80–96; Koselleck, 1988). For Oakeshott, depoliticization takes the form of conceiving the state, not as a civil association to be governed, but as an enterprise to be managed (Oakeshott, 1975a, pp. 203–6 and 214–16). For all three the degenerative process had its roots in the Enlightenment, accelerated by the proliferation of utopian, or rationalist, ideologies, rendering rule, or governance, ineffective and corrupted. The common assumption they make is that the constitution of a government, such as monarchy, aristocracy or liberal democracy, or the binary division between despotism and republicanism, had to be distinguished from the offices of governing and the mode of association, that is, the bond by which citizens or subjects believed themselves to be associated.

At the level of mere resemblance there are certainly identities between Schmitt, Koselleck and Oakeshott, which have led interpreters, such as Duncan Bell, to claim very close affinities between them (2015, pp. 185–213). It is in terms of the mode of association, however, that we may fundamentally deny a common identity between Schmitt and Koselleck, on the one hand, and Oakeshott on the other. For both Schmitt and Koselleck it is the obedience/protection nexus that provides the bond of association. Authority is dependent upon and inextricable from power. Obligation is dependent on power. The power of the sovereign is imperative, and threats to this power constitute for them the crisis of civilization. Power and the political is eroded by the substitution of the rule of law for the rule of man. For Oakeshott power and authority are categorially distinct and obligation rests not on the expectation of protection, but upon the common acknowledgement of the authority of a system of law, that is, the idea of the rule of law, which does not specify substantive conduct, nor require approval of the substantive conditions it prescribes, but instead specifies the relationship which constitutes the bond between citizens.

Ideal-Types and History

Each takes a present condition to be indicative of a corruption of consciousness, the culmination of misunderstandings, misinterpretations, misappropriations and almost negligent optimism, the result of an irrational, or 'rationalist', obsession with progress, which has its origins in the seventeenth century.

Schmitt, Koselleck and Oakeshott may not, however, be accused of writing what Herbert Butterfield pejoratively termed 'whig' history, even though what they offer are abridgements, that is, selective readings in which all roads lead to the present. In a review of Butterfield's *The Origin of Modern Science*, Oakeshott criticizes those writers who have 'too often read the story backwards, finding significant in the past only that which led subsequently to positive achievement' (2007, p. 298, and Buttterfield, 1949 and 1965).

All three philosophers rejected the principal assumption of the whig interpretation of history, namely progress, which in Oakeshott's words 'stands for a habit of reading the course of events backwards, and in this manner making history a success story' (2004, p. 220). Schmitt, Koselleck and Oakeshott are, on the contrary, philosophers of crisis and portray history as a series of degenerative ideas and events responsible for the present malaise of politics. The type of 'history' in which they engage is what Schmitt called 'extraordinary history' which he believed was 'written not by the "winners" but by the "vanquished"' (cited in Olsen, 2011, p. 198). They stood as the vanquished against the tide of European history.

They were immersed in the form of inquiry that Ferenc Feher claims was Europe's mainstream political tradition, namely hermeneutics, and whose foremost exponent was Karl Marx. Marx, Feher claims, 'was the ultimate hermeneutician of the European project: with unfailing eye, he re-read all of its texts and found in the "deep texts", the "real meaning" beneath them' (Feher, 1989, p. 82).

Our philosophers of crisis were without doubt immersed in and influenced by continental hermeneutics. Koselleck was personally acquainted with and influenced by Heidegger and Gadamer, but most significantly by Schmitt (Olsen, 2004, pp. 61-4), who had been a student of Heidegger's. Oakeshott certainly studied Heidegger's *Being and Time* (O'Sullivan, 2003, p. 208), but made it clear that, in addition to Aristotle, it was from Hegel and Dilthey he had learnt the most (Oakeshott, 1965, p. 90). While Schmitt, Koselleck and Oakeshott are sensitive to the finer points of hermeneutics, they all nevertheless present us with idealtypes in their characterizations of the past. Max Weber used the term 'ideal-type' not as a normative concept, but instead as a heuristic device to give emphasis to certain characteristics, or collections of occurrences common to most cases of a given entity, in order to construct a coherent whole for explanatory purposes. They refer to worlds of ideas, or mental images that assist us in making sense of what may appear a chaotic coincidence of characteristics (Weber, 1949, p. 173).

Ideal-types denote different entities, such as types of action, and institutions or concepts. He distinguishes authority, for example, into traditional, rational-legal and charismatic ideal-types (Weber, 1970, p. 228; Weber, 1994 and 2004; McCormick, 1997; Waters and Waters, 2015). Schmitt, who was a student of Weber's in Munich explicitly recommends the use of ideal-types as historical devices for making sense of contemporary political and legal theory (Bell, 2015, pp. 191-2; Schmitt, 2011, pp. 122, 183; 2005, pp. 27, 42, 65). Koselleck draws on Schmitt's ideal-type framework at the beginning of *Critique and Crisis* to characterize the development of world history from the French Revolution to the present. Koselleck refers to his theoretical framework as an 'ideal typically constructed context into which detailed events and findings can be put', not merely for historical curiosity, but because the problems raised continue to require answers (Koselleck, 1988, pp. 3-4).

While historical understanding in terms of ideal-types does not meet Oakeshott's exacting standards for historical inquiry as it should be practised (Callahan, 2007, p. 59), he does concede they offer a certain degree of historical intelligibility (Oakeshott, 1983, p. 65). Ideal characters, or types, are aids to reflection, or instruments of inquiry, in discerning, for example, the character of a modern European state, and no 'historic state' will correspond exactly to them because there are always contingent conditions which have to be considered (Oakeshott, 1975a, pp. 192 and 247).

Myth and the Subversion of the Political

For Schmitt, Koselleck and Oakeshott the importance of myth in the self-understanding of a society was an important and imperative counterweight against rationalism, which sought to eradicate and ridicule superstitious beliefs that emerged from what the rationalists believed to be irrational and unreflective habitual practices, based not on reason but prejudice.

Each understood the power of myth in the formation of social self-identity. Each people creates its own stories, legends or myths about how it came into existence; and how it came to acquire its shared values and ideals. Such stories rarely have a solid foundation in fact, nor do they have the veracity to be submitted to historical verification, because they acquire characters of transhistorical importance in building social cohesion. Schmitt, for example, praises the irrationalism of myths because of their intellectual power to sustain our political practices and institutions. Myth, which need not conform to 'reality', generates the vital strength to foster national enthusiasm, legitimize great causes, and harness the energy of a nation to achieve heroic heights (Schmitt, 1988, p. 75; Oakeshott, 2006; 2008, O'Sullivan's Introduction, p. 26; Frohnen, 1990, pp. 789–809; Boucher, 2015, pp. 123–52; Riendeau, 2014). Koselleck is clear that, for him, myth is an imperative component in ensuring that the political retains and maintains its character, and which does not allow a private realm of morality to flourish and stand in judgement of it (Hoffman, 2006, p. 475; Koselleck, 2004, pp. 255–76; Oakeshott, 2004, pp. 245–54).

However, in the view of Schmitt, Koselleck and Oakeshott, the critics of the Enlightenment and their followers among the *Illuminati* misguidedly attacked the very foundations of knowledge, and, instead of dispelling our civilizational myths, were the purveyors of counterfeit myths. Counterfeit myths, Oakeshott argues, are enemies of civilization (Oakeshott, 1975b, p. 153). The proliferation of such myths serves to destroy the solidarity of a community: 'The last remnants of solidarity and a feeling of belonging together will be destroyed in the pluralism of an unforeseeable number of myths' (Schmitt, 1988, p. 76), perpetrated on the world by utopian rationalists.

Schmitt, Koselleck and Oakeshott share a common endeavour to expose and articulate the counterfeit myths that threaten the 'genuine' civilizational myths. The site on which the struggle for ascendancy takes place is the modern European state, which for all three has become transformed by the encroachment upon, or importation into, its values, ideas and practices, which are alien to its 'true' character as state. The competition for ascendancy, between the genuine and the counterfeit, constitutes the crisis that each, in their different ways, try in vain to avert. The crisis may be summarized as the neutralization and depoliticization of the political. Liberal rationalism, the purveyor of utopian dreams, constructed a gulf between the space of experience—

the world as we know it—and the horizon of expectations—the world as we would like it to be.

Schmitt, Koselleck and Oakeshott share the assumption that the state has become perverted by utopian ideologies such as liberalism, socialism and fascism, which project utopian horizons of expectation, or counterfeit myths, disconnected from lived experience, giving rise to exaggerated expectations that overreach the ability of their proponents to deliver them, but which nevertheless generate conflict and crisis in the attempt. Koselleck argues that rationalists consciously separate the 'space of experience and horizon of expectation [making] ... the task of political action to bridge this difference' (Koselleck, 2004, p. 272). The offer of multiple horizons of expectation promises numberless unrealizable utopias, relying on the implementation of political programmes formulated in the French Revolution, and the revolutions of 1848 and beyond. The promise of such utopias has proliferated conflicts, even civil wars, which may directly be related to Enlightenment rationalism (Schmitt, 2005; Oakeshott, 1991; Koselleck, 1988).

The practice of politics and the art of the political constitute a discrete area of activity, requiring distinctive skills and talents, governed by different considerations from those appropriate to other activities. Schmitt, Koselleck and Oakeshott regard the political as a specialist practice, whose practitioners are public servants, politicians and statesman, thoroughly inducted into the political institutions, relying not on abstract theoretical knowledge for an understanding of the limitations and constraints on what may be achieved, but on their practical experience, finely tuned to the intimations indicating a direction of travel. Politics is not the pursuit of utopian dreams, but of intimations that may sometimes be elusive, and subject to 'gross errors of judgment', but far fewer, 'less frequent and less disastrous if we escape the illusion that politics is ever anything more than the pursuit of intimations; a conversation, not an argument' (Oakeshott, 1991, pp. 57–8).

The tragedy for Schmitt, Koselleck and Oakeshott is not in the often irresolvable dilemmas with which we are confronted by politics, but in the belief that emanated from Enlightenment rationalism, or utopianism, bereft of experience, that perfect solutions populate and are achievable within our contemporary horizons of expectation (Koselleck, 2004, pp. 255–75; Oakeshott, 1993, p. 109). While ideologies were all in differing degrees expressions of rationalism, liberalism in particular was the most complete expression of these defects in reasoning (Schmitt, 2007, pp. 69–79; Schmitt, 1988, p. 76; Koselleck, 1988, pp. 5–12; Oakeshott, 1993, pp. 99–100; McIntyre, 2004, pp. 4, 155–7). Rationalism is the manner of reasoning which believes that every problem has a rational solution, and that when based on first principles, unencumbered by tradition or prejudice, we may achieve certainty in politics. The danger of rationalism in politics is that it is a form of depolitization that commits the category error of defying the boundaries of the civil condition in which politics legitimately operates and instead obsesses with planning and instrumental policy-making in the belief that a new Jerusalem may be attained (Oakeshott, 1975a, pp. 183–4). Koselleck disdainfully declares: 'The lesser the experience, the greater the expectation: this is a formula for the temporal structure of the modern, to the degree that it is rendered a concept by "progress"' (Koselleck, 2004, p. 274).

For Schmitt, Koselleck and Oakeshott the Enlightenment gives impetus to the modern attitude to politics that is anti-political in character. Standing in the antechamber, to use a term both Schmitt and Koselleck employ, of the degenerative process, appears the ghostly figure of Descartes. Doubting all things that could be doubted, he reconstructed both science and philosophy as a protest which championed the individual against the oppressive hand of tradition (Sorley, 1926, p. 5). Koselleck argued: 'In the course of unfolding the Cartesian *cogito ergo sum* as the self-guarantee of a man who has dropped out of religious bonds, eschatology recoils into Utopianism. Planning history comes to be just as important as mastering nature' (Koselleck, 1988, p. 11).

The Crisis of Civilization and the Critique of Liberalism

What they found pernicious and contributory to the crisis was, however, quite different. Each explanation was itself a political intervention, a diagnosis, prognosis and remedy. Schmitt, Koselleck and Oakeshott identified trends evident for centuries manifest in modern European history. For all three the crisis was the affliction of liberal democracy and a diffusion and erosion of executive authority. In essence, Schmitt's diagnosis of the crisis afflicting modern society was expressive of his opposition to individualism, liberalism, parliamentarianism, democracy and the rule of law, all of which were the drivers behind the trends culminating in the modern malaise of state power and authority, which for him were indistinguishable. The liberal rule of law was a hindrance to governing. Its basic principle that the individual cannot be controlled, is not itself a form of state or constitution, but instead a mode of association, of which he disapproves because it is a system of restraints designed to tether the state, destructive of the realm of the political because of its hostility to all formative initiatives. Typically, the liberal rule of law is manifest in parliamentary democracies, which are a mixture of forms of constitution, including monarchy and democracy. The sovereign who decides on the exceptional may place law in abeyance, ignore it or eliminate it in an emergency, without undermining the authority of the state. The decision on the exception is not that of the people, but of the ruler, or sovereign. Schmitt's constitutional theory puts the state and the rule of law in confrontation. The rule of law, for him, was in fact anti-political, in that it constrained and undermined the state. The idea of the rule of law was vulnerable to manipulation by parties and groups, as Schmitt claimed it had been in the Weimar Republic (Christi, 1998, pp. 123–5). The unity of the state takes priority over the people who comprise it, in that the president, or sovereign, is almost unconstrained by law.

The triumph of liberalism constituted the demise of the political, that is, the ability decisively to distinguish friends from enemies. It distinguishes politics from ostensibly neutral domains, such as morality in which the key distinction is between 'good and evil'; in aesthetics, 'ugly and beautiful'; and in economics, 'profitable and unprofitable' (Schmitt, 2007, p. 26). Each antithesis belongs to a separate domain and is not reducible to each other. Pluralist doctrines of the state place it on an equal footing with these other entities, diminishing its capacity to act, and eliminating its distinctiveness and power. Schmitt contended: 'the political becomes evident by virtue of its being able to treat, distinguish, and comprehend the friend–enemy antithesis independently of other antitheses' (Schmitt, 2007, p. 27). The other domains may, nevertheless, transform their antitheses into the political if they are a cohesive and strong enough group of people to organize effectively in terms of friends and enemies (Schmitt, 2007, p. 37).

The foundational principles of liberal democracy are the sanctity of the rights of the individual; the separation of powers; the unlimited freedom of the individual; and the constrained power of the state (Schmitt, [1928] 2002a, p. 296). There is an unlimited sphere of opportunities for individuals, and a comprehensive system of checks and balances on the activity of the state. Just as the liberal bourgeoisie is apolitical, the liberal state is anti-political. Because democracy is based on the principle of majority decisions, liberalism is designed to destroy the political decision. The secret ballot itself serves to isolate people from each other, putting decisions in the hands of 'politically irresponsible people' (Schmitt, 2002a, p. 299), invariably leading to the predominance of the politically uninterested over politically responsible. Majority rule minimizes the political decision (Schmitt, 2002a, pp. 296–8). Parliamentary democracy, in Schmitt's view, is not consistent with a political state because of its inability or unwillingness to distinguish between friend and enemy. Every democracy, he argued, needed a homogeneous unified people, because only then could it assume political responsibility. The problem with liberal democracies in general was their heterogeneity. They were socially divided by class, culture, race and religion. Pluralism was the enemy of the state (Schmitt, 2002a, p. 299). What had previously been the neutral domains of religion, culture, education and the economy ceased to be neutral, and in response appeared the 'total state' that embraced them all, resulting in a complete identification between the state and society. Everything is therefore at least potentially political, rendering it impossible to assert for the 'total state' a specifically political character (Schmitt, 2007, pp. 22-3). The universal state, however, is separate from and stands above society (Schmitt, 2007, pp. 22 and 80-96).

Schmitt's answer was for the state, or sovereign, to rescue back the sphere of the political from the forces of depoliticization which neutralized its monopoly of political power. They were to be replaced by authentic democratic constituents of the assembled crowd signifying acceptance or rejection by acclamation. In other words, the manipulation of the masses. Technological advances, such as radio and film, which could be used to manipulate the masses had to be controlled by the state, and political parties had to be banned because they manipulated the rules of liberal democracy to acquire power legally, with a view to denying the same right to other parties (Schmitt, 2004).

For Koselleck, the Age of Enlightenment was indelibly marked by two social structures, the Republic of Letters and the Masonic Lodges. Their legacy from the outset was the attainment of rational understanding cloaked in mystery. The cult of secrecy endemic in the Masonic Lodges generated moral criticism from novel social spheres outside state politics (Koselleck, 1988, p. 62). The allure of the bourgeois lodges consisted not so much in their social equality, but in their freedom from the state. Their internal legitimacy, freedom and independence were premised not on the removal of ecclesiastical authority but on the avoidance of political interference by state power. Protection by the state was replaced by protection from the state. The secrecy and mystery of the lodges had the dual function of rejecting the state and protecting themselves from it (Koselleck, 1988, p. 73). The criticisms, oblivious to the constraints of political conflict, were responsible for the replacement of the political with the moral (Hoffman, 2006, pp. 76-7).

The space of experience, that is, the range of experiences open to us, gives rise to the possibility of differing expectations, which may in certain circumstances encourage the creation of concepts that contain a prognostic potential, and which no longer 'register experience' but instead generate it (Koselleck, 2004, p. 272). Political societies were now subject to appraisal in terms of utopian standards that largely ignore the constraints under which political actors are able to respond to political problems. The moralistic and utopian alternatives offered by modern ideologies are unrealistically speculative and offer no credible alternatives to the existing institutions and practices. The process of anti-statism that had begun with the Enlightenment created a perpetual crisis, which pitched one utopian ideology against another, destabilizing the political and resulting in the extremes of twentieth-century totalitarianism and the ideological stand-off of the Cold War. Koselleck similarly rejects the liberal idea of the rule of law whose origin he finds in Hobbes: 'his consistently Absolutist theory of the State already contains the nucleus of the bourgeois notion of a government of laws' (Koselleck, 1988, p. 22).

Koselleck's aim is to re-politicize contemporary discussions of politics and infuse them with a sense that conflict is endemic in public life, unavoidable in all political decision making. The constraints of political life are inescapable and the conflicts irreducible to mere differences of opinion. To ignore the constraints invites the condition about which Hobbes warned—the war of all against all. His prescriptive alternative viewpoint is to accept the imperfection of the social order and the permanence of conflict in the political. This is a view close to Schmitt, although Kosselleck does not want to enter into any ideological debate, nor is he interested in politicizing Schmitt's formalized differentiation between 'friend' and 'enemy'. Plural histories are his way of countering modern temporality (Ewning, 2016, p. 14).

Like Schmitt and Koselleck, Oakeshott is sceptical of liberalism because it had become infected with rationalism—not pluralism—a trend that undermined individualism rather than encouraged it. The important difference between Oakeshott and the Germans is that he differentiated 'liberalism' and 'parliamentary government' (Oakeshott, 1993, p. 109). What 'may now be meant by the word "liberal" is anyone's guess' (Oakeshott, 1991, pp. 439–40). It is clear that Oakeshott distanced himself from classical liberalism, especially in its Lockean form. He rejected, for example, as did Schmitt and Koselleck, the idea that the legitimacy of government derives from contract, in which individuals are understood to possess rights prior to political society, and where the purpose of the state is conceived to protect them. Agreeing with Schmitt and Koselleck, Oakeshott maintains that liberalism is concerned with the menace of sovereign authority and with constitutional devices to contain and diminish it (Oakeshott, 1975a, p. 245 n.2). Parliamentary democracy, *pace* the view of Schmitt, does not derive from, and is not a manifestation of, rationalist ideology. Oakeshott contends: 'British democracy is not an abstract idea. It is a way of living and a manner of politics which began to emerge in the Middle Ages' (Oakeshott, 2006, p. 321).

While Oakeshott is critical of classical liberalism for its extreme individualism, modern liberalism, or the philosophy of Representative Democracy, while in need of a radical restatement had the advantage of its rivals such as Communism, Catholicism, National Socialism and Fascism in being less rigid in its capacity for change over a long period of time; and in comprising a tradition of thinking more coherent than its rivals (Oakeshott, 1947, pp. xxviii–xxix). The central principles of representative democracy, for Oakeshott, *pace* Schmitt and Koselleck, far from undermining government, are to be valued. They are: 'that a society must not be so unified as to abolish vital and valuable differences, nor so extravagantly diversified as to make an intelligently co-ordinated and civilized social life impossible, and that the imposition of a universal plan of life on a society is at once stupid and immoral…' (Oakeshott, 1947, p. xxix). The danger is rationalism, and misconceiving the mode of association as enterprise rather than civil association.

In contrast to Schmitt and Koselleck, the rule of law is a safeguard against the state, especially against misconceptions of its purpose, such as that of the rationalist in politics who understands society as a joint enterprise, and ruling a form of managerialism. By referring to the rule of law as an ideal characterization, he means that the moral relationship of the rule of law is glimpsed throughout early modern European history. It is not ideal in that it presents us with the perfect condition, but because it is 'abstracted from the contingencies and ambiguities of actual goings-on in the world' (Oakeshott, 1975a, p. 109). It does not provide a portrait of the modern European state. The rule of law is not the product of liberal democracy. It had its origins in ancient Rome and Medieval Europe. The rule of law is a mode of association integral to civil association, referring to non-instrumental rules appropriate to the relationship in which individuals stand to each other, and is the guarantor of individuality. For Oakeshott the rule of law, and not central planning, is the safeguard against *laissez-faire* society because of its insistence on duties at least as much as rights between citizens (Oakeshott, 2007, p. 208).

Hobbes, the Problem?

For Schmitt, Koselleck and Oakeshott, Hobbes is the principal thinker for understanding the emergence of the modern sovereign state in early modern Europe (Edwards, 2006, p. 432). He is paradigmatic in the ideal-types that Schmitt, Koselleck and Oakeshott offer as instruments of inquiry. For the Germans, Hobbes recognizes the importance of the obedience/protection nexus (Schmitt, 2008, pp. 72, 83, 96; Koselleck,

1988, p. 33; Hobbes, 1991, pp. 153, 230, 484–5, 191). Both Schmitt and Koselleck contend there can be no legitimacy or legality, no absolute power constituting a stage 'without protection and obedience' (Schmitt, 2007, p. 52; cf. Schmitt, 2008, p. 96, and Koselleck, 1988, p. 33).

Individuals give consent to power always because they need protection and they seek this protection from power. Seen from the perspective of the humans, a linkage between protection and obedience is the only explanation of power. He who does not have the power to protect someone does not have the right to require obedience. Conversely, anyone who receives has no right to withhold obedience. Power and authority are inextricable combined (Schmitt, 2015, p. 31). Schmitt maintains that 'in front of every chamber of direct power an antechamber of direct influences and powers constructs itself, a path of access to the ear, a corridor to the soul of the holder of power. There is no human power without this antechamber and without this corridor (Schmitt, 2015, p. 35). For Schmitt and Koselleck, Hobbes is the philosopher of power and protection, who undermined his own theory by allowing freedom of conscience, a private sphere, which eventually served to dissipate power, and neutralize the political.

For Oakeshott, Hobbes is the least equivocal and intrepid account of civil association understood in terms of the common acknowledgement of the authority of the laws, independent of their approval or relation to power (Oakeshott, 1975b, p. 252). What for Koselleck and Schmitt was a fatal flaw generating individualism, was for Oakeshott one of Hobbes's remarkable achievements preserving men's individuality. Authority could control only men's actions, not their intellect or conscience (Oakeshott, 2007, pp. 120–1).

The conflation of authority and power is a category error. 'There is no more fundamental distinction to be made in political thought than that between "might" and "right"'; force (*potentia*) or violence, which is physical, and authority (*potestas* or *auctoritas*), which is mental. Power and authority may each establish order, but in qualitatively different ways. Power or violence may compel obedience by making it physically impossible to disobey, but authority requires obedience in virtue of the right to be obeyed (Oakeshott, 2006, p. 293).

Authority in Hobbes, for Oakeshott, is based on nothing more than the opinions of those who consent to it, and has to be conceptually distinguished from 'an apparatus of power, and a mode of association' (Oakeshott, 2008, p. 233). A ruler may have both authority and power, but authority is not based on power, but on whatever is believed to be his 'right to rule' (Oakeshott, 2006, p. 293). The power available to an office of rule is conceptually independent of its authority (Oakeshott, 2008, p. 230). An office of authority may have allied to it the power of enforcing compliance and penalizing non-compliance; but these are not conditions of recognizing the office to be authoritative. The absence of the apparatus of power, or its ineffectiveness, is no ground for denying its authority (Oakeshott, 2008, p. 239). Recognizing power may be a good reason for complying with a demand, but it provides no reason for acknowledging an obligation to do so. A bandit and his fearful victim stand in relation to one another in a relationship of power (Oakeshott, 1991, pp. 445–6).

Both Schmitt and Koselleck attributed the depoliticization of politics to the impetus Hobbes gave to the development of individualism (Koselleck, 1988, p. 24), which for Schmitt and Koselleck emanated from a tiny facture in Hobbes's theory, namely private conscience (Koselleck, 1988, p. 26; Schmitt, 2008, pp. 55–7), independent of the state, which subsequently flourished, challenged and dominated the political (Koselleck, 1988, p. 24). The public interest, which is alone the prerogative of the sovereign, no longer falls within the jurisdiction of conscience. By relegating conscience to the private sphere it becomes alienated from the state and turns into private morality (Koselleck, 1988, p. 31). Koselleck argues that conscience, far from being the judge of good and evil, is in fact the source of evil itself: 'Instead of being *causa pacis*, the authority of conscience in its subjective plurality is a downright *causa belli civilis*' (Koselleck, 1988, p. 29). In the view of both Schmitt and Koselleck there was a direct line of descent from Hobbes's distinction between the public and private, faith and confession, to the rise of the liberal constitutional state and the neutralization of politics (Schmitt, 2008, p. 56; Koselleck, 1988, p. 28).

Both Schmitt and Koselleck attributed the demise of politics to the waning of mass man and the impetus to individualism that the tiny fracture in Hobbes's political theory made possible. For Oakeshott, it is not individualism that has subverted and depoliticized politics, but the rise of mass man, manipulated by the rationalist, possessing exactly those powers that Schmitt and Koselleck (to a lesser degree) deemed necessary for the protection of the integrity and purity of politics (Hoffman, 2006).

Conclusion

There is little agreement, among historians, or indeed physicians to whom the concept initially belonged, on what constitutes a crisis, and even less upon *the* crisis (Starn, 1971, p. 22). Koselleck maintains that the 'concept remains as multi-layered and ambiguous as the emotions attached to it' (Koselleck, 2006, p. 358).

The reasons Oakeshott gives for his conclusions are almost diametrically opposed to those of Schmitt and Koselleck. All of those elements that Schmitt and Koselleck identify as pernicious, Oakeshott views in a positive light. He applauds individualism; deplores 'mass' man; extols the virtues of the rule of law, whereas both Schmitt and Koselleck deplore them; and unlike them Oakeshott emphasizes, not the friend/enemy distinction, nor the decisionism of the sovereign, nor the mutual dependence of power and authority in Hobbes, but the importance of distinguishing authority as a moral relationship in which individuals stand to each other in civil association under the rule of law. In essence, for Schmitt and Koselleck, Hobbes is the philosopher of power, politics and Absolutism *par excellence*; while for Oakeshott, Hobbes is the philosopher of governance and authority. For Oakeshott, it was the enhancement of the state's ability to act decisively, to set aside the rule of law, exacerbated by the propensity to go to war (Oakeshott, 1975b, p. 273) that constituted the problem. This suppression of individualism which Schmitt and Koselleck thought necessary, Oakeshott abhorred and instead praised Hobbes as the philosopher of individuality.

In all three of our philosophers of crisis we are presented with ideal-types, instruments of interrogation into which they place selective evidence, or idealizations, which support a degenerative decline, the exact opposite of 'whig' history. Each extols the virtues of myths that have the power to sustain their favoured, and idealized, political practices and institutions. The authenticity of the myths depends upon our acceptance of the propositions that politics constitutes a discrete area of activity, reserved for specialists, skilled in the art of the political. The inauthenticity of the counterfeit myths depends upon our acceptance of the view that anything of an alien character that impinges upon what is stipulated to be the political is necessarily destructive of it. Oakeshott's method of arresting the decline is to draw out the catastrophic consequences of counterfeit myths, such as the Tower of Babel in which man challenges the authority of God who wreaks his revenge (Oakeshott, 1983, pp. 164–94). Schmitt and Koselleck (to a lesser degree) want us to face up to the inevitability of conflict and wish to reintroduce the illiberal into politics, revert to the rule of man by subverting the rule of law, and banish private conscience from the public business of successfully distinguishing between friends and enemies, with the capacity and will of the sovereign to respond decisively to the exception. Modern trends, exemplified by parliamentary democracy and the rule of law had impaired the ability of the state to act decisively.

The difficulty with which all three philosophers of crisis present us is by what criteria are we to determine the present space of experience – the range of activities for which governments now take responsibility

— on the basis of which our horizons of expectation have expanded, to be pronounced illegitimate, or inauthentic? The mode of association — protection/obedience, on the one hand, and civil, on the other — elevate an aspect of the political to the level of what Onora O'Neill terms idealization (1996), the identification of the part for the whole, just as Marx reinterpreted the great European canon of texts, in identifying economic factors as the decisive drivers, Schmitt, Koselleck and Oakeshott, in their different ways, do the same, as in, for example, their reinterpretation of Hobbes, as on the one hand the philosopher who recognized the importance of the obedience/protection nexus, but inadvertently gave rise to an invidious individualism, and on the other the philosopher who distinguished clearly between power and authority, and preserved the individuality that rationalism and the rise of mass man threatened.

References

Bell, D. (2015) Reconfiguring reason of state in response to political crisis, in Dyzenhaus, D. & Poole, T. (eds.) *Law, Liberty and State: Oakeshott, Hayek and Schmitt on the Rule of Law*, pp. 185–213, Cambridge: Cambridge University Press.

Boucher, D. (1989) *The Social and Political Thought of R.G. Collingwood*, pp. 231–243, Cambridge: Cambridge University Press.

Boucher, D. (2015) Schmitt, Oakeshott and the Hobbesian legacy in the crisis of our times, in Dyzenhaus, D. & Poole, T. (eds.) *Law, Liberty and State*, pp. 123–152, Cambridge: Cambridge University Press.

Butterfield, H. (1949) *The Origins of Modern Science, 1300–1800*, London: Bell and Son.

Butterfield, H. (1965) *The Whig Interpretation of History*, London: Norton.

Callahan, G. (2007) Ideal types and the historical method, *Collingwood and British Idealism Studies*, **13**, pp. 53–68.

Christi, R. (1998) *Carl Schmitt and Authoritarian Liberalism: Strong State, Free Economy*, pp. 123–125, Cardiff: University of Wales Press.

Edwards, J. (2006) Critique and Crisis today: Koselleck, Enlightenment and the concept of politics, *Contemporary Political Theory*, **5**, pp. 428–446.

Ewning, A.B. (2016) Conceptions of Reinhart Koselleck's theory of historical time in the thinking of Michael Oakeshott, *History of European Ideas*, DOI: 10.1080/01916599.2015.118331.

Feher, F. (1988) Crisis and crisis-solving in the Soviet system under Gorbachev's new course, *Thesis Eleven*, **21** (1), pp. 5–19.

Feher, F. (1989) Hermeneutic as Europe's mainstream political tradition, *Thesis Eleven*, **22** (82).

Frohnen, B.P. (1990) Oakeshott's Hobbesian myth: Pride, character and the limits of reason, *The Western Political Quarterly*, **43**, pp. 789–809.

Hobbes, T. (1991) *The Leviathan*, Cambridge: Cambridge University Press.
Hoffman, S.L. (2006) Reinhart Koselleck (1923-2006): The conceptual historian, *German History*, **24** (3), pp. 475-478.
Koselleck, R. (1988) *Critique and Crisis: Enlightenment and the Pathogenesis of Modern Society*, Cambridge, MA: MIT Press.
Koselleck, R. (2004) *Futures Past: On the Semantics of Historical Time (Studies in Contemporary German Social Thought)*, New York: Columbia University Press.
Koselleck, R. (2006) Crisis, *Journal of the History of Ideas*, Richter, M.W. (trans.), **67** (2), pp. 357-400.
McCormick, J.P. (1997) *Carl Schmitt's Critique of Liberalism: Against Politics as Technology*, Cambridge: Cambridge University Press.
McIntyre, K. (2004) *The Limits of Political Theory*, Exeter: Imprint Academic.
Oakeshott, M. (ed.) (1947) *The Political Doctrines of Contemporary Europe*, American edition with five prefaces by Frederic A. Ogg, Cambridge: Cambridge University Press.
Oakeshott, M. (1965) *Rationalism in Politics*: A reply to Professor Raphael, *Political Studies*, **XIII**, pp. 89-92.
Oakeshott, M. (1975a) *On Human Conduct*, Oxford: Clarendon Press.
Oakeshott, M. (1975b) *Hobbes on Civil Association*, Oxford: Blackwell.
Oakeshott, M. (1983) *On History and Other Essays*, Oxford: Blackwell.
Oakeshott, M. (1991) *Rationalism in Politics and Other Essays*, new ed., Fuller, T. (ed.), Indianapolis, IN: Liberty Fund.
Oakeshott, M. (1993) *Religion, Politics and the Moral Life*, Fuller, T. (ed.), New Haven, CT: Yale University Press.
Oakeshott, M. (2004) The Whig interpretation of history, in *What is History? And Other Essays*, pp. 217-223, Exeter: Imprint Academic.
Oakeshott, M. (2006) *Lectures in the History of Political Thought*, Exeter: Imprint Academic.
Oakeshott, M. (2007) *The Concept of a Philosophical Jurisprudence: Essays and Reviews 1926-1951*, O'Sullivan, L. (ed.), Exeter: Imprint Academic.
Oakeshott, M. (2008) *The Vocabulary of a Modern European State*, Exeter: Imprint Academic.
Oakeshott, M. (2014) *Notebooks, 1922-1986*, O'Sullivan, L. (ed.), Exeter: Imprint Academic.
O'Neill, O. (1996) *Towards Justice and Virtue: A Constructive Account of Practical Reasoning*, Cambridge: Cambridge University Press.
O'Sullivan, L. (2003) *Oakeshott on History*, Exeter: Imprint Academic.
Olsen, N. (2004) 'Of all my teachers Schmitt was the most important': Reinhart Koselleck's intellectual and personal relations with Carl Schmitt, *Historisk Tidsskrift*, **104** (1), pp. 61-64.
Olsen, N. (2011) Carl Schmitt, Reinhart Koselleck and the foundations of history and politics, *European History of Ideas*, **37**, pp. 197-208.

Olsen, N. (2012) *History in the Plural: An Introduction to the Work of Reinhart Koselleck*, Oxford and New York: Berghahn Books.

Riendeau, N. (2014) *The Legendary Past: Michael Oakeshott on Imagination and Political Identity*, Exeter: Imprint Academic.

Schmitt, C. [1926] (1998) *The Crisis of Parliamentary Democracy*, Cambridge, MA: MIT Press.

Schmitt, C. [1930] (2002a) State ethics and the pluralist state, reprinted in Jacobson, A.J. & Schlink, B. (eds.) *Weimar A Jurisprudence of Crisis*, pp. 303-312, Berkeley, CA: University of Los Angeles Press.

Schmitt, C. [1925] (2002b) The status quo and the peace, reprinted in Jacobson, A.J. & Schlink, B. (eds.) *Weimar: A Jurisprudence of Crisis*, Chicago, IL: University of Chicago Press.

Schmitt, C. [1928] (2002) The liberal rule of law, reprinted in Jacobson, A.J. & Schlink, B. (eds.) *Weimar: A Jurisprudence of Crisis*, Berkeley, CA: University of Los Angeles Press.

Schmitt, C. (2004) *Legality and Legitimacy*, Seitzer, J. (ed. & trans.), Durham, NC: Duke University Press.

Schmitt, C. (2005) *Political Theology: Four Chapters on the Concept of Sovereignty*, Schwab, G. (trans.), with a Forward by Strong, T.B., Chicago, IL: Chicago University Press.

Schmitt, C. (2007) *The Concept of the Political*, Schwab, G. (ed.) with a Foreword by Strong, T.B., and Notes by Strauss, L., Chicago, IL: Chicago University Press.

Schmitt, C. (2008) *The Leviathan in the State Theory of Thomas Hobbes*, Chicago, IL: Chicago University Press.

Schmitt, C. (2015) *Dialogues on Power and Space*, Cambridge: Cambridge University Press.

Sorley, W.R. (1926) *Tradition*, The Herbert Spencer Lecture Delivered at Oxford, 19 May 1926, Oxford: Clarendon Press.

Starn, R. (1971) Historians and 'crisis', *Past and Present*, **52** (1), pp. 3-22.

Waters, T. & Waters, D. (2015) *Weber's Rationalism and Modern Society*, London: Palgrave Macmillan.

Weber, M. (1949) The logic of the cultural sciences, *The Methodology of the Social Sciences*, New York: Free Press.

Weber, M. (1970) *From Max Weber*, Gerth H. & Wright Mills, C. (eds.), London: Routledge.

Weber, M. (1992) *The Protestant Ethic and the Spirit of Capitalism*, London: Routledge.

Weber, M. (1994) *Political Writings*, Lassman, P. & Speirs, R. (eds.), Cambridge: Cambridge University Press.

Weber, M. (2004) *The Vocation Lectures*, Owen, D. & Strong, T.B. (eds.), Indianapolis, IN: Hackett.

Wendell John Coats, Jr.

Michael Oakeshott as Philosopher of 'the Creative'

> ...[T]he characteristic developments of modern political theory have depended on the displacement of the concept of information by that of creation as the highest practical activity ... the same displacement has influenced the modern concept of artistic activity. — M.B. Foster (1935)

This chapter advances the argument that the work of the twentieth-century political philosopher Michael Oakeshott may be coherently viewed as an increasingly explicit appreciation of what I am calling 'the creative' in human thought and action, and what Oakeshott himself alluded to as 'the poetic character of human activity'. I have advanced this thesis for many years, but never attempted a comprehensive statement of it showing both its meaning across Oakeshott's various works, as well as how it fits in the context of Western philosophy from Plato to the twenty-first century. Thus, this chapter is an attempt to show not only the presence of a unifying theme across Oakeshott's various works beginning with *Experience and Its Modes* (1933), but also how this theme fits in and helps to elucidate and advance the various philosophic and political themes of Western modernity and post-modernity. In brief, and to get ahead of ourselves, I shall be trying to show that the general drift and outline of Western philosophy and political philosophy can be manageably perceived from the late medieval period onward as an increasingly explicit argument between the cosmological, ontological and ethical assumptions of ancient Greek rationalism and the implied assumptions of the Judaic and Christian biblical inheritance over the issue of 'the creative' in cosmology, history and conduct, to the increasing favour by late modernity of the latter, whether explicitly so or not; and that Oakeshott's is an important twentieth-century voice echoing for the most part in and within the tones and perspective of 'the creative' *versus* the Greek rationalist side of the debate.

The case for this argument will be laid out in stages. The first will be to contrast the differences between (1) the Greek rationalist (especially Platonic) view of the eternity of the universe, and its implications for politics and ethics, and (2) the biblical (especially Maimonidian) view of the creation of the universe and its implications for ethics and politics. The second stage will be to show how the conception of the creative in human experience appears in Oakeshott's writing with increasing explicitness in and after the essays of the 1940s and 1950s collected in *Rationalism in Politics*. The third stage of the argument will be to show how Oakeshott's understanding of the poetic or creative character of human thought and activity compares and contrasts with the views of other twentieth-century thinkers such as Charles Taylor, Friedrich Hayek, Alasdair MacIntyre and Leo Strauss.

'The Creative'

Since the aim of this chapter is to fit Oakeshott's work into a 'meta-narrative' about the tensions *between* the Greek rationalist and biblical inheritances of Western civilization, it will be necessary to reach back and summarily indicate the salient issues here. At stake here will be the answers to three broad questions: (1) what kind(s) of activities may be done for their own sake; (2) are there any antecedently existing ideas, or is intellect always and inextricably entwined with previous experience and action; and (3) given the answers to these questions, what is the basis for sound and skilful human moral and political practice?

Let us begin by summarily contrasting the Greek and biblical inheritances on these kinds of questions by focusing on the difference between a created and an eternal, teleologically purposive universe; and between a created and a crafted object (including a human being). The best place to start is with the Jewish philosopher Moses Maimonides' twelfth-century Arabic language masterpiece, *The Guide of the Perplexed*. (Maimonides is better suited for our purposes than Aquinas in the *Summa Theologica* who is generally concerned to minimize the differences between the Greek and biblical inheritances in order to synthesize them.) Maimonides is explicit about the way in which the biblical account of wilful creation *ex nihilo* denies the possibility of an eternal, teleological universe ordered toward a final end, as in the Greek rationalist accounts. On the biblical account of the universe ('the All'), the only thing which can be said of God's creation is that it is God's volition and is created 'for no other purpose' than God's glory:

> Thus ... the quest for a final end of all collapses. For we say that is virtue of this will He has brought into existence all of the parts of the world, some of which have been intended for their own sakes. (Maimonides, 1963, p. 452)

And Maimonides also distinguishes the biblical account of creation *ex nihilo* from the Platonic account of a divine craftsman in *The Timaeus* who moulds or crafts pre-existing matter into pre-existing forms – the believer in the Law of Moses and Abraham 'is to believe that there is nothing eternal in any way ... with God', and that 'the bringing into existence out of non-existence is for the deity not an impossibility...' (Maimonides, 1963, p. 285).

Let us draw out more fully the (implied) differences between the Greek rationalist and the biblical accounts in this connection. As is generally known, on the Greek rationalist worldview, both form and matter are given eternally; the essence of any object is its 'detachable' form; matter adds nothing positive to form; and both thinking and making are purposive and involve discovering and copying pre-existing forms or models. By contrast, as we have just noted in Maimonides' text, the account of cosmological creation in the sacred Hebrew and Christian texts entails the ideas that creation is not purposive in the Greek sense, that is, it is not directed toward a distinctively conceived and antecedently existing form or end in advance of the act of wilful creation; and, by implication, in creation, and in a created (versus a crafted) object there is no intellectively graspable form distinguishable from its accidental embodiment.

Several more implications follow. Creation is an act of will which can exceed regulations prescribed by reason. Contingency is an important aspect of created objects (including physical nature and human beings), that is, their 'accidental' embodiments are not necessitated by, nor can be deduced from, their form or idea. And, finally, there can be no degrees of being in creation as there are in the Greek idea of substance (*ousia*): if something is created *ex nihilo*, 'it must be entirely present as soon as it has ceased to be wholly absent' (Foster, 1934, p. 464).

To continue this accelerated narrative, Maimonides' account of divine, creative will is taken to an extreme in the thought of the late medieval British voluntarist thinkers, Duns Scotus and William of Ockham, in which both divine and human will become pure, unlimited, indeterminate power without finality (distinguished from the older views of both Aristotle and Augustine that human willing is naturally directed toward what is good). In the words of the contemporary Swiss medieval scholar, Andre de Muralt, with reference to Scotus and Ockham, 'it is between 1250 and 1350 ... that the premise of the contemporary intellectual situation appears as well as the decline of a unified philosophic conception of possible human knowledge...' (de Muralt, 1991, p. 39, my translation). And in the case of Ockham, the voluntarist claim is partnered with the nominalist claim that universals are not real but are merely names: *universalia sunt nomina*. This single sentence arguably killed the work of five hundred years of scholasticism as the view spread that there are meanings and representations in the mind but only things in the world, displacing the idea that the 'beings of the world' were in the soul.

Additionally, in the thought of Ockham, the seeds are sown of the modern Liberal view of liberty as the freedom to act short of harm to another, and of governmental authority as merely an external limit to infinite, individual freedom. Over time, the idea of the infinite freedom of human will (based on a claim of its univocity with divine will) arguably issues in 'creative' political alternatives to the Platonic *techne* model of political rule, in which rulers form inert citizen subject matter into pre-existing political forms, as exemplified in great detail in *The Republic*. These alternatives became clearer in the work of Hobbes and Rousseau. In the case of Hobbes, human art imitates divine art (nature) in wilfully constructing the great *Leviathan*; in the case of Rousseau, in direct opposition to Plato and the *techne* model of rule, a sovereign people create, or give themselves, their own political or constitutional forms. In Rousseau's surface vision, people cease to be inert, passive subject matter formed by rulers, and creatively generate and impose upon themselves their own political forms (albeit while being secretly manipulated by philosophy and religion).

The idea of the autonomy of the human spirit will follow Ockham to Germany where he emigrated, and appears in its present form there centuries later in Kantian ethics and its ascription of categorical duties toward others, transcending any claims of the empirical ego; and also in the thought of Hegel who argues that the human spirit can override all antecedent and genetic inheritance. However, it is in the nineteenth-century German neo-Kantian explorations of the disintegrations of the medieval synthesis (in the increasing differentiation and fragmentation of knowledge) that we can see the long-term effects of the spread of the medieval voluntarist conception of the creative will. For it is this conception of a created and contingent reality, the implications of which we saw identified by Maimonides, which makes impossible a teleological conception of the world and of nature since all sorts of so-called 'lower' beings and purposes are now equally _real_, and not simply diluted forms of reason and intellect, as in the Greek rationalist view. This viewpoint about the reality of matter and the contingency of physical nature not only makes possible modern empirical science, but also modern epistemological and ethical pluralisms, since all sorts of mundane activities can now be done (*contra* Aristotle) for their own sake, and all sorts of knowledge claims can be made for their own sake.

To unpack this idea briefly, it involves a transformation and broadening of the Aristotelian idea of activity done for its own sake. For the ontological dualist, Aristotle, the only activity which can be done purely for its own sake is thought thinking thought, an activity of the Unmoved Mover which thinks itself, and which can be approximated by human beings in philosophic contemplation. And even though Aristotle is more appreciative of the reality of material and practical life than his teacher, Plato, in the end for him matter is still a diminution of Being understood as pure thought. Now, for historically complex reasons involving biblical ideas such as creation and incarnation and sacred history read and discussed in the light of Greek logic, the idea slowly evolved that activities other than *Theoria* could be done and enjoyed for their own sake, owing to the reality of the material and mundane world which in the Christian (especially Augustinian) worldview becomes not a diminution of Being, but an arena for spiritual engagement and growth. One of the first and clearest instances of the view that mundane activity could be done for its own sake and enjoyment (and not simply as a diversion as in the ancient Epicurean view) is to be found in the three volumes of Montaigne's *Essays*. As is well known, at the age of thirty-eight Montaigne retired to his estate and his study in order to construct a private life where he could avoid instrumental purposes as much as practically possible, and engage in various mundane activities such as conversation and friendship for their own sake and enjoyment. And where this was not realistically possible owing to practical obligations, Montaigne preferred to focus on the ritualistic aspects of activity and relationships, since these are more easily thought of as existing for their own sake even where they issue in some practical benefit. (One waits one's turn to speak not merely for the order it produces, but because it is the polite or civil thing to do.) By implication, Montaigne clearly sees himself as a unique (created) individual in whom 'essence' and 'accident' cannot be meaningfully separated, as in the ontologically dualist, Greek rationalist account, an individual for whom the most important thing in life is to learn how to belong to himself and cultivate his own ruling form (*formemaitresse*).

Montaigne's cultivation of the diversity and plurality of life for its own sake becomes an epistemological and ontological issue in German philosophy of the nineteenth and early twentieth centuries, especially in neo-Kantianism, where the phenomenon of the radical plurality of modernity is recognized as a problem to be analysed for the difficulties it creates for any unified theory of knowledge and experience. Heinrich

Rickert, for example, in *Kant as Philosopher of the Modern Age* argued that the relative autonomy of thinking, willing and feeling in Kant's three critiques made him *the* philosopher of a modernity characterized by the claims of each of the three to exist for its own sake, although Rickert himself called for a unified theory of knowledge which could preserve the 'many-sidedness' (*Vielseitigkeit*) of reality (Rickert, 1924, p. 150). And in the same generation the highly original thinker, George Simmel, expounded an 'aesthetic' view of modernity as historically transcending the more primitive purposive orientation of the teleological or pragmatic human stage in the achieved capacity to pursue various forms or modulations of the whole of experience (such as art, science and practice) for their own sake (Podoksik, 2015), in an almost ritualistic sense reminiscent of Montaigne's approach to appropriate and contented living. And what is now known as postmodernism, in all its varieties, might be summarily characterized as the attempt at 'validation' of all 'difference' and particularity, through 'deconstruction' of the inherited philosophic, scientific and political forms of modernity, at whatever cost to structures of authority and stability.

Now, before moving on to an attempt at placing Oakeshott's work in the context of this narrative of the fortunes of the 'creative' in Western philosophy and political thought, let us briefly rehearse its themes. Western philosophy is not just a footnote to Plato, because since at least the second century before Christ, Greek philosophy has been in a dialogue with Hebraic creation doctrines;[1] and since the second century after Christ, with Christian creation and incarnation doctrines, i.e. with ideas that the cosmos and the world are not eternal; that divine creative will can create in advance of positing intellective forms and purposes; and that the divine *logos* could somehow be amplified, rather than diminished, through material incarnation. In philosophic terms, this would be to say that the material world is no less real than the intellective world, and hence to deny the possibility of an ascending chain of teleological purposes culminating in a final cause. As we have seen, in a created world and in created objects (including human beings), intellective essence cannot be separated from material 'accident' and used as a standard by which to judge various historical instantiations. Summarily speaking, in a created (versus an eternal, teleological) universe, contingency will be essential to the idea of physical nature; creativity will be essential in accounting for human thinking and acting, which will not be seen as purposive in the Greek sense of copying distinctively conceived and antecedently existing intellective models; and, by implication, positivity (versus

---

[1] For more on this, see Dihle (1982).

mere rationality) will be essential to the idea of law. I have been suggesting that it has been the tension between these two inheritances — the Greek and the biblical, the 'intellectual' and the 'creative' — which has characterized Western philosophy and science for roughly the best part of two millennia, and that, since about the thirteenth century, it has been the 'creative' account which has increasingly gained dominance, or at least alternating dominance, over teleological modes of thinking (Thomism and eighteenth-century Enlightenment rationalism to the contrary notwithstanding).

This chapter will now attempt to place Oakeshott's work in the context of this compact narrative, but before doing so it is important to note that it is possible to come to some of the insights about the creative fluidity of reality and about human skill and moral balance in this light from non-Western sources, in particular, from classical Chinese Daoist thought (in its contentions with Confucian rationalism), a source which we shall see Oakeshott drew upon in formulating his critique of rationalism in morals and politics.[2]

Oakeshott as Philosopher of the Creative

In order to proceed with an investigation for contemporary readers of the theme of the creative or poetic character of human activity throughout Oakeshott's work, it is first necessary to address and declare a position on a major issue in Oakeshott scholarship. This is the question of whether Oakeshott after the 1950s *abandoned* the philosophic idealism of *Experience and Its Modes* (1933), and its conception of philosophy as experience without arrest on presupposition, continually *en voyage* to the ultimate satisfaction of full coherence, for 1) either a Hobbesian-like nominalism; or 2) a modified form of Personal Idealism asserting the primacy of the finite or practical individual; or 3) a sort of neo-Kantian embrace of the modern and postmodern 'fragmentation' of a unified knowledge of any kind.[3] My own view, and the assumption of the analysis which follows, is that there is no compelling reason to assume that Oakeshott did change his fundamental orientation in *Experience and Its Modes*, although his emphasis often changed depending on the subject being investigated, and/or rhetorical considerations *vis-à-vis* potential readerships. Even the 1958 essay on the voice of poetry and its orientation of image-making within the 'conversation of mankind' can be read as metaphorical or even as a view of the whole from a poetic perspective, distinguished from the focus of

---

[2] For more on this see Coats and Cheung (2012).
[3] For the first view, see Bhuta (2015); for the second, see Podoksik (2012); for a refutation of the third, see Boucher (2012).

Experience and Its Modes on the progression of thought itself. The only clear change in his thought after the 1958 essay (which Oakeshott himself obliquely acknowledged) is the recognition of aesthetic experience as a distinct modality or arrested view of the whole of experience itself. And even these who think Oakeshott did abandon Absolute Idealism can hopefully profit from the following investigation which provides a way of looking at the developmental issue in Oakeshott scholarship, from the standpoint of the increasing prevalence of the 'creative' in Oakeshott's thought over time. In different words, I will be suggesting that the unifying perspective in Oakeshott's entire *corpus* is arguably the poetic or creative structure of experiential reality; and that the 'developmental' change in Oakeshott's view of aesthetic experience may have come from the increasing realization that his own account of the evolution and structure the various modalities of experience was dependent on the 'creative' idea that the form and content of experience arise simultaneously and fluidly, and that there are no ascertainable degrees of reality in various determinate modulations of the experience as in a teleological worldview.

With that as a point of departure then, let us take up several salient ways in which Oakeshott's work (increasingly) reflects the insight that the structure of human experience is creative. First to be considered is the 'creative' way in which the various modalities of experience (science, history, practice, art) arise and exist for Oakeshott. Next, how Oakeshott uses this insight to criticize rationalism in morals and politics. Finally, how Oakeshott's conception of civil association (vs. enterprise association) better accommodates the creative or poetic structure of reality. And, finally, how the theoretical perspective Oakeshott calls 'theorizing contingency' reflects the medieval theological insight that in a created being content is not accidental to form, by providing a theoretical perspective capable of explaining an event in human conduct 'without explaining it away'.

I would like to suggest that Oakeshott's 1933 account of experience and its modalities is a 'creativist' account in two important ways—the relationship between and among modalities of experience, and the way in which determinate modalities arise in human experience. As is now generally known, for Oakeshott in *Experience and Its Modes* the drive of human consciousness and experience is toward complete coherence (even if never achieved) and various 'modalities' of experience such as 'science' and 'history' are seen as incomplete assertions, of the whole of reality based upon some mediating principle such as 'quantity' or 'contiguity'. What distinguished Oakeshott's account from those of other idealist thinkers such as Hegel and Bosanquet and Collingwood was his view that there could be no teleological-like ascending chain of modes of experience distinguished by their increasing logical coherence. Although perhaps a logical possibility, human intellect was not up to the task of establishing or demonstrating this, Oakeshott thought, and, moreover, focusing on this problem directed attention away from the more important idea that each mode of arrest in experience was an assertion about the whole of reality, rather than simply non-entity, and formally equal to other such modes in this respect.

Now, it is here that we can see in Oakeshott's account the similarity and perhaps influence of the medieval voluntarist, 'creationist' cosmological account (vs. the rationalist, teleological account). As we saw in the chapter's first section, in a created universe, there are no degrees of being as there are in the Greek concept of *ousia*—'if something is created *ex nihilo*, it must be entirely present as soon as it has ceased to be wholly absent' (Foster, 1934, p. 464). Now, this implied the reality of matter (as well as thought), a point which the idealist Oakeshott would not unqualifiedly admit. Yet, in fact, he approximates this insight in asserting that each modality of experience (such as science) is an assertion about the whole of experience or reality. Since science for Oakeshott mediates experience upon the principle of quantity, and since matter is especially susceptible to conceptualization through quantity, and since human intellect is not up to the demonstrating degrees of failed assertions of reality, assertions about the reality of quantifiable matter must at least be taken as formally equal to the claims of other determinate modes of experience such as those of history and practice. And even philosophy, the unachievable pursuit of full coherence, cannot, on Oakeshott's account, take the place of arrest or failed attempts in the pursuit of coherence. The implication is that Oakeshott's account of the human experience is structured in such a way as to confirm an important insight from 'creationist' theological accounts—reality is not teleologically ordered, and that various assertions of reality must be taken upon their own terms, rather than as diminution of Being understood as pure thought as in the Greek rationalist inheritance.

Another way in which Oakeshott's account of experience reflects the creative structure of experiential reality is the way in which determinate modalities arise even though all experience for Oakeshott is viewed as conceptual, with even sense experience simply as incipient form of judgement. For Oakeshott the form and content (not matter) of experience arise fluidly and spontaneously in tension with one another, with neither more important in creating the modal identity. The formal aspect is the mediating principle (e.g. quantity) and the content is an unidentifiable something until given conceptual identity by the mediating principle. (As Oakeshott would later put it in an essay on teaching and learning, activity arises in a tension between a how and what of experience, between its form and content.) This is why the logical error of irrelevance (*ignoratio elenchi*) is salient with Oakeshott. That is, various modalities of experience (or later voices in the conversation of mankind) cannot address one another directly because they have no common subject matter to discuss—each determinate modality of experience *creates* its own distinctive subject matter in the way it mediates experience. A scientist, for example, does not study a falling apple, but first resolves it into an abstraction with universal properties called 'mass'. Or, an historian studies a new subject matter called the historical past, not a commonsensical practical past. And so on. And individual conceptual identities within determinate modes of experience arise in the same 'creative' way, not as antecendently existed forms or models to be copied, as in the Platonic *techne* model.

It is this view of the creative structure of experiential reality (what Oakeshott later calls the 'poetic character of human activity') which provides the basis for Oakeshott's critique of rationalism in morals and politics in the essays of the 1950s and 1960s. The 'blindness' of rationalism (ancient, medieval and modern) is precisely its failure to perceive the 'poetic character' of human activity, that is, the insight that the form and content of all activity, *how* we think or do something and *what* we think or do, arise simultaneously, and condition one another reciprocally, distinguished from the rationalist view that the mind can grasp intellectively antecedently existing forms or models and then prosaically copy them in thought and action. In failing to appreciate the 'fluidity' of the relationship *between* moral and political ideals *and* action, rationalism overestimates the capacity of conscious thought to control, and *elevates* what should properly provide a critical facility in times of moral and political crises and disruption into the source of action itself. In failing to appreciate that it is part of a 'process' that reciprocally influences it, rationalism corrodes the moral balance and political skill which grow when the spring of action is largely unreflective. It also corrodes political and other skills when it irrelevantly attempts to apply models derived in one activity or sphere of knowledge to another in the mistaken belief that they have a common subject matter.

This insight is a version of the medieval insight that in a created universe (and object, including a human being) the essence and existence of something are of equal importance, neither able to claim ontological priority. Yet, in Oakeshott's thought, there is an additional source for this insight in the classical Chinese Daoist critique of Confucian rationalism, especially in the composite work Oakeshott knew as *Chuang-tzu*. This is the insight that both practical skill and moral balance depend not on 'rationally' applying antecedently formulated codes and models, but by acting appropriately and spontaneously in a particular context, and employing analytic intellect only as the protective critic, not instigator, of action. The problem with the former 'rationalist' approach, says Oakeshott, is that 'self-consciousness is asked to be creative' and 'its rule is misrule' (Oakeshott, 1962, p. 75). The rationalist approach to both practical skill and moral balance Oakeshott calls a denial of 'the poetic character of human activity'. We may also observe that the Daoist account of skill and appropriate thought and action is in accord with Oakeshott's account of the way the form and content of particular modalities of experience evolve fluidly and reciprocally, with neither more important than the other.

Let us now consider my claim that Oakeshott's conception of civil (versus enterprise) association better accommodates what he calls the poetic character of human activity. The reason is, quite simply, that since civil association imposes no unifying, substantive purpose upon a society, it leaves free a realm of activity in which diverse activities can arise spontaneously and 'creatively', and in which governmental policy can pursue small, slow changes in accord with a society's 'intimations'. This is also Oakeshott's defence of institutions of private property and market-economics—civil association, rule of law and dispersed economic arrangements all nurture the latitude for 'creative' responses to the ordeal of consciousness, and, hence, also nurture cultivation of practical skill and moral balance in a society, as well as habits of peace. (For Oakeshott, enterprise association and collectivism arise in conditions of war and tend to perpetuate it.)

Finally, let us consider Oakeshott's account of 'theorizing contingency' as a reflection of the medieval insight that in a created being content is not accidental to form, and as a theoretical perspective capable of explaining an event in human conduct without 'explaining it away'. In *On Human Conduct* Oakeshott articulates a theoretical perspective which makes explicit an evolved Western understanding of the human ordeal, in which individual actions and utterances are understood as intelligent (or not so intelligent) responses to understood (or misunderstood) situations, distinguished from explanation and understanding in terms of teleological, nomological and causative processes. Within this realm of *meaning* called 'human conduct' Oakeshott also articulates a theoretical perspective capable of explaining particular, individual events without 'explaining them away' as they are when explained as effects of teleological processes or as examples of causative processes. Events in the context of 'human conduct' are seen as contingently related, that is, related and given meaning and intelligibility by being understood *historically*, that is, understood as 'touching', or related in being understood responses to similar antecedent events, rather than as examples of some sort of qualitatively different covering law, or teleological process, or organic process. This extraordinarily refined theoretical perspective articulates a view of writing history as the telling of a story with no external meaning, in which events in human conduct are given a conditional intelligibility by being shown to be understood responses to what came before. And I am suggesting that Oakeshott's account of writing history or 'theorizing contingency' is a most refined culmination of the medieval insight that contingency is an unavoidable component of a created universe, where contingency is understood to mean that the particulars are not 'accidents' of form, nor can be deduced from antecedently existing forms, but arise coevally with form, and hence can only be accounted for *historically* in human conduct.

Oakeshott and Some Contemporaries

The aim of this section is to illustrate the tensions between the rationalist and creativist inheritances and how Oakshott fits in here, by comparing and contrasting his thought with four other twentieth-century thinkers—Charles Taylor, Friedrich Hayek, Alasdair MacIntyre and Leo Strauss. We shall see that Oakeshott has more in common in this connection with Taylor and Hayek, less with MacIntyre, and least with Leo Strauss, who fixes on the spread of the idea of the 'creative' (the extension of the theoretical into the mutable and material) as the source of 'modern darkness'.

Oakeshott and Charles Taylor share an Hegelian occupation in finding and accounting for the place of the subjective in human experience and history, but in the end Oakeshott is simply less Hegelian and rationalist than Taylor. What does this mean? Arguably, Hegel incorporates in his thought a secularized version of the Christian Trinity and the Incarnation, but not the Hebraic theme of creation, and its implication that will is essential in human action, contingency in nature, and positivity in law.[4] In different words, Hegel remains strongly on the side of the Greek rationalist inheritance on the importance of Reason in human experience except possibly for his historical accounts which still have at least a temporal *telos*, i.e. human freedom.

Now, Taylor does incorporate the modern insight into the 'creative' as part of an historical reconstruction of what he calls the ethics of authenticity, but he does so in an account of eighteenth-century German Romanticism's shifting the 'human centre of gravity' from *logos* to *poiesis*: 'The artist becomes in some way the paradigm case of

---

[4] For development of this view, see Foster (1935).

the human being as agent...' And, later, 'no longer defined ... by *mimesis* of reality ... art is understood now more in terms of creation' (Taylor, 1992, p. 62). By contrast, as I have been attempting to show, Oakeshott incorporates the idea of the creative into his entire account of the structure of all experiential reality, and, in turn, in his accounts of appropriate and skilful activity in all aspects of life.

In the end, Taylor is simply more Hegelian than Oakeshott in characterizing human beings as rationally purposive beings, and in articulating forms of community congenial to rational purposiveness. Although both Oakeshott and Taylor are respectful of the Hegelian theme of 'social-situatedness' of the individual, their differences on individual–community relationships have to do with the fact that Oakeshott shows more influence of the Hobbesian ('Will and Artifice') paradigm of thought and its emphasis on the importance of authority in preserving both order and individual moral autonomy: 'It is Reason, not Authority, which is destructive of individuality', wrote Oakeshott in introducing *Leviathan* (Oakeshott, 1975a, p. 63). Taylor, by contrast, in trying to rescue his ethics of authenticity from charges of egoism and narcissism, is led to strong defences of community as highly constitutive of individual identity, to the point of implying wholesale endorsement of what Oakeshott calls enterprise or teleocratic association, or association in terms of a common substantive purpose.

Another twentieth-century thinker who shares some similarity with Oakeshott on what I am calling the 'creative' is the twentieth-century economist and philosopher Friedrich Hayek. (The two even corresponded in the 1960s when Oakeshott was formulating his account of teleocracy vs. nomocracy.)[5] Detailed comparisons and contrasts of Oakeshott and Hayek on especially the critique of modern rationalist planning (including economic planning) have been made by others[6] and there is perhaps little new ground to break in this connection. They share a view of the limits of conscious intellect and an appreciation of the implicit rationality embodied in evolved or 'spontaneous orders' (to use Hayek's terminology) in contrast to consciously crafted political, social and economic institutions and organization, as well as an appreciation of the importance of *general* rules of law to ground and channel 'spontaneously' evolving orders such as markets based on the interplay of forces of demand and supply. In both cases this orientation derives from an appreciation of the *complexity* of both human experience and of the practical tasks facing large political and social entities. Insight into what I am calling the 'creative' aspects of experience, in

---

5   Cited in Boyd and Morrison (2007, p. 102, n.1).
6   See, for example, Cheung (2014), and Boyd and Morrison (2007).

particular the awareness that the form and content of all human activity arises creatively, i.e. arises simultaneously, fluidly and reciprocally, conditions their respective critiques of rationalism in morals, politics and economics.

Perhaps what is most to be gained in comparing the two thinkers on the limits to rationalist planning is perspective on the different ways such critiques can be mounted, and how they re-enforce one another. For example, Hayek's psychological studies (Hayek, 1952) on the limits of the human mind's ability to know itself delve into areas of cognitive research which Oakeshott never addresses, but which support his philosophic scepticism. Perhaps the largest difference between the two thinkers is that Oakeshott remains even more sceptical than Hayek on the possibilities for human 'progress' inherent in nurturing creative forces such as markets, and in the unwavering conviction that all civilizational achievements are highly complex and historically contingent and might have been otherwise, and could be again. Oakeshott's work is also generally more theoretically consistent than is Hayek's, given the diversity of subjects Hayek addressed over a lifetime, and in his pressing practical concern to foster markets and limited government under general rules of law.

It is appreciation of the 'creative' in experience which sets off the thought of Oakeshott, Hayek (and even Taylor) from the 'virtue ethics' of Alasdair MacIntyre. We might say that where Oakeshott has chosen to emphasize the creative side of the medieval inheritance, MacIntyre, following Aquinas, has followed its Aristotelian side by attempting to re-incorporate in morality a *telos* or final purpose tied to the performance of a human function (MacIntyre, 1981). While Oakeshott and MacIntyre do share an Aristotelian-like view of morality as skilful participation in inherited practice and traditions, Oakeshott's appreciation of the creative structure of experiential reality and the corresponding limits of conscious intellect to direct practical and moral life lead him, as we have seen, to reject any sort of teleological thinking in human affairs as simply confused. In defence of MacIntyre on this score, we might observe that his political realism leads him to reject the possibility that notions of a common purpose could ever intelligently and moderately be the basis for large modern states, and could only thrive in small, local associations as the basis for community in an instrumentalist liberal-capitalist age.

As for MacIntyre's account of the incommensurability of modern versions of morality owing to competing conceptions of rationality (MacIntyre, 1988), we might observe that MacIntyre's account rests on an intellectual move that the early Oakeshott employed in establishing the separateness of various modalities of experience such as practice, science and history, and which, it has been suggested, crystallized in Oakeshott's attempts in the 1920s to mediate between the claims of science and religion. This intellectual move is the invocation of the logical error of *ignoratio elenchi* or irrelevance. But for Oakeshott this move led to the view that there could be no scientific or natural proof or disproof of the practical claims of the Christian religion since the two were dealing with categorically different subject matters. By implication, this would entail a rejection as confused of the attempted Aquinian synthesis of Aristotelian reason and Christian revelation which MacIntyre extols as the most coherent and best model for regeneration of communities of rational morality in the contemporary world. And, more specifically, Oakeshott rejects as confused the attempt to inject 'rationality' directly into morality by way of *telos* of shared, common purposes, natural or transcendental, grounded in an essentialist view of human beings as matrices of specifiable and hierarchically arranged functions, in favour of a more creative or Daoist-like and fluid conception of the individual self *vis-à-vis* the world, depending on the particular way the self is being active at any moment. In brief, all about all that Oakeshott and MacIntyre share is a view of the importance of evolved shared practices in the generation of the self and concomitant rejection of Rawlsian-like accounts of 'antecedently-situated' subjects or agents.

Oakeshott's differences with Leo Strauss here are profound since Strauss propounds the view that creativity, which he identifies with making, production and the temporalizing of Being, has been the cause of 'modern darkness' (Emberly and Cooper, 1993, pp. 65–6). Let us look closely at what Strauss is saying in this regard, and how Oakeshott's analysis differs from it, especially his critique of rationalism in morals and politics, extending back to Plato.

Strauss's viewpoint in this regard is that 'modern derailments' have come from the confused 'creative' attempt to conflate the theoretical, practical and productive lives (which the ancient Greeks kept separate) by extending theorizing into the realm of the mutable and material, and privileging the latter over the former, with the effect of privileging productive and instrumentalist aims over questions of truth and right and wrong (Strauss, 1952, p. 572).[7] The real meaning of 'creativity' for Strauss has been the historicizing of both Being and knowledge (Strauss, 1989, pp. 227–70), which he traces to at least Descartes, obscuring the fact that voluntarist medieval thinkers such as Avicenna

---

[7] To see the contrast between Strauss and Oakeshott on these points, see my essay, 'Theory and Practice in Oakeshott, Strauss and Voegelin', Coats (2012).

and Duns Scotus admitted the possibility of a theoretical knowledge of the strictly human, and, in the case of Scotus, even saw practical knowledge as an extension of theoretical knowledge (Lobkowicz, 1967, pp. 78-9). Strauss also insisted, like the exoteric Maimonides, that the philosophic and biblical ways of life were incompatible, especially creation and incarnation doctrines (Strauss, 1989, p. 260). However, another way of viewing all of this is to say, as we saw Andre de Muralt maintain in the first section of this chapter, that modernity begins in the late medieval period with the voluntarist, nominalist univocal equation of divine and human willing.

To summarize here, the exoteric[8] Strauss uses the idea of creativity, not to distinguish a created from a crafted object, but to designate the entire view that thinking is making and dependent on history, or 'the making of other men'; or, in Kantian terms, that Reason understands that which it produces after a plan of its own; and to suggest this has been the source of modern ideological fanaticisms, modern instrumentalism and modern public immorality.

In contrasting Oakeshott and Strauss on the origins of modern, rationalist ideological thinking we might summarily say the following. For (the exoteric) Strauss it is an outcome of a misguided, enthusiastic, 'creative' attempt to extend the certainty of rational knowledge into the realm of human mutability and time, and turn knowing into making; for Oakeshott it is a consequence of failure to perceive the creative structure of experiential reality through overestimation of the powers of conscious intellect, a development incipient as well in Platonic rationalism and its view of creation as imitative copying of antecedently conceived models, including models for reforming cities (Oakeshott, 1962, pp. 219-21). And in defence of Oakeshott on this point one might cite the ancient Daoist critique of Mohist and Confucian rationalist attempts to 'live by precept', a critique in no way influenced by a creationist and incarnationist religious symbolism. Oakeshott (like the Daoist writers he occasionally cites in footnotes to his critique of rationalism) proceeds by clear-sighted inspection of the basis for skill and balance in all activity, one reason he is appreciative of Aristotelian *phronesis* as a form of knowing. One might also observe, in criticism of Strauss's narrative on this point, that its implication is an indictment as well of the empirical side of all of modern science, a

---

[8] Stanley Rosen (1987, pp. 125-6) argues by logical implication that Strauss's defence of Greek rationalist philosophy is a salutary rhetorical posture, and that Strauss's own views are closer to those of Kant and Nietzsche. That claim is to one side of this chapter's argument which simply engages Strauss's critique of creativity at face value.

development which in combination with its Greek rationalist inheritance has arguably achieved deep insights into knowledge of physical reality, insights which Greek rationalist science could never have achieved *by itself* given its elitist denigration of the material realm.

What Oakeshott and Strauss may be said to have in common in this connection is the view that *theoria*, or the activity of understanding and explaining, has an oblique relationship to practical (political and moral) activity, although less oblique for Plato and Strauss than for Oakeshott. In Straussian terms, 'theory' for Oakeshott still remains more 'seeing' than 'making', in spite of Oakeshott's recognition of the creative character of experiential reality; philosophy for Oakeshott is not practice or production, and 'the theorist of conduct' is not a 'doer' (Oakeshott, 1975, p. 35).

By way of rehearsing this chapter's themes I offer the following summary. I have articulated a point of view about the creative or dynamic tension of Western civilization which is especially congenial for characterizing the life-work of the twentieth-century English philosophical essayist, Michael Oakeshott. It is the tension between its Greek and biblical inheritances as historically mediated by those consummate pragmatists, the Romans and neo-Romans, who couldn't see the contradictions and kept trying to synthesize them, quintessentially in Aquinas. This tension is that between the Greek rationalist view of the primacy of logic in discerning an eternal, teleologically ordered cosmos, and a biblical, creationist account of the universe privileging temporality, will and contingency, a tension manifest in the rational and empirical aspects of modern science, for example. I have suggested that Oakeshott's work is a rather unique take on this tension, in that it uses philosophic reason to identify the constructivist structure of all experiential reality as creative or poetic; and then uses this creative structure as a basis for his contingent preferences with regard to a plurality of subjects from morality, politics and art, to philosophic and historical theorizing. I have tried to illustrate *both* the cogency of this large narrative for understanding the Western intellectual and social progression from unity and compactness to increasing differentiation and plurality, *as well as* its aptness in providing a degree of unity for Oakeshott's wide-ranging *opus*.

One practical implication of this chapter's argument is that the modern and postmodern ascendancy of the pole of creative differentiation in this dynamic tension may have reached its apex in the anarchic rush to 'validate all difference' and now calls out for the re-appearance of its opposite, if the animating tension of the West is not to be drained. Arguably, Oakeshott's account of 'the creative' in human experience provides a sustainable and cogent view for a unified diversity grounded in a theoretically satisfying narrative of historically evolved forms generating identity and meaning from the sheer flux of contingency and particularity.

References

Bhuta, N. (2015) The mystery of the state: State concept, state theory and state making in Schmitt and Oakeshott, in Dyzenhaus, D. & Poole, T. (eds.) *Law, Liberty and the State*, pp. 18-19, Cambridge: Cambridge University Press.

Boucher, D. (2012) Oakeshott in the context of British idealism, in Podoksik, E. (ed.) *The Cambridge Companion to Oakeshott*, pp. 259-268, Cambridge: Cambridge University Press.

Boyd, R. & Morrison, J.A. (2007) F.A. Hayek, Michael Oakeshott, and the concept of spontaneous order, in Hunt, L. & McNamara, P. (eds.) *Liberalism, Conservatism and Hayek's Idea of Spontaneous Order*, New York: Palgrave Macmillan.

Cheung, C. (2014) The critique of rationalism and the defense of individuality, *Cosmos & Taxis*, **1** (3).

Coats, W.J., Jr. (2012) Theory and practice in Oakshott, Strauss and Voegelin, in Coats, W.J. & Cheung, C., *The Poetic Character of Human Activity*, Lanham, MD: Lexington Books.

Dihl, A. (1982) *The Theory of Will in Classical Antiquity*, Berkeley, CA: University of California Press.

Emberly, P. & Cooper, B. (eds.) (1993) *Faith and Political Philosophy: The Correspondence between Leo Strauss and Eric Voegelin, 1934-1964*, University Park, PA: Penn State University Press.

Foster, M.B. (1934) The Christian doctrine of creation and the rise of modern natural science, *Mind*, **43** (Oct.), p. 464, n.1.

Foster, M.B. (1935) *The Political Philosophies of Plato and Hegel*, Oxford: Clarendon Press.

Hayek, F. (1952) *The Sensory Order: An Inquiry into the Foundation of Theoretical Psychology*, London: Routledge.

MacIntyre, A. (1981) *After Virtue*, Notre Dame, IN: University of Notre Dame Press.

MacIntyre, A. (1988) *Whose Justice: Which Rationality?*, Notre Dame, IN: University of Notre Dame Press.

Maimonides, M. (1963) *The Guide of the Perplexed*, Pines, S. (trans.), Chicago, IL: University of Chicago Press.

de Muralt, A. (1991) *L'Enjeu de la Philosophie Medievale*, Leiden: E.J. Brill.

Oakeshott, M. (1933) *Experience and Its Modes*, Cambridge: Cambridge University Press.

Oakeshott, M. (1967) Learning and teaching, in Peters, R.S. (ed.) *The Concept of Education*, pp. 156-176, London: Routledge.

Oakeshott, M. (1975a) *Hobbes on Civil Association*, Berkeley, CA: University of California Press.
Oakeshott, M. (1975b) *On Human Conduct*, Oxford: Clarendon Press.
Oakeshott, M. (1962) *Rationalism in Politics and Other Essays*, London: Methuen and Co.
Podoksik, E. (2013) From difference to fragmentation, in Henkel, M. & Lembcke, O. (eds.) *Praxis und Politk – Michael Oakeshott im Dialog*, pp. 101-104, Tübingen: Mohr Siebeck.
Podoksik, E. (2015) Neo-Kantianism and George Simmel's interpretation of Kant, *Modern Intellectual History*, September 2015, pp. 1-26.
Rickert, H. (1924) *Kant als Philosoph der Modernen Kultur*, Tübingen: Mohr Siebeck.
Rosen, S. (1987) *Hermeneutics as Politics*, New York: Oxford University Press.
Strauss, L. (1952) On Collingwood's philosophy of history, *The Review of Metaphysics*, **5** (4).
Strauss, L. (1989) *The Rebirth of Classical Political Rationalism*, Pangle, T. (ed.), Chicago, IL: University of Chicago Press.
Taylor, C. (1992) *The Ethics of Authenticity*, Cambridge, MA: Harvard University Press.

Noël O'Sullivan

Constitutionalism, Legitimacy and Modernity in Michael Oakeshott and Leo Strauss

Amongst postwar defenders of constitutional democracy, a major division existed between thinkers like Strauss, who insisted on the need to recover ancient political wisdom as the only antidote to the relativism he sees as the main threat to modern constitutional democracy, and Oakeshott, for whom the modern world contains within itself the principal resources required to sustain a viable constitutionalism in the form of an ideal of civil association based on the rule of law. Only a concept of constitutionalism shaped by this ideal, Oakeshott maintains, can solve the modern problem of legitimacy, for which ancient thought offers no answer. This chapter examines the rival positions of a leading defender of the ancients and a notable defender of the Moderns from the standpoint of the problem of constitutional legitimacy.

Strauss

For Strauss, the greatest danger confronting contemporary liberal democracies is an internal rather than an external one, consisting of a moral relativism which means that 'the principles of cannibalism are as defensible or sound as those of civilized life' (Strauss, 1953, p. 3). The result is that the modern ideal of constitutional government rests on nothing more than 'our blind preferences' (Strauss, 1953, pp. 4–5). An excellent example of this malaise is provided by the contemporary American liberal intelligentsia, whose members no longer believe that the self-evident truths proclaimed in the Declaration of Independence are based upon unchanging principles of natural right but are merely 'an ideal, if not an ideology, or a myth' (Strauss, 1953, p. 2). Although relativism does not automatically doom modern constitutional democracy, it does mean that it lacks a foundation which can protect it against totalitarianism and, ultimately, nihilism (Strauss, 1953, pp. 4–5).

The advent of moral relativism is attributed by Strauss to the gradual erosion of the pre-modern natural right conception of the human condition by three successive waves of intellectual development which destroyed the classical political philosophy that enshrined knowledge of natural right. The first wave, which is represented by Machiavelli and Hobbes, involved a 'lowering of sights' in politics due to the rejection by both thinkers of the idealism characteristic of traditional political philosophy in favour of a realism based on 'how men [actually] live' (Strauss, 1989a, p. 86). This lowering of standards was accompanied by the rejection of the pre-modern belief that chance or *fortuna* is the ultimate determinant of political success. In Machiavelli's case, for example, an outstanding man can, in principle at least, overcome chance (Strauss, 1989a, p. 85). Machiavelli's rejection of the ancient belief in the insuperability of chance was shared by Hobbes, for whom political science is the art of creating a rational structure in which chance has no place by basing that structure entirely on the right of self-preservation (Strauss, 1989a, p. 88). It was in this way that Hobbes promoted the lowering of political standards that culminated in the modern doctrine of the rights of man found, for example, in the 'right of comfortable self-preservation which is the pivot of Locke's teaching' (Strauss, 1989a, p. 89) as well as being a central concern of Locke's liberal successors.

The main characteristic of the second wave, represented for Strauss by Rousseau, is an intensification of the break with classical political philosophy due to a new concept of freedom as self-determination, expressed in Rousseau's case by the concept of the general will. For Strauss, this concept of freedom marked the final rejection of a moral order independent of man's will (Strauss, 1989a, p. 91) which was completed by Hegel's replacement of the concept of nature by history, conceived of as a process in which freedom is inevitably actualized in modern Western democracies.

In the third wave of modernity, represented by Nietzsche, the sense of historicity inaugurated by Hegel is retained, but belief in progress is replaced by a tragic perspective according to which history is intrinsically meaningless. The loss of historical meaning is accompanied, however, by an intensified belief in man's potential creativity (Strauss, 1989a, p. 96). It is this belief, Strauss notes, which links Marx and Nietzsche, despite their radical opposition in other respects, in so far as they both regard modernity as finally ending the rule of chance.

Modernity, that is, is the first age in which man replaces God by entirely shaping his own existence: man becomes, in short, 'the master of his fate' (Strauss, 1989a, p. 97). Since the sense of historicity remains deep-seated, however, the third wave is characterized not only by extraordinary faith in the power of will but also by the triumph of relativism.

The political conclusion Strauss draws from his account of the three waves is that while 'The theory of liberal democracy, as well as that of communism, originated in the first and second waves of modernity', the political implication of the third wave 'proved to be fascism' (Strauss, 1989a, p. 98). He emphasizes, however, that the collapse of the old natural law vision does not inevitably lead to the collapse of liberal democracy because, unlike communism and fascism, it has continued despite the three destructive waves to derive 'powerful support from a way of thinking which cannot be called modern at all—the premodern thought of our western tradition' (Strauss, 1989a, p. 98). Before considering the ways in which Strauss believes pre-modern thought has continued to support liberal democracy, however, it is necessary to consider the difficulties created by his relentlessly negative view of modern political thinkers.

The first difficulty concerns Strauss's claim that Machiavelli is guilty of a 'lowering of sights' by maintaiining that 'political life is not subject to morality' (Strauss, 1989a, p. 86). What Machiavelli maintains, however, is entirely different, which is that there is a difference between private and public morality that was not adequately acknowledged by ancient and medieval thinkers. As Federico Chabod put it, Machiavelli's 'true and essential contribution to the history of human thought [is] the clear recognition of the autonomy and the necessity of politics' (Chabod, 1965, p. 116). Strauss is incorrect, then, to present Machiavelli as rejecting morality. Machiavelli's concern is, rather, with a deeper appreciation of the complexity of political morality.

Perhaps the most serious instance of Strauss's misrepresentation of modern thinkers, however, relates to Hobbes. Above all, Strauss's desire to emphasize Hobbes's lowering of moral standards and elimination of chance from political science means that he simply ignores the central feataure of Hobbes's thought, which is an ideal of sovereign authority intended to accommodate individual freedom and moral pluralism. Why is it, one must ask, that the central position of sovereignty in the modern state is, as Pippin remarks, 'not even a problem for [Strauss]' (Pippin, 1997a, p. 187; cf. Fuller, 1997a, p. 185)?

One reason is Strauss's 'perfectionist' perspective which echoes the classical Greek concern with politics as a means of promoting the good life, rather than the modern concern with the conditions for legitimate authority (Mewes, 1997, p. 189). Closely related to this is Strauss's sympathy for the ancient assumption that practical wisdom is a condition for the possession of authority (Strauss and Cropsey, 1981, p. 49). In the modern constitutional state, in contrast, sovereign authority comes not from the wisdom of rulers but from their occupancy of an office recognized as authoritative by those within its sphere of jurisdiction. As Hobbes puts it, the source of authority lies in the fact that those subject to it 'own' the acts of their representative. It is because of the impersonal nature of the office that the modern view is able to reconcile individual freedom with acknowledgement of authority. In itself, the possession of practical wisdom by rulers, in other words, can never render their authority compatible with freedom.

In addition to the reasons just mentioned for Strauss's neglect of sovereignty, there is yet another which is perhaps the most important of all. This is his central concern with modern relativism. With this in mind, Strauss identifies the principal task of political philosophy as the 'foundationalist' one of locating an objective standard of rationality by means of which, as he put it in *Natural Right and History*, 'we can [not only] distinguish between genuine needs and fancied needs' but also 'discern the hierarchy of the various types of genuine need' (Strauss, 1953, p. 3). Where, then, did Strauss think such a standard of rationality might be found?

Although Strauss turns in the first instance to Plato for guidance, he does not turn to the well-known Plato of *The Republic* who favours rule by philosophers who grasp the eternal ideas of things. Instead, Strauss emphasizes the need for a standard of rationality shaped by practical rather than theoretical reason. With this in mind, he turns in particular to the Plato of *The Laws* (Strauss, 1981, pp. 51–2). There, Plato specifically rejected the claim of theoretical reason to provide the sole title to rule and maintained instead that 'The viable regime must be [not only] mixed', but 'mixed wisely' (Strauss, 1981, p. 56). What then is the 'right mixture'? Plato's answer, according to Strauss, is that it consists 'of wisdom and freedom, of wisdom and consent, of the rule of wise laws framed by a wise legislator and administered by the best members of the city, and of the rule of the common people' (Strauss, 1981, p. 56). It is because *The Laws* settles for an ideal of mixed or balanced government derived from practical reason that Strauss describes it as Plato's 'only political work' (Strauss, 1975, p. 1).

Although Strauss's quest for an objective standard of rationality emphasizes practical rather than theoretical reason, the very fact that he conceives of the political problem in terms of such a standard inevitably means that constitutionalism of the modern, essentially juridical, kind is an irrelevance to him: what really matters for him, as it did for Plato, is education. This, however, immediately poses the question of what kind of education can provide the rationally grounded form of constitutionalism Strauss seeks. His answer is that it must be an education based in the first instance on the restoration of common sense to the fundamental position in moral and political education assigned to it by classical thought. Since Strauss's concept of common sense is diametrically opposed to the one familiar in popular usage today, it is necessary to clarify what he means by it.

In ancient thought, common sense referred to the reflective practical wisdom of mature and experienced citizens, rather than the uninformed *doxa* (opinion) of the mass. In practice, Strauss maintains, restoration of it requires the recovery of the classical ideal of liberal education—an ideal now lost because education is largely in the hands of technocratic elites who have reduced it to 'hardly more than the interplay of mass taste with high-grade but ... unprincipled efficiency' (Strauss, 1989b, p. 23). Above all, the restoration of liberal education requires rejection of the contemporary conception of a university as primarily a centre for specialized research. For Strauss, the essence of liberal education consists, rather, in studying 'the great books which the greatest minds have left behind'—books he defines as those written by the few teachers who have ceased to be pupils (Strauss, 1989b, p. 3). The great books in Strauss's sense, it may be added, do not comprise a canon, or provide a doctrine or a programme: they consist, rather, in what Timothy Fuller aptly describes as 'hints of a connoisseur to initiates as to what to look for' (Fuller, 1997b, p. 71, n.12).

The aim of an education of this kind, Strauss explains, is to 'found an aristocracy within democratic mass society' which will permit us to 'ascend from mass democracy to democracy as originally meant' (Strauss, 1989b, p. 5). It is, then, to an elite of liberal gentleman, rather than to philosophers, that Strauss turns in order to provide enlightened political leadership. Unlike the philosopher, Strauss stresses, the gentleman is not an intrinsically subversive figure because he realizes that in politics 'it is a sound rule to let sleeping dogs lie or to prefer the established to the nonestablished or to recognise the right of the first occupier. Philosophy [in contrast] stands or falls by its intransigent disregard of this rule' (Strauss, 1989b, pp. 14-15). The city, then, can more easily accommodate the practical wisdom of the gentleman than the inevitably subversive speculations of the philosopher.

To the charge that there seems to be little likelihood of finding any Straussian gentlemen to rule us in an era characterized by the loss of contact with the natural order outlined in the three-waves essay discussed above, Strauss gives a somewhat surprising reply. It is that, despite the ubiquitous character of moral relativism, a significant body of gentlemen endowed with classical wisdom nevertheless still survives, in England and America at least. In the case of England, Strauss maintained in a 1941 lecture on 'German Nihilism', it was the very English thinkers who were responsible for the loss of contact with natural right who 'were at the same time versed in the classical tradition' and helped to preserve it (Strauss, 1999, p. 372). In the American case, Strauss refused to adopt the contemptuous attitude displayed by fellow émigrés like Adorno and Marcuse, for whom the United States exemplified mass society at its worst. Despite his reservations, Strauss wrote that 'I share the hope ... and faith in America' (Strauss, 1989c, p. 233). Even if Bonnie Honig's sceptical remark that the America Strauss admired was really a 'reflecting pool' into which he projected a vision of his own has a certain truth, Strauss's sympathy for the US remains an important qualification to his general tendency to regard the story of modernity in terms of a spiritual fall (Honig, 1997, p. 178).

It is Strauss's optimism about the survival of liberally educated gentlemen rooted in the classical tradition of natural right, then, which explains his otherwise puzzling claim (in *What is Political Philosophy?*) that modern constitutional democracy 'comes closer to what the classics demanded than any alternative that is viable in our age' (Strauss, 1988, p. 113). Even if a form of constitutionalism based on rule by gentlemen is regarded as feasible in an era of moral relativism, however, such an ideal provides no solution to the problem of legitimating sovereignty which any theory of the modern European state must confront. What it offers is, instead, only a theory of power — power placed, it is true, in the hands of intelligent and well-intentioned rulers who claim to be guided by an objective standard of rationality, but who do not on that account exercise anything more than power. They have, that is, no claim to be entitled to obligate those over whom they rule in a way which constrains their freedom. By focusing attention on the need for a rational standard for identifying genuine need, in short, Strauss's version of constitutionalism merely by-passes the problem of legitmating sovereignty.

The two major problems presented by Strauss's philosophy so far considered relate to his unduly negative assessment of modern political thinkers, on the one hand, and his apparent indifference to the nature of sovereignty, on the other. The third problem concerns the concept of nature on which his entire philosophy rests. If there is indeed a natural order which is simultaneously an ethical one, as Strauss claims, then not only does his largely negative assessment of modern political thinkers gain plausibility; what also follows is that he can claim that the issue of legitimacy he appears to neglect is in fact automatically solved, in so far as the natural order comprises an ethically based hierarchy that can be defended without resort to concepts such as a public realm and a representative system of government.

Strauss fully acknowledged the difficulty facing modern readers who wish to understand the classical conception of nature (or, more precisely, his interpretation of it), attributing their problem in part to modern historicist and positivist assumptions which have in effect dug what he describes in *Persecution and the Art of Writing* as a second cave beneath the natural one originally outlined in *The Republic* (Strauss, 1952, pp. 155–6). But in addition to the difficulty created by the new sub-cave, Strauss argued, the problem of regaining classical knowledge of nature is made still more difficult by the tendency of pre-modern philosophers to mask their true thoughts in order to avoid persecution for challenging the existing social order (Strauss, 1953, p. 33). Although both of Strauss's claims have provoked a large literature, they will not be examined in the present context since that would shed no light on the ultimate problem his thought presents. This is the problem of whether knowledge of a natural order, as Strauss conceives it, is in fact logically possible. If it is not, then to pursue ancient philosophy in the hope that it will yield such knowledge is a wild goose chase.

The principal difficulty posed by Strauss's conception of classical natural right is apparent as soon as one of the most remarkable features of his three-wave account of modernity is noticed. This is that it ignores Kant. The omission is crucial since Kant, as Richard Kennington remarks, is the thinker who 'more than any other [modern thinker] ... emptied "natural right" of meaning by asserting that the moral law must be a law of reason and not a law of nature' (Kennington, 1981, p. 57). Echoing Kennington, Robert Pippin has forcefully emphasized the incoherence at the centre of Strauss's philosophy created by his failure to respond adequately to Kant. It is 'essential ... to the critical force of Strauss's position', Pippin observes, 'that we be able in some way to identify the "natural order of things"'. Yet precisely this identification, Pippin adds, 'is what is so incompatible theoretically with post-Kantian critical philosophy', the significance of which is that it renders impossible the kind of unmediated or uninterpreted knowledge of reality that Strauss attributes to the classical conception of the natural order (Pippin, 1997b, pp. 150–1).

The philosophical difficulty presented by Strauss's concept of the natural order means, it need hardly be said, that his interpretation of Plato must be called into question in so far as he regards Plato's philosophy as the key to the classical concept of nature. In particular, Strauss's claim that he finds in Plato only what Plato himself intended to say is impossible to sustain in view of the fact that what Strauss turns to Plato for is an answer to an essentially modern problem unknown to Plato—the problem, that is, of nihilism posed by Nietzsche, Heidegger and Strauss himself.

The last major problem presented by Strauss's political philosophy which will be considered here is his claim that what characterizes modernity is a potentially disastrous relativism, in the sense of unqualified moral subjectivism. As Strauss put it in a sentence quoted above, we confront today a situation in which 'the principles of cannibalism are as defensible or sound as those of civilized life' (Strauss, 1953, p. 3). Many contemporary philosophers have pointed out, however, that the absence of belief in a timeless, universally valid natural order of the kind Strauss has in mind does not entail relativism in his sense. As an eminent admirer of Hume, Simon Blackburn concluded in a compelling critique of relativism (Blackburn, 1998, pp. 306-7), it is foolish to forget Hume's salutary reminder that even a 'peevish delicacy' can never 'be carried so far as to make us deny the existence of every species of merit, and all distinctions of manners and behaviour' (Hume, 1975, p. 242; see Long, 1998). The core of the relativist error, Blackburn notes, is the assumption that, if we cannot appeal to universal principles, we are left with nothing more than our own opinions as the only ground of the rightness and wrongness of things. What this disregards is the fact that 'Cruelty is not bad because I think it is bad, but because it exhibits the intention to cause pain' (Blackburn, 1998, pp. 307-8). Strauss's indictment of modernity in terms of relativism, then, seriously misrepresents the moral situation of the contemporary world.

When the difficulties outlined above are taken into account, the conclusion must be that Strauss's attempt to construct a defence of modern constitutional democracy based on the universal and timeless foundations he believed existed in classical political thought is flawed in important respects. It would be unfortunate, however, if the defects of that defence were allowed to obscure the fact that several major revisions in contemporary political science which Strauss calls for on the basis of classical political thought remain relevant to any defence of constitutionalism, even though they fail to provide the ambitious underpinnings Strauss sought.

The first revision Strauss advocates is a recovery of the ancient realization that politics is an essentially endless activity. Unlike modern radical ideologies which characterize the good society as one in which power and conflict (and therefore politics itself) have been abolished, that is, classical political philosophy acknowledges ineliminable problems at the heart of human existence to which the only appropriate response is openness to their reality, rather than dreams of a final solution (Strauss, 1989b, p. 14).

The second revision Strauss desires is a recovery of classical awareness of the extremely limited role abstract reason can play in politics. The key to this awareness is a distinction between theoretical and practical knowledge which modern political science, under the influence of positivism, fails to make. Positivism identifies the aim of political science as the accumulation of facts, in the interest of making generalizations and predictions. Unlike ancient political science, it has no regard for the practical wisdom which only actual involvement in political activity itself can provide (Strauss, 1989b, p. 205). More generally, indifference to practical wisdom has opened the door to the modern world of ideological politics, in which abstract visions without roots in the common sense world of concrete practice have dominated much political thought.

The third revision for which Strauss calls is closely connected to the second: it is the realization that classical political philosophy had no place for the fact/value dichotomy on which modern political science is based. That dichotomy only appeared when contemporary political science, under the influence of natural science, rejected the common sense perspective in which classical moral and political thought was rooted on the ground that common sense is wholly subjective and must be replaced by supposedly 'value free' empirical data that can be quantified. But precisely because modern political science claims to be value-free, Strauss contends, it lacks a criterion of political relevance, of the kind inherent in the practical wisdom (incorporated in the common sense of mature citizens) upon which classical political science was based. In short, instead of the political wisdom offered by classical political thought, all that is offered by contemporary political science is quantitative methods which claim to predict political events but inevitably fail to do so since the world is too complex to permit this (Strauss, 1989b, pp. 203–23).

The final revision of contemporary political science proposed by Strauss as fundamental to the defence of modern constitutionalism involves a recovery of a truth about the nature of the good life which was central to classical political philosophy but has been rejected by modern totalitarian ideologies. This is that the good life is extra-political. For Strauss this life is, as it was for Plato, the life of philosophy, the inescapably subversive nature of which means that it cannot possibly be the life of the citizen. The problematic aspect of Strauss's defence of this truth arises not so much from his conviction that the good life is extra-political as from his desire to identify the philosophic life with the highest life. The defence of constitutionalism in either its ancient or modern forms requires only the more modest proposition that the highest good is not to be found in politics.

These, then, are instructive lessons from classical thought which Strauss seeks to incorporate into modern political science in order to strengthen the defence of modern constitutionalism. It must be repeated once again, however, that no matter how compelling such revisions may be, they are contributions to the theory and practice of good government, rather than to the modern problem of legitimacy. More precisely, the revisions Strauss proposes are intended to further the quest for rulers who possess an objective standard of rationality with which to distinguish genuine from fancied needs, rather than to explain how citizens who value freedom may nevertheless acknowledge an obligation to obey laws with which they may not only disagree, but which may be made by rulers whose virtue and rationality they may not aknowledge. The only solution, Hobbes suggested, is the mutual acknowledgement by all citizens of the authority of a sovereign, in the form of an impersonal, legally constituted office whose occupant is authorized to make rules which do not impose a substantive purpose, doctrine or vision of any kind. Since this response to the problem of legitimacy will be considered more fully in connection with Oakeshott's thought, further consideration of it may be postponed. For the moment, it is appropriate to conclude the review of Strauss by highlighting an unresolved tension at the core of his political thought which has already been touched upon but which warrants more emphasis.

The tension in question is between Strauss's desire, on the one hand, to retrieve from ancient political philosophy a deeper concept of the political than has been common in Western progressive thought since the Enlightenment by acknowledging, in particular, the open and unending nature of political activity (see Honig, 1993; Mouffe, 1993; Newey, 2001); and his desire, on the other hand, to overcome modern relativism by underpinning his position with a timeless, universally valid foundation which would yield a completely objective standard of moral and political truth. In the end, it was the latter—profoundly antipolitical—desire which gained the ascendancy, as is evident, for example, in Strauss's debate with Carl Schmitt.

According to Schmitt, much modern liberal political theory has been especially guilty of indulging in a flight from politics into an apolitical vision of the good society inspired by the utopian hope that the spread of enlightenment will gradually remove all major sources of conflict from the social order. Although Strauss rightly accused Schmitt of exaggerating the place of conflict in politics to such an extent that Schmitt was unable to distinguish between politics and war, this well-founded criticism did not invalidate Schmitt's identification of much liberal thought as a depoliticization project (Meir, 1995, pp. 116–17). What is relevant at present is the fact that, ironically, Strauss himself succumbs to that depoliticization project in so far as he shares the liberal dream of grounding constitutionalism, as has been noticed above, on a rational, extra-political standard for distinguishing genuine from fancied needs. It is the claim to possess such a standard, for example, which entitles Strauss's elite of gentlemen rulers to dismiss those who disagree with them as benighted cave-dwellers caught up in the pursuit of fancied needs.

In order to avoid misunderstanding, it must immediately be added that Strauss's version of the 'depoliticization' project did not entail anything as crude as predicting the end of the state. On the contrary, Strauss was highly critical of Alexandre Kojève for sympathizing with the Hegelian vision of history as a struggle for recognition which would eventually bring about the end of the state by creating an harmonious condition of universal equality. For Strauss, in contrast, universal recognition, should it (*per impossible*) ever occur, would not mean the end of the state but only a condition he describes as the state of the Final and Universal Tyrant (Strauss, 1991, p. 211).

Strauss does not, then, foresee the end of the state. What has been suggested, however, is that he nevertheless shares the liberal depoliticization project in so far as he attempts to by-pass the issue of legitimacy by relying upon a ruling elite that can eliminate political conflict by deploying an objective standard of rationality to distinguish genuine from fancied needs.

Oakeshott

For Oakeshott, as for Strauss, the kind of constitutionalism which characterizes contemporary liberal democracies provides an inadequate foundation for freedom. In Oakeshott's case, the source of this inadequacy is not the relativism criticized by Strauss but consists, rather, in an ineradicable tension between two fundamentally different ways of thinking about the state which lies at the heart of modern European politics, with the result that the meaning of every word in the modern Western political vocabulary is ambiguous, including the concept of a constitution itself.

One way of thinking about the state, which Oakeshott describes as an 'enterprise' or 'managerial' model, involves conceiving of it as held together by a common purpose, religion or ideology which it is the task of government to promote. Within this way of thinking, a constitution is merely a tool for imposing a substantive interpretation of the good society. An example is the Soviet constitution of 1936 which appeared on paper to be one of the most democratic constitutions ever adopted by a modern state. In reality, the constitution was merely a tool used by Stalin to implement a totalitarian ideology.

The other way of thinking about the state conceives of it as held together solely by the formal bond of non-instrumental rules which do not involve the imposition by government of a substantive vision of social order. Oakeshott describes a state of this kind as a civil association. Constitutionalism, in the context of civil association, therefore has a very different meaning to the one it possesses in an enterprise conception of politics. To be precise: in civil association, a constitution is not a device for promoting the good society, however that may be understood. It determines, rather, an identity—specifically, the identity of citizenship.

In this respect, Oakeshott maintains, the rule of law in civil society is like the rules of a game: the rules of chess, for example, are not an instrument for playing chess but define what it *means* to play chess and to be a chess-player. As Oakeshott puts it, the rules of a game do not

> procure a wished-for future satisfaction. [Nor] are they guides to the effective use of power ... Nor [are they] commands to do or to forbear ... To be related in terms of these non-instrumental rules is to be related in a mutual obligation to observe the conditions which themselves constitute the game, an obligation which ... may be symbolically expressed in deference to their custodian: an umpire or referee. (Oakeshott, 1983, p. 126)

An important implication of Oakeshott's comparison of the rules of a game with those of civil association is that a constitution in civil association must not be narrowly understood, as it often is, as referring to a written constitution. In civil association it consists, rather, in an ongoing acknowledgement of the rule of law, expressed in an unending concern for preserving the integrity of the non-instrumental procedures which define civil identity and, by so doing, confer legitimacy on those who hold office according to the rules of the particular civil association in question.

Unless the two different meanings of constitutionalism in the 'civil' and 'enterprise' ways of interpreting politics are borne in mind, Oakeshott maintains, the result will be a continuation of the deep-seated confusion about the conditions for legitimacy which has characterized European political thought since the very beginning of the modern period. The result of this confusion, he observes, has been that what are often referred to as the 'constitutional histories' of European states have often been little more than 'stories of somewhat confused and sordid expedients for accommodating the modern disposition to judge everything from the point of view of the desirability of its outcomes in policies and performances and to discount legitimacy'

(Oakeshott, 1975, p. 193). Confusion of this kind, Oakeshott emphasizes, is not of merely academic significance: what is at stake is a dangerous inability to distinguish clearly between legitimate authority, on the one hand, and arbitrary (albeit more or less benign) power, on the other.

It is likely to be objected at this point that Oakeshott's use of the model of civil association to interpret the meaning of constitutionalism in a free society creates serious difficulties, of which the first is that it is surely impossible to interpret *any* state solely in terms of a formal system of rules of the kind that comprise civil association. Oakeshott does not, however, maintain that a *complete* account of a constitutional state can be given in terms of civil association; on the contrary, he insists that *every* state inevitably displays some characteristics of enterprise association, of which levying taxation is the most obvious. In addition, no state can operate solely through rules: it must inevitably issue specific directives or commands that cannot be analysed in terms of the rule-bound activities of legislating and adjudicating (Oakeshott, 1975, p. 144). But if that is so, what then is the point of the model of civil association, if it cannot provide a comprehensive account of the state?

The answer is the realization that a free society always involves a *tension* between the civil and managerial (or enterprise) aspects of government. Since Oakeshott's acknowledgement of the inescapable nature of this tension is fundamental to his thought, his concern is not the utopian one of purging modern European politics of the ambiguity which is the source of the tension. He is not concerned, that is, to advocate the (impossible) transformation of the state into a pure civil association. His concern is, rather, to warn against glossing over the tension instead of confronting it.

In this connection, Oakeshott is critical, in particular, of the social democratic belief that a 'middle way' can be found which offers the best of all worlds. During the decades since the Second World War, indeed, the dangerous complacency encouraged by this belief may plausibly be regarded as the greatest threat to the preservation of constitutionalism of the 'civil' kind.

A second objection, closely related to the first, likely to be made to Oakeshott's commitment to civil association as the core of a free society is that it is wholly unrealistic because it is incompatible with the enterprise-type functions of government now regarded as fundamental to social democracy. This is not so, however. In the course of outlining the duties of contemporary politicians Oakeshott explicitly acknowledges that they must compromise with social democracy by acting to prevent 'fear of unemployment' as well as to alleviate ignorance and disease, concessions which potentially pave the way for extensive government managerial activity. In addition, he referred approvingly to Quintin Hogg's view that economic freedom requires the diffusion of property 'as widely as possible throughout the community' (Oakeshott, 2007, pp. 216-17). If it is asked how far Oakeshott's compromise between civil association and social democracy could go, the answer seems to be that any compromise must satisfy two conditions. One is that the government must wherever possible avoid central planning which imposes a unitary purpose on citizens and operate instead through fiscal and regulatory methods. The other is that government activity must not pursue projects which inevitably threaten the rule of law.

A third possible objection to Oakeshott's identification of the conditions for legitimacy with those of civil association is that it rests on a narrowly legal conception of civil identity which ignores the reality of multiculturalism. John Gray, for example, has maintained that 'insofar as a policy is held together by little else than allegiance to [the] abstract principles or procedural rules [of civil association], it will be fragmented and weak' (Gray, 1991, p. 24). To this criticism it may be replied that what Oakeshott is committed to is not so much an 'abstract' (to use Gray's term) concept of legal identity which ignores cultural identity, as a concept of sovereignty which permits no appeal to some higher (cultural) authority such as reason, natural law, God or Allah. This is of course a politically demanding requirement, as Oakeshott himself fully acknowledges, but one which is entirely compatible with mutlticultural minorities committed to mutual toleration.

Finally, an objection to Oakeshott's model of civil association that is more difficult to rebut concerns his concept of the self, which is open to the charge of resting upon a narrowly existentialist emphasis on choosing as the primary expression of human identity. This criticism carries weight, since narrowness is particularly evident, for example, in a simplistic portrait Oakeshott gave of modern European history as a struggle between two different kinds of self, *viz*. the individual who relishes personal responsibility, on the one hand, and the 'individual manqué' (or anti-individual) who turns to government in order to escape responsibility for choosing his own life, on the other (Oakeshott, 1991, pp. 363-83). Even if this picture is oversimplified, however, it is possible to argue in response that Oakeshott's model of civil association can be detached, in some degree at least, from his concept of the self, in a way which permits revision of the latter whilst still retaining the civil model as a formulation of the conditions for constructing a public realm (*respublica*) in a way compatible with individual freedom.

Conclusion

For Strauss, the great danger confronting liberal democracy is relativism, which has destroyed contact with the natural order and left modern forms of constitutionalism without a solid moral foundation. For Oakeshott, in contrast, the danger is an instrumental perspective which pervades modern Western culture and makes it almost impossible to appreciate the non-instrumental conditions for political legitimacy entailed by the model of civil association—the conditions, that is, on which the preservation of a free society depends. It has been argued that Oakeshott's view offers the most coherent interpretation of the present situation of liberal democracies. I will conclude by considering very briefly the main practical problem posed by Oakeshott's analysis of that situation, which is whether the concept of constitutional legitimacy embodied in the ideal of civil association is viable in modern Western liberal democracies.

Oakeshott himself provided a disturbing answer to this problem in his late work, in which he argued that the greatest challenge to the preservation of a free society is the fact that the non-instrumental perspective upon which civil association depends is only possible in a culture which has at its core a sense of play. Without this, a regard for forms and procedures which serve no extraneous purpose is almost impossible, since they will be seen as merely veils for privilege and obstacles to 'modernization', rather than the guardians of liberty. In modern European technological culture, however, Oakeshott maintains that the sense of play has been almost completely destroyed by a concern with control. In this respect, it may be noticed, Oakeshott sympathized with the cultural pessimism of notable continental conservative contemporaries like the Spanish philosopher Ortega y Gasset (1961) and the Dutch historian Johan Huizinga (1970), as well as with radical thinkers like Adorno and Horkheimer (Adorno and Horkheimer, 1972).

The implication of Oakeshott's pessimism is that the concern for legitimacy upon which civil association depends will simply cease to exist. This is, I think, a more plausible vision of the future of liberal democracy than Strauss's concern with the dangers of relativism. It is worth emphasizing that Oakeshott's misgivings would not be allayed by the survival of the outward institutional forms often associated with civil association—institutions, that is, such as parliaments, general elections and parties—since the reality will be that only a language of power, rather than an ethical language of law, authority and obligation, is left with which to defend them. If Oakeshott's misgivings in this respect prove to be well founded, then his fate as a political thinker may ultimately be the one Hegel suggested befalls all great political theorists when he remarked that the owl of Minerva takes wing only at dusk. Oakeshott may have clarified the constitutional requirements of legitimacy, that is to say, at the very time when the course of history has begun to turn decisively away from the model of civil association upon which they depend.

References

Adorno, T. & Horkheimer, M. (1972) *Dialectic of Enlightenment*, New York: Seabury Press.

Austin, J. (1873) *Lectures on Jurisprudence, or the Philosophy of Positive Law*, London: Murray.

Blackburn, S. (1998) *Ruling Passions*, Oxford: Oxford University Press.

Chabod, F. (1965) *Machiavelli and the Renaissance*, New York: Harper and Row.

Cooper, B. (1996) Introduction to E. Voegelin, in *Political Religions*, New York: Edwin Mellen Press.

Drury, S. (2005) Postmodernity: Plato or Nietzsche?, in *The Political Ideas of Leo Strauss*, London: Macmillan.

Dunn, J. (1969) *The Political Thought of John Locke*, Cambridge: Cambridge University Press.

Ferry, L. (1990) *Political Philosophy 1. Rights: The New Quarrel between the Ancients and the Moderns*, Franklin, P. (trans.), Chicago, IL: Chicago University Press.

Fuller, T. (1997a) Discussion: The influence of German philosophy, in Kielmansegg, P.G., Mewes, H. & Glaser-Schmidt, E. (eds.) *Hannah Arendt and Leo Strauss: German Émigrés and American Political Thought after World War II*, Cambridge: Cambridge University Press.

Fuller, T. (1997b) Reflections on Leo Strauss and American education, in Kielmansegg, P.G., Mewes, H. & Glaser-Schmidt, E. (eds.) *Hannah Arendt and Leo Strauss: German Émigrés and American Political Thought after World War II*, Cambridge: Cambridge University Press.

Gray, J. (1991) Oakeshott as a liberal, *The Salisbury Review*, **10** (1).

Honig, B. (1993) *Political Theory and the Displacement of Politics*, New York: Cornell University Press.

Honig, B. (1997) Discussion: The influence of German philosophy, in Kielmansegg, P.G., Mewes, H. & Glaser-Schmidt, E. (eds.) *Hannah Arendt and Leo Strauss: German Émigrés and American Political Thought after World War II*, Cambridge: Cambridge University Press.

Huizinga, J. (1970) *Homo Ludens*, London: Paladin.

Hume, D. (1975) *Enquiries Concerning Human Understanding and Concerning the Principles of Morals*, Selby-Bigge, L.A. (ed.), 3rd ed. revised by Nidditch, P.H., Oxford: Oxford University Press.

Kelsen, H. (1964) Foundations of democracy, in Stankiewicz, W.J. (ed.) *Political Thought Since World War II: Critical and Interpretive Essays*, New York: Free Press of Glencoe.

Kennington, R. (1981) Strauss's natural right and history, *Review of Metaphysics*, **35** (September).

Long, G. (1998) *Relativism and the Foundations of Liberalism*, Exeter: Imprint Academic.

Machiavelli, N. (1950) *The Prince*, New York: Random House.

Meir, H. (1995) *Carl Schmitt and Leo Strauss: The Hidden Dialogue*, Chicago, IL: University of Chicago Press.

Mewes, H. (1997) Discussion: The influence of German philosophy, in Kielmansegg, P.G., Mewes, H. & Glaser-Schmidt, E. (eds.) *Hannah Arendt and Leo Strauss: German Émigrés and American Political Thought after World War II*, Cambridge: Cambridge University Press.

Mouffe, C. (1993) *The Return of the Political*, London: Verso.

Newey, G. (2001) *After Politics*, Basingstoke: Palgrave.

Oakeshott, M. (1975) *On Human Conduct*, Oxford: Clarendon Press.

Oakeshott, M. (1983) *On History and Other Essays*, Oxford: Blackwell.

Oakeshott, M. (1991) The masses in representative democracy, in *Rationalism in Politics and Other Essays*, Indianapolis, IN: Liberty Press.

Oakeshott, M. (2004) The new science of politics, in O'Sullivan, L. (ed.) *What is History? And Other Essays*, Exeter: Imprint Academic.

Oakeshott, M. (2007) Contemporary British politics, in O'Sullivan, L. (ed.) *The Concept of a Philosophical Jurisprudence*, Exeter: Imprint Academic.

Ortega y Gasset, J. (1961) *The Revolt of the Masses*, London: Unwin.

Pippin, R. (1997a) Discussion: The influence of German philosophy, in Kielmansegg, P.G., Mewes, H. & Glaser-Schmidt, E. (eds.) *Hannah Arendt and Leo Strauss: German Émigrés and American Political Thought after World War II*, Cambridge: Cambridge University Press.

Pippin, R. (1997b) The modern world of Leo Strauss, in Kielmansegg, P.G., Mewes, H. & Glaser-Schmidt, E. (eds.) *Hannah Arendt and Leo Strauss: German Émigrés and American Political Thought after World War II*, Cambridge: Cambridge University Press.

Strauss, L. & Cropsey, J. (eds.) (1981) *History of Political Philosophy*, Chicago, IL: University of Chicago Press.

Strauss, L. (1952) *Persecution and the Art of Writing*, Glencoe, IL: Free Press.

Strauss, L. (1953) *Natural Right and History*, Chicago, IL: University of Chicago Press.

Strauss, L. (1975) *The Argument and Action of Plato's Laws*, Chicago, IL: University of Chicago Press.

Strauss, L. (1981) *History of Political Thought*, Chicago, IL: University of Chicago Press.

Strauss, L. (1988) *What is Political Philosophy?*, Chicago, IL: University of Chicago Press.
Strauss, L. (1989a) The three waves of modernity, in Gildin, H. (ed.) *An Introduction to Political Philosophy: Ten Essays by Leo Strauss*, Detroit, MI: Wayne State University Press.
Strauss, L. (1989b) *Liberalism Ancient and Modern*, Chicago, IL: University of Chicago Press.
Strauss, L. (1989c) *The Rebirth of Classical Political*, Chicago, IL: University of Chicago Press.
Strauss, L. (1991) *On Tyranny*, Gourevitch, V. & Roth, M.S. (eds.), New York: Free Press.
Strauss, L. (1999) German nihilism, *Interpretation*, **26** (3), Spring 1999.
Voegelin, E. (1966) *The New Science of Politics*, Chicago, IL: University of Chicago Press.

Chor-yung Cheung

Oakeshott, Hayek and the Conservative Turn of Chinese Liberalism

Oakeshott and Chinese Liberalism

As far as I know, Professor Zhang Rulun (張汝倫) of Fudan University is the first scholar who reflects on Oakeshott's relevance to Chinese liberalism. At the inaugural Michael Oakeshott Association conference held in 2002, he presented a paper entitled 'Oakeshott and Chinese Liberalism', a revised Chinese version (〈歐克肖特和中國自由主義〉) of which was subsequently published in his *Conscience and Theory* (《良知與理論》).[1]

In that paper, Zhang observes that judging from Oakeshott's critique of modern rationalism, Chinese liberalism is rationalist through and through. Zhang argues that there are clear family resemblances between the six common positions identified by a leading Chinese liberal Yin Haiguang (殷海光)[2] (namely: against Confucianism;

---

[1] Guangxi Normal University Press (廣西師範大學出版社), 2003, pp. 176–89. I am using the Chinese published version of Zhang's paper here. The English translation of the Chinese text in this paper, unless otherwise specified, is mine.

[2] Yin is one pivotal figure in Chinese liberalism. See his *Prospect of Chinese Culture* (《中國文化的展望》), 2 Vols. (Taiwan: National Taiwan University Publishing Centre (台大出版中心), 2011), for a detailed discussion of the six common Chinese liberal positions stated in the main text as quoted by Zhang Rulun. Born in 1919, Yin is regarded as one of the last leading liberals of the pre-war generation who were directly influenced by China's May Fourth Movement (which heralded the intellectuals' new culture campaign for the introduction of science and democracy to China and against Confucianism), and helped keep the ideal of liberalism alive in postwar China in the 1950s–1960s by his moral integrity and fight for democracy in Taiwan. Yin fled with the Nationalist Party to Taiwan in 1949

promoting science; pursuing democracy; advocating freedom; believing in progress; and, using the vernacular language to replace classical Chinese, which are adopted by many Chinese liberals) and modern rationalists' insistence on the sovereignty of technical knowledge, the authority of reason and reason alone, radical doubt over unexamined experience and traditional practices, and preferring things that are eternal and universal to things that are temporary and partial.

In other words, according to Zhang, Chinese liberals, when confronted with the political and cultural challenges from Western imperial powers since the Qing Dynasty was forced to open up China after a series of military defeats in the nineteenth century, believe that what is required is a rational blueprint to help China modernize. In particular, they think that there must be a comprehensive plan to revitalize China's national strengths, to develop a scientific culture and to establish democracy in the modern Chinese state.

To the Chinese liberals, traditional Chinese culture, with its emphasis on feudalistic, hierarchical and collectivist values, resistance to change and aversion to modern and scientific scholarship, is more a fundamental barrier than a pool of resources for China to achieve those modernization goals. Although Chinese liberalism is not as successful as Chinese communism in wielding political power to implement its modernization programmes, it is no less radical in believing that the outdated Chinese tradition must be replaced in a wholesale manner by the 'universal' culture of modernity, and the key to this is to use scientific knowledge and a rational plan to help transform China both politically, economically, technologically and culturally, and the model to follow is the modern states in the West, not the intimations of the conventional practices within her own tradition.

Oakeshott's relevance to Chinese liberalism in this regard is that his philosophical insights could help us understand the follies of the

---

after the latter was defeated by the communists in the civil war. Since then, Chinese liberalism could not be openly discussed (except as a main target of criticism in political prosecution) on the Chinese mainland under the rule of the Chinese Communist Party until China opened up to the world again in the 1980s. Yin's liberal ideas were very influential in post-1949 Taiwan and were instrumental in inspiring the opposition forces in Taiwan to fight against the ruling Nationalist Party, leading to the introduction of democracy in Taiwan in the 1990s. His experience and ideas are also enthusiastically studied on the mainland after the Chinese Communist Party has loosened its ideological control since the1980s. For a recent book-length study on Yin's liberalism by a mainland Chinese scholar, see He, Z., (何卓恩), *Yin Haiguang and Modern Chinese Liberalism* (《殷海光與近代中國自由主義》) (Shanghai: Shanghai Joint Publishing (上海三聯), 2004).

rationalistic pretension of Chinese liberalism if one finds Oakeshott's analysis persuasive; or conversely, for the Chinese liberals, what amounts to the same logic though with an opposite substantive conclusion from the above position, Oakeshott is totally irrelevant and unconvincing, since they strongly disagree with Oakeshott's claim that 'political crisis (even when it seems to be imposed upon a society by changes beyond its control) always appears *within* a tradition of political activity; and "salvation" comes from the unimpaired resources of the tradition itself.'[3]

More recently, Zhang has revisited some of the issues he raised in his 2002 paper in 'Oakeshott in China'.[4] In this 2015 published article, Zhang further observes that since the Chinese liberals would very much like to import constitutional democracy to China to save her from the tyrannical rule of totalitarianism under the one-party state or despotism under the traditional dynastic emperors, Oakeshott's stricture over the illusion of putting theory into practice makes it difficult for the Chinese liberals to use his theory of civil association as a guide to convert China into a liberal state. Oakeshott's emphasis on the importance of the authority of the state as a postulate in his philosophical idea of the rule of law also puzzles the ideological liberals in China, since they have already put freedom and democracy as premediated purposes for the construction of a legitimate state for a modern China. Freedom, therefore, must be protected by human rights, which are more or less universal. Laws are instruments to constrain the government from infringement against the rights of the citizens, and the model of separation of powers must be accepted as a prime principle for constitutional democracy in China.

In a nutshell, what Zhang is saying is that while the Chinese liberals' plan to resist the socialists' central planning or totalitarian rule is laudable, they nevertheless are not sceptics but rationalists, holding a highly ideological view of a liberal state the style of which is the same as the socialists and advocates of totalitarianism. Chinese liberals in the end believe that the way to introduce constitutional democracy to China is by reason and rational design, with tradition playing little part in this undertaking.

Zhang's Oakeshottian arguments against Chinese liberalism are powerful and illuminating. Broadly speaking, there is much truth in his

---

[3] Oakeshott, M., 'Political education', in *Rationalism in Politics and Other Essays*, foreword by Fuller, T., new and extended edition (Indianapolis: Liberty Press, 1991), p. 59, emphasis in the original.

[4] In Nardin, T. (ed.), *Michael Oakeshott's Cold War Liberalism* (London: Palgrave MacMillan, 2015), pp. 137–51.

critique of Chinese liberalism. However, his is not the whole story. The relationship between tradition and Chinese liberalism is richer than what Zhang has described in his two essays discussed above, and a closer look at the development of postwar Chinese liberalism reveals that more and more Chinese liberals increasingly come to realize that to cope with the challenges of modernity, 'even the help we may get from the traditions of another society (or from a tradition of a vaguer sort which is shared by a number of societies) is conditional upon our being able to assimilate them to our own arrangements and our own manner of attending to our arrangements.'[5] But before the Chinese liberals came to appreciate Oakeshott's insights, they went to Hayek first in the 1950s, since Hayek as a theorist of civil association does have a plan to resist all planning by whittling down the arrogance of synoptic rationalism with emphasis on the role performed by traditional practices in the spontaneous development of a liberal society.

Hayek and Chinese Liberalism

The publication of *The Road to Serfdom*[6] in 1944 not only made Hayek famous (or notorious) in the West, it also attracted the attention of many Chinese liberals in Taiwan, particularly from the 1950s onwards, some of whom have since become increasingly Hayekian in their liberalism, which was quite an important departure from pre-war Chinese liberalism.

In his excellent *The Intellectual Foundations of Chinese Modernity*,[7] Edmund S.K. Fung rightly observes that 'from May Fourth on, liberalism and socialism were intimately intertwined in the minds of many liberal [Chinese] intellectuals.'[8] In particular, Fung's analysis shows that while the pre-war Chinese liberals were at one with their Western counterparts in upholding individual freedom, constitutionalism and the like, 'they were not opposed to ... the exercise of state initiative to

---

[5] See Oakeshott, M., 'Political education', in *Rationalism in Politics and Other Essays*, foreword by Fuller, T., new and extended edition (Indianapolis: Liberty Press, 1991), p. 59.

[6] Hayek, F.A., *The Road to Serfdom* (Chicago: University of Chicago Press, 1944/1972).

[7] Fung, E.S.K., *The Intellectual Foundations of Chinese Modernity: Cultural and Political Thought in the Republican Era* (Cambridge: Cambridge University Press, 2010).

[8] Fung, E.S.K., *The Intellectual Foundations of Chinese Modernity: Cultural and Political Thought in the Republican Era* (Cambridge: Cambridge University Press, 2010), pp. 191–2.

develop the economy and to regulate the market simultaneously.'⁹ Hu Shih (胡適),¹⁰ one of the leading protagonists of the May Fourth Movement for a new culture for China and the leading liberal thinker in modern China until his death in 1962, recalled that, in the 1930s, he believed that 'socialism is a logical sequence of the democratic movement.'¹¹ Even Yin Haiguang said this in 1948: 'In the search for a bright road for China's future ... the consensus is that China must go down the "democratic socialist" road. For democratic socialism is the child born in wedlock between democracy and socialism, having the blood of democracy and the blood of socialism. It combines the best of both worlds to create an ideal society.'¹² But after having read Hayek's *The Road to Serfdom*, many leading Chinese liberals in postwar Taiwan changed their mind.

Hayek's thought was introduced to Taiwan by his first Chinese student at the London School of Economics, Zhou Dewai (周德偉), who studied monetary theory under Hayek there in the 1930s. It was through the influence of Zhou that Yin Haiguang subsequently translated most of *The Road to Serfdom* into Chinese in the mid-1950s, while Zhou himself translated Hayek's *The Constitution of Liberty*¹³ in the early 1970s with a preface written by Hayek in English for this edition. It was in the process of translating *The Road to Serfdom* that Yin started to query his previous belief that so long as nationalized and strategic enterprises are ultimately accountable to a democratically elected government, it is right for the state to have control over these enterprises.¹⁴ He now came to realize that without economic freedom for the

---

9   Fung, E.S.K., *The Intellectual Foundations of Chinese Modernity: Cultural and Political Thought in the Republican Era* (Cambridge: Cambridge University Press, 2010), p. 259.
10 For an excellent discussion of Hu Shih's liberalism, see Grieder, J.B., *Hu Shih and the Chinese Renaissance: Liberalism in the Chinese Revolution, 1917–1937* (Cambridge: Harvard University Press, 1970).
11 This was taken from Hu Shih's 24 November 1953 diary entry, and I quote this from Lin Jiangang's (林建剛) 'From Laski to Hayek: Western scholarship in Hu Shih's changing thought' (〈從拉斯基到哈耶克：胡適思想變遷中的西學〉), in *Theoretical Perspective* (《理論視野》), October 2013, pp. 61–3.
12 Quoted from *The Intellectual Foundations of Chinese Modernity*, p. 253. The English translation here is Fung's.
13 Hayek, F.A., *The Constitution of Liberty* (Chicago: Chicago University Press, 1960).
14 Yin still held this view in 1950, as shown in his article 'Russell on authority and the individual' (〈羅素論權威與個體〉), see *Essays by Mr. Yin Haiguang, Volume 1* (《殷海光先生文集(一)》) (New York: Laurel Publishing (桂冠出版社), 1982), p. 37.

individual and the protection of private property, the so-called political freedom under democracy would be increasingly undermined, and the people would unwittingly be slipping down the slope into serfdom in the end.¹⁵ Hu Shih, after having read *The Road to Serfdom*, also remarked in his diary that 'Hayek's book argues that socialism and liberty cannot co-exist at the same time and I found this persuasive ... I am a liberal, and liberalism believes in a healthy and proper individualism. So I will not accept socialist doctrine of any kind.'¹⁶

While the Chinese liberals in Taiwan were persuaded by Hayek's theoretical arguments in the 1950s, many mainland intellectuals, when they were able to read Hayek for the first time in the 1980-1990s, found *The Road to Serfdom* nothing short of prophetic, though paradoxically in a somewhat retrospective manner, since what Hayek analysed in the book in 1944 was corroborated more than once in their tragic personal experience during the great famines in the 1950s and the political upheavals of the Great Cultural Revolution from 1967–1976. 'This book had a huge impact on me', said Yang Jisheng (楊繼繩), a leading liberal journalist, now retired, on the mainland whose prize-winning book *Tombstone: The Great Chinese Famine 1958–1962*¹⁷ chronicles the first major man-made catastrophe in China that led to an estimated 36 million people dying of starvation under the totalitarian rule of the Communist Party. Yang remembers vividly Trotsky's statement quoted by Hayek in the book: 'In a country where the sole employer is the State, opposition means death by slow starvation.'¹⁸

Hayek's social and political philosophy is naturally far more profound than just a defence of the free market and a demonstration of the incompatibility of individual freedom and socialism, and his devastating critique of constructivistic rationalism, his insight into the concurrent development of mind and civilization, as well as his enrichment of the Scottish Enlightenment's thesis that social institutions are

---

15 See his Preface to the translated edition of *The Road to Serfdom* (《到勞役之路》) (Taiwan: National Taiwan University Publishing Centre, 2011), pp. 1-2.
16 See note 11 above.
17 Jisheng, Y., *Tombstone: The Great Chinese Famine 1958–1962*, Mosher, S. & Jian, G. (trans.), Friedman, E., Mosher, S. & Jian, G. (eds.), (New York: Farrar, Straus and Giroux, 2012).
18 Hayek, F.A., *The Road to Serfdom* (Chicago: University of Chicago Press, 1944/1972), p. 119. Yang's book *Tombstone* won the Manhattan Institute's Hayek Prize in 2013, and his views on Hayek and China can be seen in the interview he gave to *The Wall Street Journal* in 'Reading Hayek in Beijing', 24 May 2013, by Stephens, B., online at http://www.wsj.com/articles/SB10001424127887324659404578501492191072734, accessed on 20 August 2015.

the result of human action but not human design, all started to influence many Chinese liberals in Taiwan. Thinkers like Yin Haiguang, who had been very critical of Chinese tradition and regarded it as a barrier to China's development of science and democracy, began to be mindful of the danger of turning science into scientism by synoptic rational social planning. Yin was also aware of the role of the rule of law as a bulwark for democracy after studying Hayek. More importantly, Hayek's emphasis on the importance of traditional practices and evolutionary rationality had convinced liberals like Yin that a modern China could not be developed without revitalizing her own tradition, and from that time onwards we can see that Chinese liberalism, at least in Taiwan, has started to lose its wholesale radical rejection of traditional culture. Since then, the proper relationship between liberty and tradition in China's pursuit of modernization has accordingly become an unavoidable question to be reflected on by Chinese liberals.

I have elsewhere examined this transition in Chinese liberalism and criticized an influential liberal like Yin Haiguang for still failing properly to assimilate Hayek's complicated theoretical insights into his Chinese liberalism, since the former's adherence to the radicalism and rationalism of the May Fourth Movement was too strong for him to make a smooth U-turn to Hayek's classical liberalism.[19] It was also unfortunate that Yin died at the relatively young age of 50 in 1969, and was thus deprived of the possibility of further developing his more tradition-sensitive kind of Chinese liberalism. But his student Lin Yu-Sheng (林毓生), who also went to Chicago to study under Hayek in 1960, has continued this intellectual pilgrimage in Chinese liberalism and has since contributed to a more profound and convincing reflection on the proper relationship between liberty and tradition under Chinese liberalism.

Liberalism and the Creative Transformation of Chinese Tradition

Lin, in my view, is one of the more profound Hayekian Chinese liberals whose ideas are immune from many of the Oakeshottian criticisms against Chinese liberalism raised by Zhang Rulun. In the limited space of this chapter, I will not be able to do justice to many of Lin's carefully considered and nuanced arguments, nor to give a systematic critical overview of his liberal thought. What I can manage to do here is to

---

[19] See my forthcoming Chinese book *Political Thinkers Series: F.A. Hayek* (《政治思想家：海耶克》) (Taiwan: Linking Books (聯經出版事業), 2017), particularly chapters 10–11.

briefly examine how, through the influence of Hayek and other classical liberals, Lin comes to appreciate the limits of reason, the mutual dependence of freedom and authority, and the need to creatively transform those unimpaired resources of Chinese tradition to help provide a moral foundation allowing democracy and the rule of law, which are foreign to traditional Chinese culture, to take root in China as she faces the challenges of modernity.

First of all, it is of interest to note that in his devastating critique of the May Fourth's anti-traditional intellectual radicalism, Lin finds that despite the fact that leading radical intellectuals of the May Fourth like Hu Shih, Chen Duxiu (陳獨秀, the founder of the Chinese Communist Party who turned Trotskyist in the end and was expelled by the Party) and Lu Xun (魯迅, the most prominent left wing literary figure in China during the May Fourth period) all adopted an explicit totalistic rejection stance against the Chinese cultural heritage (Lin calls this 'totalistic iconoclasm'), their frame of mind ultimately was powerfully though unconsciously influenced by the deep-rooted traditional Chinese mode of holistic thinking, which assigns primary responsibility to cultural and intellectual ideas in social and moral changes, though this time round the 'ideas' concerned were a wholesale adoption of science and democracy from the West.[20] This should remind us of Oakeshott's observation that 'The Russian Revolution (what actually happened in Russia) was not the implementation of an abstract design worked out by Lenin and others in Switzerland: it was a modification of *Russian* circumstances. And the French Revolution was far more closely connected with the *ancien regime* than with Locke or America.'[21] If Oakeshott were in a position to reflect on the May Fourth era, he probably would agree that the radical intellectuals' 'totalistic iconoclasm' was largely a modification of the dominant traditional Chinese mode of holistic thinking, the emphasis of which is more on

---

[20] See Lin, Y., *The Crisis of Chinese Consciousness: Radical Antitraditionalism in the May Fourth Era* (Madison: University of Wisconsin Press, 1979). See also Lin's 'Radical iconoclasm in the May Fourth period and the future of Chinese liberalism', in Schwartz, B.I. (ed.), *Reflections on the May Fourth Movement: A Symposium* (Cambridge: Harvard University Press, 1973), pp. 23-58, in which Lin argues that while there may be some ambiguity as to whether one can derive this traditional mode of thinking from classical Confucianism, it is certain that post-classical Confucianism since the Song and Ming dynasties has embodied this mode up to the present day.

[21] Oakeshott, M., 'Political education', in *Rationalism in Politics and Other Essays*, foreword by Fuller, T., new and extended edition (Indianapolis: Liberty Press, 1991), p. 59, n.6, emphasis in the original.

abstract ideas than on actual concrete practices. To Oakeshott, this is very much in line with the nature of ancient Confucian thought:

> Ren [仁] in the Confucian morality was an abstraction from the filial piety and respect for elders which constituted the ancient Chinese habit of moral behavior. The activity of the Sages, who (according to Zhuangzi) *invented* goodness, duty and the rules and ideals of moral conduct, was one in which a concrete morality of habitual behavior was sifted and refined; but, like too critical anthologies, they threw out the imperfect approximations of their material and what remained was not the reflection of a literature but merely a collection of masterpiece.[22]

I do not think that Lin arrives at the above conclusion under the influence of Oakeshott, but the conclusion nevertheless is in line with one important common ground shared by the respective critiques of rationalism by Hayek and Oakeshott: that the abstract Cartesian type of reason is wrong to think that one can go beyond one's traditional practices to start afresh *intoto* for rational planning for reform or revolution.[23]

Hayek's critique of Cartesian rationalism is based on his sophisticated theory of knowledge,[24] in which the mind is characterized as essentially a mechanism of classification in which external stimuli one has perceived are related to other stimuli or to one's past experience remembered within the classificatory structure of one's mental order, in relation to which one makes sense of human interaction and the external environment, and also in relation to which one derives meanings and values which guide one's actions. Like all classificatory structures, the mind cannot classify itself and it is therefore logically impossible for it to fully explain itself or to go outside itself to give a

---

[22] See Oakeshott, M., 'Tower of Babel', in *Rationalism in Politics and Other Essays* (Indianapolis: Liberty Press, 1991), p. 480, n.2, emphasis in the original. I have discussed Oakeshott and classical Chinese thinking in 'Skepticism, poetic imagination, and the art of non-instrumentality: Oakeshott and Zhuangzi' and 'Learning and conversation: Oakeshott and Confucius', both in Coats, W.J. & Cheung, C., *The Poetic Character of Human Activity: Collected Essays on the Thought of Michael Oakeshott* (Lanham: Lexington Books, 2012), pp. 19–40 and pp. 57–78, respectively.

[23] For a comparison of Hayek's and Oakeshott's critique of rationalism, see my 'The critique of rationalism and the defense of individuality: Oakeshott and Hayek', in *Cosmos and Taxis*, 1 (3), 2014, pp. 3–9.

[24] For a fuller discussion of this, see my 'Beyond complex: Can *The Sensory Order* defend the liberal self?', in Marsh, L. (ed.), *Hayek in Mind: Hayek's Philosophical Psychology, Advances in Austrian Economics*, 2011, pp. 219–39.

full and synoptic view of the mind. That is why Hayek contends that 'The mind can never foresee its own advance.'[25]

Furthermore, in a market or a society there exists numerous diverse and dispersed 'knowledge of particular circumstances of time and place',[26] the contents and possible use of which are only known to each and every concerned individual. Also, the nature of this type of knowledge (such as personal preferences) is contextual and fleeting, changeable in accordance with the anticipated or perceived results of the interaction amongst the participating individuals, whose respective perceptions and decisions made under the circumstances will not be known in advance by any single mind. With these logical and circumstantial limitations in mind, it is absurd to assume that rationality can be based purely on certain clear and distinct premises which have survived the test of universal doubt and are therefore conceptually absolutely certain, from which one can deduce a system of certain knowledge to design the most rational result for all. That is why Hayek says,

> Man did not simply impose upon the world a pattern created by his mind. His mind is itself a system that constantly changes as a result of his endeavor to adapt himself to his surroundings ... [T]he growth of the human mind is part of the growth of civilization; it is the state of civilization at any given moment that determines the scope and the possibilities of human ends and values.[27]

In a number of essays written in the 1980s,[28] Lin essentially adopted the above Hayekian understanding of rationality. In these essays, following in the footsteps of Hayek, he also cited Polanyi's ideas of 'focal awareness' and 'subsidiary awareness'[29] to argue that, in every rational thinking process, both types of awareness are needed since subsidiary

---

[25] Hayek, F.A., *The Constitution of Liberty* (Chicago: Chicago University Press, 1960), p. 24.
[26] See Hayek, F.A., 'The use of knowledge in society', in his *Individualism and Economic Order* (Chicago: University of Chicago Press, 1948/1980), pp. 77-91.
[27] Hayek, F.A., *The Constitution of Liberty* (Chicago: Chicago University Press, 1960), pp. 23-4.
[28] See Lin's *The Creative Transformation of Chinese Tradition* (《中國傳統的創造性轉化》) (Joint Publishing (生活‧讀書‧新知三聯書店), 1988); in particular, see 'What is rationality' (〈什麼是理性〉), pp. 43-64, 'On the relationship between freedom and authority' (〈論自由與權威的關係〉), pp. 65-75, and 'Further discussion on the relationship between freedom and authority' (〈再論自由與權威的關係〉), pp. 76-87.
[29] See Polanyi, M., *Personal Knowledge: Towards a Post-Critical Philosophy* (London: Routledge & Kegan Paul, 1958/1978), particularly chapters 4-5.

awareness provides us with the context to make sense of our focal attention (e.g. the meaning of a particular word in a text depends on the sentence the word is in as its context, and the meaning of the sentence or the full text depends on certain general grammatical and linguistic rules and practices and so on) even though we are not fully conscious of the former or able to articulate it in full.[30]

The concurrent development of mind and civilization not only points to the implausibility of the Cartesian understanding of rationality, it also draws Lin's attention to the importance of existing and accepted institutions and practices embedded in a stable but evolving civilization for the possible growth of knowledge. Lin calls these institutions and practices 'authorities' and only when we subscribe to these 'authorities' can we learn the skills and acquire the necessary knowledge for those practices or ways of doing things. This of course does not mean that 'authorities' are fixed once and for all, since we as individuals and civilization as a whole always face new challenges and the environment we are in is changing all the time. But innovations or new ways of doing things to cope with these new challenges will not come from the void, they must come as improvements or modifications of existing and accepted rules and practices, be they scientific, social, cultural or aesthetical, which proven to be more effective, agreeable or desirable and hence have become new 'authorities'. Naturally, without freedom, people cannot explore new possibilities to find out innovative solutions and to make mistakes. Equally, without subscribing to 'authorities' in the first place, people simply cannot act at all, not to say inventing new measures. In the light of this, Zhang Rulun's criticism of Chinese liberalism in his 'Oakeshott in China' is not completely applicable to Lin's liberalism to say the least, since the latter does not think that freedom and 'authority' are antithetical; instead, properly understood, they are mutually dependent.

One fundamental problem facing Chinese liberals like Lin is that since democracy and the rule of law are foreign to Chinese tradition, how can they subscribe to accepted institutions and practices that are conducive to the protection and enhancement of liberal values, yet at the same time preserve their identification with Chinese culture? To Lin, the only way to go about this is by the creative transformation of Confucian humanism such that a moral foundation can be created out of the unimpaired resources of Chinese tradition to support the political and legal institutions of democracy and the rule of law in the Chinese context.

---

[30] *The Creative Transformation of Chinese Tradition*, p. 50, and pp. 71-2.

Lin accepts that democracy and the rule of law cannot be found in the tradition of China, but this does not entail that the liberal values these institutions support, such as respect for the intrinsic worth of the individual, are necessarily incompatible with certain core Confucian values such as *ren*, which still command respect and acceptance by the Chinese. To Lin, while institutions and cultural values are mutually reinforcing, they are also mutually irreducible in the sense that each sphere has its own relatively autonomous status. 'One can reject all the evils in Chinese traditional society', says Lin, 'without necessarily attacking traditional Chinese culture as a whole.' To him, 'It does not seem far-fetched to say that the formal structure of classical Confucianism is quite compatible with liberal humanism. The concept of *ren* is not identical with the belief in the worth of the individual. But ... in a creative re-interpretation of Confucianism ... there is plenty of room for creative integration of Confucian moral idealism and Western liberal humanism.'[31]

In this respect, Edward Shils is in agreement with Lin. Like Lin, Shils argues that while 'Confucianism ... does not have a concept of civil society [understood as a society of the rule of law] as a complex of institutions and patterns of activities different from those of the family and the state', there are nevertheless elements of civil society in ancient Chinese philosophy because, for example, Confucius's idea of *ren* contains important virtues like 'Moderation, serenity, tranquility, modesty, equanimity, courtesy, resistance to any impulse toward anger' that are 'required in a civil society if the individualism, ambition, and acquisitiveness in the economic sphere are to be held in check'.[32] Nevertheless, we should be reminded of Lin's qualification in this respect: 'One cannot foretell what the outcome of this integration will be; but only on such an integration ... can liberal individualism take root in the consciousness of the Chinese intellectuals. This new liberal individualism will certainly not be the same as that of the West. But it will converge with Western liberal individualism on many important points.

---

[31] See Lin's 'Radical iconoclasm in the May Fourth period and the future of Chinese liberalism', in Schwartz, B.I. (ed.), *Reflections on the May Fourth Movement: A Symposium* (Cambridge: Harvard University Press, 1973), p. 57 and p. 58.

[32] See Shils, E., 'Reflections on civil society and civility in the Chinese intellectual tradition', in Tu, W. (ed.), *Confucian Traditions in East Asian Modernity: Moral Education and Economic Culture in Japan and the Four Mini-Dragons* (Cambridge: Harvard University Press, 1996), pp. 38–71. The first quote in the main text is from p. 46, and the second and third quotes are both from p. 67.

Working for this new synthesis may ... discover a new sense of identity [for the Chinese intellectuals].'[33]

Of course, to Oakeshott, the claim that one must create a 'moral foundation' for the adoption of Western institutions in the process of creative transformation of Chinese culture is still too much for a sceptic to accept, since that is a symptom of the politics of the 'felt need' rather than the politics of sound reason. But a sympathetic reader of Lin's proposal may argue that this is no transcendental foundation of any sort. It simply acts as a cultural anchor for assimilation in the Chinese context. At one point, Lin compares his proposed creative transformation of Chinese tradition as analogous to Weber's *The Protestant Ethic and the Spirit of Capitalism*.[34] I take this to mean that, like the Protestant ethic, Confucian humanism, a kind of traditional value, has to be developed during the transformation process so that it can help sustain the emergence of a new kind of social institution or practice, the exact outcome of which cannot be foretold. However, one should remember that Weber's classical work is a masterpiece of explanation, not a practical guide to transform Middle Ages Christian Europe into capitalism. In the case of Lin's creative transformation proposal, however, it acts more like a plan, albeit one that is immune from the arrogance of Cartesian rationalism and is mindful of the role played by tradition, with a clearly pre-mediated purpose.

Tradition, 'Guided Pursuit of Intimations' and Conservative Liberalism in China

Theoretical contributions to Chinese liberalism made by people like Lin are one reason that helps the Chinese intellectuals become receptive to the kind of conservative liberalism they have encountered since China opened up from the 1980s onwards. Hayek's influence, of course, has been significant. In addition to *The Road to Serfdom*, his lifelong critique of socialism of various kinds turned out to be hugely vindicated by the collapse of the USSR and her Eastern bloc socialist allies since 1989. China's own failed socialist experiment since 1949 played a dominant role in the conservative turn of the Chinese intellectuals too. By the time Liu Junning (劉軍寧), a leading conservative liberal in China, published his article 'Classical Liberalism Catches On in China'[35] in

---

[33] Lin, Y., 'Radical iconoclasm in the May Fourth period and the future of Chinese liberalism', in Schwartz, B.I. (ed.), *Reflections on the May Fourth Movement: A Symposium* (Cambridge: Harvard University Press, 1973), p. 58.
[34] *The Creative Transformation of Chinese Tradition*, p. 64.
[35] Liu, J., 'Classical liberalism catches on in China', *Journal of Democracy*, 3 (11), July 2000, pp. 48–57.

2002, he could claim that 'Classical liberalism now dominates China's intellectual landscape. No other school of political thought enjoys greater popularity in the Chinese intellectual community.'[36]

Of course it would be wrong to think that classical liberalism is now the only brand of liberalism that is influential in China. This, however, is not the place to give a comprehensive account of the development of liberalism in China since the Chinese government has loosened its ideological control. For the purpose of this paper, I intend to briefly examine the works of two leading conservative liberals in present day China, Liu Junning and Qiu Feng (秋風), to see how they have benefited from the insights of classical liberalism and Western conservatism to further develop a kind of Chinese liberalism that pays due regard to traditional practices in its pursuit of freedom and constitutionalism in the Chinese context.

Unlike their fellow liberals during the May Fourth era, Chinese conservative liberals like Liu and Qiu have a far more nuanced and positive view of tradition. In his book *Conservatism* (《保守主義》),[37] Liu argues that, properly understood, tradition is open, evolving not static, covering past, present and future and is structurally pluralistic with possible internal tensions. Tradition is necessarily ambiguous but concrete; and our attitude to tradition must be selective, since no one can embrace tradition as a whole. With these attributes, tradition, to Liu, is capable of self-correction; and the richer a tradition is, the more it may have internal conflicts yet at the same time the more resources it may have to use for assimilation or adaptation.[38] While Liu has not cited Oakeshott for this account of tradition, it is clear that it shares many of the characteristics of Oakeshott's conception of a tradition of behaviour.[39]

---

[36] Liu, J., 'Classical liberalism catches on in China', *Journal of Democracy*, 3 (11), July 2000, p. 54. I should also mention that the late Deng Zhenglai (鄧正來) spent eight years in China translating Hayek's works into Chinese and writing many in-depth commentaries on Hayek, which have helped promote Hayek's social and political philosophy to the Chinese intellectual community. See Deng's *Rules, Order, Ignorance: Studying Hayekian Liberalism* (《規則・秩序・無知：關於哈耶克自由主義的研究》) (Hong Kong: Joint Publishing, 2004), as an example.

[37] Liu, J., *Conservatism*, 3rd edition (Singapore: Oriental Publishing (東方出版社), 2014). This book was first published in 1997.

[38] Liu, J., *Conservatism*, 3rd edition (Singapore: Oriental Publishing (東方出版社), 2014), pp. 264–72.

[39] See Oakeshott, M., 'Political education', in *Rationalism in Politics and Other Essays*, foreword by Fuller, T., new and extended edition (Indianapolis: Liberty Press, 1991), pp. 61–2. I cannot resist the temptation to reproduce this beautifully articulated paragraph of Oakeshott here: '[A] tradition of

With such an understanding of tradition, Liu argues that although Chinese tradition has no elements which strongly support liberal values and institutions, it does not follow that we cannot select those elements within the tradition that are conducive to the development of freedom and civility in order to nurture and enrich the liberality of Chinese culture.[40] As Edward Shils says, 'Tradition is not the dead hand of the past but rather the hand of the gardener, which nourishes and elicits tendencies of judgment which would otherwise not be strong enough to emerge on their own.'[41]

Two points, however, need to be made here. Unlike Oakeshottian conservatives, conservative Chinese liberals like Liu, while having developed a far more amiable conception of tradition than their forebears, still regard freedom as a sovereign ideal that needs to be promoted. Indeed, Liu tries to distinguish his conservatism from traditionalism in China by his contention that traditionalism maintains tradition for its own sake even if it is not liberal, whereas conservative liberalism is conservative because it is there to maintain and conserve

---

behavior is a tricky thing to get to know. Indeed, it may even appear to be essentially unintelligible. It is neither fixed nor finished; it has no changeless centre to which understanding can anchor itself; there is no sovereign purpose to be perceived or invariable direction to be detected; there is no model to be copied, idea to be realized, or rule to be followed. Some parts of it may change more slowly than others, but none is immune from change. Everything is temporary. Nevertheless, though a tradition of behavior is flimsy and elusive, it is not without identity, and what makes it a possible object of knowledge is the fact that all its parts do not change at the same time and that the changes it undergoes are potential within it. Its principle is a principle of *continuity*: authority is diffused between past, present, and future; between the old, the new, and what is to come. It is steady because, though it moves, it is never wholly in motion; and though it is tranquil, it is never wholly at rest. Nothing that ever belonged to it is completely lost; we are always swerving back to recover and make something topical out of even its remotest moments: and nothing for long remains unmodified. Everything is temporary, but nothing is arbitrary. Everything figures by comparison, not with what stands next to it, but with the whole. And since a tradition of behavior is not susceptible of the distinction between essence and accident, knowledge of it is unavoidably knowledge of its detail: to know only the gist is to know nothing. What has to be learned is not an abstract idea, or a set of tricks, not even a ritual, but a concrete, coherent manner of living in all its intricateness' (emphasis in the original).

[40] See de Bary, W.T., *The Liberal Tradition in China* (Hong Kong: Chinese University of Hong Kong Press, 1983), for an interesting account of certain liberal practices in Chinese tradition.

[41] See Shils, E., 'Tradition and liberty: Antinomy and interdependence', in his *The Virtue of Civility: Selected Essays on Liberalism, Tradition, and Civil Society*, Grosby, S. (ed.) (Indianapolis: Liberty Fund, 1997), p. 107.

the value of freedom in tradition.⁴² Liu also explicitly says that if tradition is in conflict with freedom, his conservatism will always stand on the side of freedom, not tradition.⁴³ While I am sure that Liu would no doubt endorse Shils' gardener metaphor in selecting and nourishing liberal elements to enrich Chinese culture, an inevitable dose of rationalism imbues his conservatism since an invariable commitment to freedom is fundamental to his concept of tradition.

Secondly, as Oakeshott says, to learn a tradition of behaviour is never to learn just the gist, but a concrete and coherent manner of living. As Oakeshott has famously argued, learning always involves the partnership of the two aspects of knowledge: the technical aspect and the practical aspect, with the technical part being demonstrable and, in a sense, acting as the gist, while the practical aspect is the detailed and concrete part which normally exists only in doing/acting.⁴⁴ In the light of this, two questions immediately come to mind. First, if, as Liu and other Chinese liberals readily admit, liberal elements within Chinese tradition are far from strong, is the gardener in the Chinese garden skilful or experienced enough to nourish freedom in Chinese culture? Even with the benefit of cross-cultural experience, it would be highly inadequate for the gardener to rely entirely on foreign books on gardening in his/her attempt to transplant liberal flowers from foreign gardens to his/her own without first-hand concrete knowledge. Second, if to know the gist is to know nothing at all in a tradition of behaviour, then even the best theoretical efforts by Chinese liberals to explicate the kind of conservatism or liberalism most compatible with tradition are all half-baked at best, since without actually engaging in a concrete way of living, one can learn and nourish little from abstract principles or arguments alone. In the light of this, would it not be better if we direct more of our attention to learning about the actual, practical and detailed experience of the Chinese in places like Hong Kong and Taiwan in order to see how the former managed to become the most liberal and open society within China and the latter the most democratic?⁴⁵

---

42 Liu, J., *Conservatism*, 3rd edition (Singapore: Oriental Publishing (東方出版社), 2014), pp. 258–60.
43 Liu, J., *Conservatism*, 3rd edition, (Singapore: Oriental Publishing (東方出版社), 2014), p. 263.
44 See Oakeshott, M., 'Rationalism in politics', in *Rationalism in Politics and Other Essays*, foreword by Fuller, T., new and extended edition (Indianapolis: Liberty Press, 1991), pp. 6–42.
45 Of course Hong Kong did have the benefit of being part of the British Empire where the rule of law was not only exported to it as a set of abstract principles, but was accompanied by skilful practitioners from the UK for

Qiu Feng is perhaps the Chinese liberal most mindful of the need to have practical knowledge that is conducive to the nourishment of liberal values in Chinese tradition. He also readily admits that non-rational and non-demonstrable knowledge of this kind can only be learned through doing and acting in contexts in which practical skills of this kind are already embedded. Therefore, he acknowledges that, in the process of learning from the liberal West, the Chinese have learned most at the abstract level of ideological and cultural values like freedom and democracy, on the one hand, and institutional arrangements like the separation of powers, a parliamentary system and an independent judiciary, etc., on the other. What the Chinese have learned least is the kind of practical and circumstantial knowledge that can only be imparted through doing in the right context.[46] However, he further observes that in modern China's political history, it is wrong to just concentrate on the increasing radicalization of Chinese politics since the late nineteenth century. This is because after every stage of radicalization or even revolution from the late Qing era to the republican and subsequent communist regimes, it was followed by a conservative turn for constitutional reform in China. Though most of these conservative turns did not succeed in establishing meaningful constitutionalism in China, the Nationalist government's constitutional enactment in 1946–1947 for the Republic of China eventually brought that constitution to Taiwan after the Nationalist Party fled there in 1949. It is on the basis of that constitution that Taiwan has developed its democratic institutions and practices since 1996 when its president was first returned by universal suffrage. Qiu therefore believes that, in fact, there is an emerging, though far from prevalent, tradition of constitutional politics in the context of Chinese culture which is understudied, and that a better and more thorough understanding of this kind of experience will not only help Chinese liberals enrich their knowledge of constitutional principles, but also their knowledge of the strengths and limits of Chinese practical experience in intimating the politics of constitutionalism in the pursuit of democracy.[47]

---

over 150 years with ample practical first-hand experience in doing and implementing it in a community.

[46] See Qui, F., 'On the conservative turn of liberalism' (〈論自由主義的保守化〉), in *Civilization Embedded: Reflections on Chinese Liberalism* (《嵌入文明：中國自由主義的反思》) (Jiangsu Literary Publishing (江蘇文藝出版社), 2014), pp. 231–306.

[47] See Qui, F., 'On conserving modern China: Thought on constitutionalism and political tradition' (〈論現代中國的保守--憲政主義思想與政治傳統〉), in *Civilization Embedded: Reflections on Chinese Liberalism* (Jiangsu Literary Publishing, 2014), pp. 173–229.

Qiu, like other Chinese liberals, admits that the elements of liberal values in Chinese tradition are weak. But he shares Liu's idea of tradition, believing that tradition is open and could be self-correcting, and that the more liberal elements within tradition can be nourished and enriched in ways that assist the development of democracy and freedom in China in a practical and concrete manner. And the study of China's practice in constitutionalism may help in this regard. Also, since Chinese liberals now mostly get their inspiration from classical liberalism instead of from that of the French Enlightenment (or what Hayek calls 'false individualism'[48]), it is to be hoped that this combination could provide a better chance of success in pursuing the intimations of freedom and democracy in Chinese culture. It is true that this perhaps is still treating freedom and democracy as independently premeditated sovereign purposes, predetermined for the evolution of Chinese tradition, but by ameliorating the arrogance of technical reason and putting more emphasis on the need for practical reason in the development of traditional behaviour towards freedom and civility, Qiu and Liu are perhaps proposing that it may be possible to have a 'guided' pursuit of intimations in order to help China overcome her challenges of modernity.

As a theorist of civil association, Hayek is distinguished by the fact that he is never short of a plan. For example, near the end of his career, he proposed a new model constitution for Western democracies aiming at rectifying their past failings. Though he thinks that one should not expect that this model can be transplanted into a state which lacks a well-entrenched tradition of the rule of law, he nevertheless believes that it can serve as a *guide* for the improvement of the nomocratic order of future democracies.[49] For Chinese liberals who are experiencing a 'felt need' created by political crises in China and the challenges of modernity, Hayek is naturally easier to understand than the sceptical Oakeshott, whose advice for political activity is 'to keep afloat on an even keel' and to use 'the resources of a traditional manner of behavior in order to make a friend of every hostile occasion'.[50] However, I hope that this chapter has shown that the theoretical insights of Hayek and Oakeshott are both relevant to Chinese liberalism, and that the

---

[48] See Hayek, F.A., 'Individualism: True and false', in *Individualism and Economic Order* (Chicago: University of Chicago Press, 1948/1980), pp. 1–32.
[49] See Hayek, F.A., 'A model constitution', in his *Law, Legislation and Liberty, Volume 3: The Political Order of a Free People* (Chicago: University of Chicago Press, 1979), chapter 17.
[50] See Oakeshott, M., 'Political education', in *Rationalism in Politics and Other Essays*, foreword by Fuller, T., new and extended edition (Indianapolis: Liberty Press, 1991), p. 60.

conservative turn of the Chinese liberalism owes not a small debt to these two Western political thinkers. Although no one can foretell what the outcome of this conservative turn will be, I am sure that Chinese liberals are likely to continue their intellectual journey to enrich the civil elements of Chinese tradition, hoping that in the end they may transform this great civilization into a liberal one.

References

Cheung, C. (2011) Beyond complex: Can *The Sensory Order* defend the liberal self?, in Marsh, L. (ed.) *Hayek in Mind: Hayek's Philosophical Psychology, Advances in Austrian Economics*, pp. 219–239, Bingley: Emerald.

Cheung, C. (2014) The critique of rationalism and the defense of individuality: Oakeshott and Hayek, *Cosmos and Taxis*, **1** (3), pp. 3–9.

Cheung, C. (張楚勇) (2017) *Political Thinkers Series: F.A. Hayek* (《政治思想家：海耶克》), Taiwan: Linking Books (聯經出版事業), forthcoming.

Coats, Jr., W.J. & Cheung, C. (2012) *The Poetic Character of Human Activity: Collected Essays on the Thought of Michael Oakeshott*, Lanham, MD: Lexington Books.

de Bary, W.T. (1983) *The Liberal Tradition in China*, Hong Kong: Chinese University of Hong Kong Press.

Deng, Z. (鄧正來) (2004) *Rules, Order, Ignorance: Studying Hayekian Liberalism* (《規則・秩序・無知：關於哈耶克自由主義的研究》), Hong Kong: Joint Publishing (生活・讀書・新知三聯書店).

Fung, E.S.K. (2010) *The Intellectual Foundations of Chinese Modernity: Cultural and Political Thought in the Republican Era*, Cambridge: Cambridge University Press.

Grieder, J.B. (1970) *Hu Shih and the Chinese Renaissance: Liberalism in the Chinese Revolution, 1917–1937*, Cambridge, MA: Harvard University Press.

Hayek, F.A. (1944/1972) *The Road to Serfdom*, Chicago, IL: University of Chicago Press.

Hayek, F.A. (1948/1980) *Individualism and Economic Order*, Chicago, IL: University of Chicago Press.

Hayek, F.A. (1960) *The Constitution of Liberty*, Chicago, IL: University of Chicago Press.

Hayek, F.A. (1979) *Law, Legislation and Liberty, Volume 3: The Political Order of a Free People*, Chicago, IL: University of Chicago Press.

He, Z. (何卓恩) (2004) *Yin Haiguang and Modern Chinese Liberalism* (《殷海光與近代中國自由主義》), Shanghai: Shanghai Joint Publishing (上海三聯).

Lin, J. (林建剛) (2013) From Laski to Hayek: Western scholarship in Hu Shih's changing thought (〈從拉斯基到哈耶克：胡適思想變遷中的西學〉), *Theoretical Perspective* (《理論視野》), October 2013, pp. 61–63.

Lin, Y. (1973) Radical iconoclasm in the May Fourth period and the future of Chinese liberalism, in Schwartz, B.I. (ed.) *Reflections on the May Fourth Movement: A Symposium*, pp. 23–58, Cambridge, MA: Harvard University Press.

Lin, Y. (1979) *The Crisis of Chinese Consciousness: Radical Antitraditionalism in the May Fourth Era*, Madison, WI: University of Wisconsin Press.

Lin, Y. (林毓生) (1988) *The Creative Transformation of Chinese Tradition* (《中國傳統的創造性轉化》), Hong Kong: Joint Publishing (生活・讀書・新知三聯書店).

Liu, J. (劉軍寧) (2014) *Conservatism* (《保守主義》), 3rd ed., Singapore: Oriental Publishing (東方出版社).

Liu, J. (2000) Classical liberalism catches on in China, *Journal of Democracy*, **3** (11), pp. 48–57.

Nardin, T. (ed.) (2015) *Michael Oakeshott's Cold War Liberalism*, London: Palgrave Macmillan.

Oakeshott, M. (1991) *Rationalism in Politics and Other Essays*, foreword by Fuller, T., new and extended ed., Indianapolis, IN: Liberty Press.

Polanyi, M. (1958/1978) *Personal Knowledge: Towards a Post-Critical Philosophy*, London: Routledge & Kegan Paul.

Qui, F. (秋風) (2014) *Civilization Embedded: Reflections on Chinese Liberalism* (《嵌入文明：中國自由主義的反思》), Jiangsu: Jiangsu Literary Publishing (江蘇文藝出版社).

Shils, E. (1996) Reflections on civil society and civility in the Chinese intellectual tradition', in Tu, W. (ed.) *Confucian Traditions in East Asian Modernity: Moral Education and Economic Culture in Japan and the Four Mini-Dragons*, pp. 38–71, Cambridge, MA: Harvard University Press.

Shils, E. (1997) *The Virtue of Civility: Selected Essays on Liberalism, Tradition, and Civil Society*, Grosby, S. (ed.), Indianapolis, IN: Liberty Fund.

Stephens, B. (2013) Reading Hayek in Beijing, *The Wall Street Journal*, 24 May 2013, [Online], http://www.wsj.com/articles/SB10001424127887324659404578501492191072734 [20 August 2015].

Yang, J. (楊繼繩) (2012) *Tombstone: The Great Chinese Famine 1958–1962*, Mosher, S. & Guo, J. (trans.), Friedman, E., Mosher, S. & Guo, J. (eds.), New York: Farrar, Straus and Giroux.

Yin, H. (殷海光) (1982) *Essays by Mr. Yin Haiguang, Volume 1* (《殷海光先生文集(一)》), New York: Laurel Publishing (桂冠出版社).

Yin, H. (2011) *Prospect of Chinese Culture* (《中國文化的展望》), 2 Vols., Taiwan: National Taiwan University Publishing Centre (台大出版中心).

Yin, H. (trans.) (殷海光譯) (2011) F.A. Hayek, *The Road to Serfdom* (《到勞役之路》), Taiwan: National Taiwan University Publishing Centre (台大出版中心).

Zhang, R. (張汝倫) (2003) Oakeshott and Chinese liberalism (〈歐克肖特和中國自由主義〉), in *Conscience and Theory* (《良知與理論》), pp. 176–189, Guilin City: Guangxi Normal University Press (廣西師範大學出版社).

Gurpreet Mahajan

Oakeshott in India
At Home or Out of Place?

A study of the history of Western political thought has been an integral part of the discipline of political science in India. In fact, for a long time, many scholars lamented that Indian traditions of political thought were not studied in classrooms; instead the focus was on concepts and ideas that emerged in the West. While political scientists looked at the British Raj and examined the views that emerged in the encounter with colonial modernity, it is Western political thinkers—from Plato to Marx —that remained central to the study of political science in India. Until the 1970s (i.e. in the first three decades after independence), the English idealist tradition, in particular the writings of T.H. Green, Bernard Bosanquet and F.H. Bradley, attracted a great deal of attention. Yet, despite the influence of English political thought in general and the idealist tradition in particular, Michael Oakeshott was not, and has not, been an important influence in India.

The reasons for this are many: an important one being that exposure to a thinker is often mediated by the representation of his thought in the public discourse. Michael Oakeshott was closely identified with the conservative and anti-rationalist tradition and, in India, this created suspicion, if not also hostility, towards his writings. At the very least these labels fostered a reluctance to engage with his work. Had Oakeshott been read more carefully it might have been evident that, even though he emphasized tradition as a condition of human existence and knowledge, he did not justify everything that existed in a given tradition. However, categories through which his work was represented created what Gadamer calls a pre-judgement, that generated a resistance (rather than willingness to open oneself to) his ideas.

Conditions of Closure and the Possibility of Engagement

In India, tradition has for a while been viewed with some misgiving. The social reform movements, which emerged in the late eighteenth century, systematically questioned several social and religious practices that were sanctioned by tradition (see Panikkar, 1990; Natarajan, 1962). The rationalists, in the nineteenth century, carried forward this task more aggressively. They blamed tradition (backed by religion) for nurturing superstitions and beliefs that were grounded in myths rather than history or reason. They raised their voice against a number of practices that were responsible for the subordination and oppression of women and the lower castes: from *Sati* and child marriage to notions of purity and pollution. Even those who spoke of the glorious past and the richness of the ancient Indian civilization acknowledged the need for a critical engagement with tradition to root out the ills of the caste-based system of stratification and other forms of social inequality.

Although only a few identified themselves as rationalists, aspects of their worldview found favour with many political leaders in the twentieth century. Pandit Jawaharlal Nehru, the first Prime Minster of independent India, held that blind faith and belief in miracles were aspects of tradition that had to be challenged through education and science. He emphasized scientific explanations of natural and social phenomena (such as disasters, epidemics, illness and disease). In this political environment, where a modern India was to be built on the rationality offered by reason and science, there could be little sympathy for ideas that were identified as anti-rational. There were of course a few alternative voices that spoke of traditional/indigenous knowledge and the value of that life-world, but they questioned the existing model of social and economic organization. That is, they critiqued centralized planning and bureaucratization but hardly ever challenged the place of reason in social and political life. Consequently, Oakeshott's analysis of the errors of rationalism in politics found few readers in India. In fact, along with the label of being a conservative political thinker, his anti-rationalism inhibited a positive reception of his work.

While the common modes of representing Oakeshott (at least in the 60s and 70s) generated prejudices that hindered his entry into the intellectual world in India, much has changed since then. Today, the revival of Aristotelian thinking has created space for exploring the limits of reason and engaging with perspectives that do not consider reason-based universal norms to be adequate for political life. Besides, the scholarship that has since emerged around the writings of Oakeshott has put to rest many of the anxieties that were engendered by his position on tradition and reason (see O'Sullivan, 2002). If that is not all, his writings are increasingly being invoked by political theorists of various ideological and political persuasions: from post-Marxists like Chantal Mouffe and postmodernists like Richard Rorty to spokespersons of deliberative democracy. In this changed environment there is today greater possibility and room in India for engaging critically and creatively with the ideas of Oakeshott.

The interest that Oakeshott can generate in India is, however, unlikely to replicate the Western experience. In case of the latter it is the idea of civil association that has received the most attention, and quite understandably so. The West is today grappling with the question of deep diversity: how can people with different moral dispositions live together? How can the freedom of the individual be protected while simultaneously ensuring peace and order? Against the growing recognition of internal plurality and the experience of totalitarian regimes, it is the idea of civil association that has captured the Western liberal imagination. Can this idea, and the notion of law embedded in it, resonate with the people of India? In the context of a globalizing and liberalizing economy, can Oakeshott's notion of nomocracy and civil association appeal to Indians? What is to be gained from an engagement with Oakeshott? Before exploring these questions let me briefly turn to the idea of civil association and what it has come to represent in modern democracies.

Civil Association as a Form of Relationship among *Cives*

Several contemporary theorists have written about and elaborated upon the idea of civil association. Almost all of them elucidate the nature and meaning of the civil relationship by differentiating it from what Oakeshott referred to as enterprise form of association. The latter is described as a relationship 'in terms of the pursuit of some common purpose, some substantive condition of things to be jointly procured, or some common interest to be continuously satisfied' (Oakeshott, 1975, p. 114). The desired end may be the creation of a classless society or social justice; preservation of a culture or some religious end, such as salvation. The relevant thing is that what binds members together in this form of association is the shared commitment to a pre-given goal or a common cause. 'The common purpose may be simple or complex, clearly identified or vaguely imagined; its achievement may be a near or a distant prospect or no prospect at all' (Oakeshott, 1975, p. 114). In contrast to this, civil association is a formal and non-purposive relationship (based not on love or affection or the pursuit of a common interest); within it members are related 'in terms of a practice or language of civil intercourse which they have not designed or chosen but within the jurisdiction of which they recognise themselves to fall and which, in subscribing to it, they continuously explore and reconstitute' (Oakeshott, 1995, p. 183). In other words, the members of civil association accept the authority of the law and agree to follow the system of rules (*lex*) while pursuing their individual interests and goals.

Oakeshott identified these two kinds of associations with two different kinds of human relationships: the enterprise model symbolizing the purposive and prudential, and the civil standing for the non-instrumental and moral (see O'Sullivan, 2012). To put it in another way, civil association is said to embody a moral relationship as it treats human beings as moral agents who are free to self-consciously reflect and pursue their individually chosen ends. In the enterprise form of association everyone is expected to pursue the identified shared goal; those who disagree and are not committed to pursuing the given end have no place in it. They can be silenced or eliminated. On the flip side, since membership of the state is not optional, all are expected to share in the commitment to pursue the shared goal. Hence, everyone is expected to do that which the authorities deem as necessary or essential for the pursuit of the common purpose; there is no space for the individual to act freely. They are merely instruments for the realization of the stipulated end.

A comparison between these two modes of association shows, quite readily, that freedom and human agency can only be protected and recognized in a civil association. Even those individuals who believe that the nation, as a mode of political organization, can be, or should be, committed to a common purpose would have to accept that there is no space for dissenters in this framework. The latter would have to endorse policies that aim to realize the shared concern. If, for instance, the desired goal is to ensure the survival of a given culture then the state may require all persons to send their children to schools where the identified vulnerable culture is the medium of instruction. The pursuit of the common end would place some restrictions upon the right of the individual to choose for her/himself. Given this propensity of the enterprise model, Oakeshott himself favoured civil association as a more desirable form of political relationship, particularly for those who wish to protect individual autonomy; and it is this potentiality of the civil mode that is being underlined by several scholars today.

Chantal Mouffe asserts that 'Oakeshott's idea of civil association as *societas* is adequate to define political association under modern democratic conditions' (Mouffe, 2013, p. 109).[1] Richard Rorty expresses a similar sentiment and argues that civil association has the capacity to nurture a society that liberal democrats would favour. It makes space for freedom of the individual by envisaging a 'band of fellow eccentrics collaborating for purposes of mutual protection rather than a band of fellow spirits united by a common goal' (Rorty, 1993, p. 59). Barber and Mapel also affirm this assessment; in different ways they claim that civil association, envisaged as a non-purposive, non-instrumental relationship, has all the features that are coherent with deliberative democracy. It allows us to combine the values of individuality, freedom, plurality (Minch, 2009, Introduction) and accommodates human beings as 'agents' (Mapel, 1990, p. 393). The idea that members of the state be bound together merely by their agreement to accept the authority of law and the willingness to abide by, and pursue, their individual purposes in accordance with law certainly offers a non-ethnic and non-cultural basis for constituting the political community—something that is essential for protecting freedom and equality for all persons within a diverse society. But does this mean that it is a model that is likely to have an appeal in all plural societies which recognize the presence of different moral dispositions? This is the question I wish to dwell upon now, particularly since Oakeshott himself recognized that the language of civil association is a contingent one—which has emerged in a context where individuals are seen as autonomous agents. If morality is not 'a matter of general principles or abstract rules but a vernacular language, made by its speakers' (Parekh, 1995, p. 174) then one would need to ask if it is indeed suitable for all societies; or more specifically, if this language is indeed suitable for a postcolonial democracy like India? Whether Oakeshott's understanding of law and rule of law is likely to be echoed in Indian democracy? Whether civil association would offer a desirable model of political and public sphere in India?

Is there a Place for Civil Association in India?

The idea of civil association would appear, at first glance, to have no place in India. The Indian Constitution was envisaged as an instrument of social transformation; the newly formed state was expected to pursue equality, both social and economic, and ensure justice for all. These were concrete ends to be followed and some specific measures,

---

[1] She however maintains that Oakeshott's idea of *respublica* along with his concept of politics needs to be changed—something that can be rectified as 'radical principles could easily be introduced here' (Mouffe, 2013, pp. 110-11).

necessary for realizing these ends, were identified in the Constitution. For instance, the practice of untouchability was abolished; temples were opened to members of all castes; bonded labour was outlawed; seats were reserved in legislative bodies for previously excluded populations. Thus, *contra* civil association, the political bond was forged around a commitment to substantive ideals—ideals that had been laid out in the preamble of the Constitution.

Besides this, civil association requires that members acknowledge the authority of the law for itself, irrespective of its content. Since the latter can be changed it is respect for legitimate authority that is a necessary condition of the civil. In India, the civil disobedience movement has left behind a somewhat different legacy. Since the law under colonial rule was an instrument of subordination and oppression of the people, political leaders, like Mahatma Gandhi, asked individuals to assess the content of law. He recognized the need for law as a condition of the political but argued that supporting or abiding by a law that was morally unjust and evil was a crime itself (Haksar, 2001, pp. 109–37). He accepted the punishment that the legitimate authority would give for breaking the law, but insisted on not complying with an unjust law. The call to look at the content of law has left a legacy in which rule of law, or obedience to the authority of law *per se*, does not fit easily.

One might of course argue that the colonial state was an enterprise state and not civil association, and hence it should not be the basis of assessing rule by a system of laws (*Lex*). Yet, historically this was the face of law in India and it justified breaking a morally unacceptable law or wilfully defying it, albeit in a non-violent and non-coercive way. This perception of law violates the basic assumptions of civil association. Add to this the fact that the Constitution of India established a formal legal authority, but it did not decisively challenge the authority of custom and religious leadership. As a result there are competing claims of legitimacy, and the recognition of multiple sites of law and authority has made it difficult for the formal relationship to law to prevail.

The civil disobedience movement was directed against an unjust alien rule. It was assumed by most political leaders then that the situation would change when Indians begin to rule themselves. They believed that the laws that will be made in independent India by a government of the people would necessarily work in the interest of the whole population. This view of a democratically elected government made the framers of the Constitution less suspicious of the interventions of the state. So they did not, unlike the civil association model, envisage a limited state.

As such, the understanding of law and the political that prevails in India defies all that civil association stands for. Over the passage of time, the early insistence on abiding by the conditions of civility that the law, or a commitment to non-violence, imposed has also been steadily eroded. The political has come to be dominated by power rather than legitimate authority. In Oakeshott's framework civil association is anchored in the mutual recognition of the authority of law and the prevalence of rule of law. The civil relationship requires individuals to subject themselves to the authority of law and assumes that the law would apply equally to all: that is, it would stipulate conditions which all members, rulers and ruled, must abide by when they act. This idea of rule of law requires the existence of strong and independent institutions, acting autonomously to uphold the law. In India this conception of rule of law is formally endorsed, but since institutions, particularly those working with the executive, do not always enjoy functional autonomy, the rule of law is often not in evidence. Law tends to be applied in a way that privileges some while coming down heavily against others. Such differential application of law is not entirely unheard of; indeed power (economic, political and ideological) is known to influence outcomes in many democratic societies today. What makes the Indian case stand out is that unequal application of law is all too pervasive, and it is visible in everyday life as well as extraordinary situations. As a result, it is an individual's capacity to access powerful social and political networks, rather than rule of law, that tends to determine his fate.

If we look at these characteristics it would appear that the civil association model has little or no resonance in India. Oakeshott, it seems, is out of place in India. This conclusion is reinforced when we take, from contemporary readings of Oakeshott, the distinction between civil association and enterprise model seriously. When the emphasis is on the dichotomy between the civil and enterprise model, it is easy to conclude that India, with its commitment to pursue substantive ends, lies on the other side of a civil association. But is there a possibility of reading Oakeshott somewhat differently? Are there other attributes present in the Indian imagination that make Oakeshott less alien in India? Are there shared concerns between the two? Should one focus merely on what exists to decide whether Oakeshott's ideas have any relevance in India? I raise these questions because ideas travel and they are open to different appropriations; and we engage with ideas not only because they resonate with our deep beliefs and traditions but because they compel us to think about them carefully. Above all, it would be methodologically naïve to arrive at what is significant or relevant merely on the basis of what exists, or has existed in the past.

History is not after all a cage in which we are placed and which binds us to act in certain predetermined ways.

History offers, without doubt, a context of experience; it also moulds our dispositions. Both these elements shape who we are, as they produce and sustain certain inclinations in us. But in giving direction to our actions we do not merely reproduce what has happened before; our inclinations may push us to act in a specific way but we do not merely do that which is a matter of habit. Actions involve reflection, or at least a consideration of what we are doing and why we are doing it. In other words, in shaping the future we reflect upon and reassess the path we have taken in the past and the consequences it has thrown up. We explore alternatives that are available to us in the present as well as those that were not explored in the past. Our history itself carries within itself residues of contrary trends and diverse understandings, some of which challenge the dominant ways of living and envisaging the political. In determining what is relevant and significant one has therefore to consider not only what exists but also what is embedded in and may be recovered and nurtured from our past.

In other words, even though what exists in India has little in common with Oakeshott's notion of civil association, one needs to see if there are traces of a political imagination in India that resonates with the concept of civil association. One needs further to ask what this concept offers for the ends and aspirations that were embodied in the Indian Constitution. It is by reflecting on these twin dimensions that one can hope to avoid the errors of path determinism and affirm the possibility of a fruitful and creative encounter with Oakeshott.

Revisiting Oakeshott

Reading and thinking about Oakeshott in India, especially his conception of civil association, it becomes evident rather quickly that contemporary readings of Oakeshott that posit a sharp distinction between the civil and the enterprise model do not offer a very fertile ground for engaging with his writings. While these interpretations are exceedingly helpful in clarifying the specificity of the civil model they deter one from considering it seriously because postcolonial societies, like India, see the pursuit of certain substantive ends—like freedom and equality—as the rationale for their existence. However, when we turn our attention to passages that are less frequently quoted in contemporary scholarship on Oakeshott then one comes up with a more suitable starting point for an encounter with Oakeshott.

While elucidating the difference between the civil and enterprise models Oakeshott maintained that he was presenting the 'ideal character' (1975, p. 109) of each of these forms of human relationships, although in reality they are not found in their pure form. In fact in certain situations, for example in case of war, the civil association may begin to look more and more like an enterprise (see Parekh, 1979, pp. 494–5). In other words, aspects of the enterprise model may well coexist with civil association; hence, the presence of the former may not always imply the absence of the civil. Then again, Oakeshott claimed that civil association may pursue such goals as peace and security. For Oakeshott these were non-substantive goals: they were far too general and many different kinds of actions and policies may be pursued within them. 'If, on the other hand, the common purpose is said to be the "security" or the *tranquillitas* of the associates, or their "peace" or moral virtue, then the identification again collapses. These are not *substantive purposes and they do not specify enterprise association*' (Oakeshott, 1975, p. 119, emphasis added). In effect this means that the pursuit of some non-specific goals may be compatible with civil association, and their pursuit may not infringe the freedom of the individual. It is only the pursuit of 'specific common want (like a sewage system or a chicken in the pot on Sundays) ... or devotion to a set of religious beliefs which prescribe substantive conduct ...' (Oakeshott, 1975, p. 119) that needs to be avoided. If commitment to some goals is indeed permissible then the notion of a civil relationship need not be dismissed out of hand in post-colonial societies. The question that would be worth asking is — which ends are indeed incompatible with the civil relationship? Does the pursuit of liberty or justice or even equality — elements that are identified as the shared goals of the political community in India — violate the conditions of a civil association?

Once we abandon thinking through binaries, and allow for a complex relationship between the civil model and the pursuit of certain ideals as goals, the idea of civil association does not appear alien to, or out of place in, India. The preamble of the Indian Constitution laid out certain ends to be pursued — namely, freedom, justice and equality. One might now ask if these cannot, like peace and security, be viewed as non-specific substantial ends that are compatible with civil association as a model of political relationship. After all, many different policies can be pursued within these ends, and providing equal rights and liberties might well be a requirement for the existence of the civil. If some are formally excluded from the domain of the political, then the basic condition of *respublica* cannot be met. To put it another way, one can now have a conversation about specific elements that go into the making of an enterprise model and how one might avoid those pitfalls without abandoning a commitment to some general ends. Reading

Oakeshott may well prove to be indispensable in this respect even for India.

Second, there are certainly elements in the Indian framework that are incompatible with the notion of a civil association, but to focus on just those aspects offers an incomplete picture of the Indian reality. There are several other dimensions of the Indian political imagination, its history and traditions, where one can find 'intimations' (to use Oakeshott's term) of the civil association. From the twentieth century onwards, when a democratic and independent India was being imagined, most of the political leadership agreed that the state in India would not endorse any one conception of good life and it would create an environment in which people of different beliefs and moral orientations would enjoy an equal degree of freedom. These sentiments echoed Oakeshott's concerns and shared, to a considerable extent, his anxieties about the enterprise mode of relationship, in which members endorse a substantial end or system of beliefs. Even the notion of civil disobedience that captured the public mood affirmed the necessity of law and accepted the authority of law. Even when the law was considered to be morally unacceptable, the protester (the *satyagrahi* as a conscientious objector) was expected to bear the punishment of violating the law. This was a way of acknowledging the authority of law *per se* (i.e. for itself), and it prepared the individual for a democratic way of life.

Besides, in independent India, the Constitution (as a system of laws/*Lex*) enjoys a special status. The Constitution has been amended more than a hundred times but through the process laid down in the Constitution. Differences of interpretation have also been settled through the available institutional mechanisms. Today there is an agreement that the 'basic structure' of the Constitution cannot be altered or amended by the parliament. A system of rules has thus been accorded primacy and one might even say that the political relationship is governed by an obligation to that constitutional law.

It is these intimations of shared concerns, in particular similar understanding of the value of law, authority and difference, that makes it both important and worthwhile to engage with Oakeshott in the Indian context. Given the difference of history and context, it is not surprising that each of the elements valued receives a different meaning and content. In Oakeshott's framework, for instance, it is individual differences that matter the most; in India differences of moral outlook, perceptions and beliefs are related to the community of which the individual is a part. Both associate freedom with a non-commitment to specific worldviews and conceptions of good but again these elements are read differently. In India the state is expected to not align itself with a conception of good that is derived from the religion and culture of any one community; it can, however, endorse general ends that are valued in modern democracies, such as freedom and respect for all. Oakeshott is not entirely averse to this way of thinking. However, clash between religious worldviews is not his only concern. Thinking about various kinds of individual differences (such as ideological differences, differences in scientific thinking, etc.) he suggests the absence of any specific substantive ends. Both formulations have their strengths and weaknesses. The Indian reading is mindful of relationships of power and historical dispositions that may be inscribed into the law; hence it considers recognition of determinate, plural ways of life as a necessary condition of the neutrality of law. The Oakeshottian view continuously reminds us of the need to give primacy to the individual even when that individual is located within a community.

One can, and indeed it may be desirable to, place these two concerns alongside each other as they are both necessary for sustaining contemporary democracies; in a way they can correct and supplement each other. In India where the individual tends to be frequently boxed into the community, and looked at as a member of that community, it is necessary to stress the individual differences between members of that community and make space institutionally for that. On the other side, where the individual tends to be abstracted from all its locations, it may be necessary to remind ourselves that the choices a person makes can, and often do, reflect his collective community preferences; as such, procedures that collate individual preferences can inadvertently privilege points of view that work to the advantage of some groups in society.

Government Action and Freedom

The civil association model is a powerful reminder of the need to protect the rights and liberties of the individual. In the Indian context where the individual is hemmed in on the one side by the community and on the other by the concerns of national interest, holding on to this maxim is of the utmost importance. However, securing the freedom of the individual in different contexts may require different kinds of actions. Many advocates of civil association maintain that freedom is best protected when the government does not maximize or extend its power. Presumably this means that the government should not seek to redistribute goods and resources or make laws compelling individuals to act in a specific way. Instead of seeing itself as a protector or promoter of a specific understanding of what is desirable, it should act only to create and sustain conditions in which individuals can make their choices.

By this reasoning all that is required of political institutions is that they protect such conditions as freedom of speech and expression, civil and political liberties. That is, they must act to protect the right of individuals to pursue a career of their choice, to marry according to their wishes, to live where they like and order their lives in a way that they deem best for themselves. In a context where the individual is taken to be the basic unit of social life, these basic liberties may well be protected by the presence of a minimal state, but in a context where the individual is severely constrained by customary practices, and the fiat of community and elders, the same goal (namely, of protecting the freedom of the individual) may require a different set of actions from the government. In India, where the social itself poses a threat to individual freedom, the state may, in addition to protecting the individual against the actions of the community and other social groups, be required to intervene and restrict or regulate practices and institutions that work to curtail the freedom of the individual. A minimalist state, that has a hands-off approach may not in these circumstances be an adequate guarantor of just those freedoms that justify a civil association.

Differences of context may require different kinds of government action. As Oakeshott reminds us, 'The system of law, if it is to serve its purpose, must, of course, be appropriate to the kind of relationships which the members of the association are apt to enter into, *and the kind of injuries they are most apt to do to one another. It, therefore, falls to government not only to administer the law, but also to see that this law is appropriate to its subjects...*' (Lectures 494 in Fuller, 2012, emphasis added). In the Indian context it is also pertinent to recall another element of Oakeshott's analysis: namely, that it is more important to focus on *how* a government acts rather than *what* it does. In a growing economy where the government is pushing for greater deregulation, liberalization of the economy and withdrawal of the state from different sectors, there is a steady clamour for less and less government. This excessive preoccupation with the quantum of government action and the extent of its intervention needs to be moderated by the Oakeshottian understanding of what matters more when it comes to government action. Less government is not by itself enough. One needs to back it with rule of law, on the one hand, and an emphasis on *how* the government acts, on the other. Non-interference is not a sufficient guarantor of freedom. What the state does is less important than the need to abide by procedures and laws, and to ensure that the law binds all persons equally. Eventually it is not the autonomy of the market that is of ultimate value but the rule of law. These are some aspects of the public and political life in India which can be enriched through an engagement with Oakeshott.

Thus far, I have emphasized the need to move beyond the binaries through which Oakeshott's work is presented and read. This needs to be supplemented with the understanding that the ideas of a political theorist, Oakeshott in this instance, may be read in two fairly different ways: we can draw from his writings a template of what civil association is and use that to decide if the political relationship is governed by those principles in a given society; or, we can get some pointers from him which can, like signposts, direct us to a mode of political organization that can protect freedom while guaranteeing security and order. The former frame of analysis is likely to offer a set of ready answers as solutions to our predicament, of what characteristics we should adopt; the latter will compel us to think about our circumstances and then determine what is relevant for us. In my view it is the second mode of approaching Oakeshott that is likely to be helpful and relevant in India. For the ideal form of civil association may be found, at least some of the time, in countries where the conditions for sustaining this political relationship have been realized; where individual autonomy is taken as the norm in society and law. In India, where these conditions do not exist, we will neither find a replica of the civil association, nor hope to reproduce that model by walking down a set path. The latter would not be possible and, even if it were, it is unlikely to yield the same results. It is therefore preferable to take the second approach and draw on the idea of civil association as a guide to what we should be cautious about, and what errors we must guard against, as we seek the same end result: namely, securing individual freedom along with the benefits of order. Not only would this be a more appropriate way of thinking about Oakeshott in India, it is likely to also help us to correct the course that India is currently taking as it moves towards greater liberalization and deregulation.

One might also add that this way of reading Oakeshott will not be entirely out of sync with his framework, as he continuously reminds us that the practical is not like the scientific or the rational. It is a different kind of activity. Reading Oakeshott we can come to appreciate that the political is the domain of the contingent; hence we cannot rely merely on adherence to a set of principles—whether they are based on an understanding what is rational, or an ideology, or some lessons from history. Thinking about freedom requires a certain flexibility so as to accord primacy to what is necessary under the circumstances instead of emulating a pre-given model.

References

Fuller, T. (2012) Michael Oakeshott on the rule of law and the liberal order, *Library of Law and Liberty*, September, 2, [Online], http://www.libertylawsite.org/liberty-forum/michael-oakeshott-on-the-rule-of-law-and-the-liberal-order/.

Gellner, E. (1990) The civil and the sacred, *Tanner Lectures on Human Values Delivered at Harvard University*, 20–21 March, [Online], utah.edu/_documents/a-to-z/g/Gellner_91.pdf.

Mapel, D. (1990) Civil association and the idea of contingency, *Political Theory*, **18** (3), pp. 392–410.

Minch, M. (2009) *The Democratic Theory of Michael Oakeshott: Discourse, Contingency, Contingency and the Politics of Conversation*, Exeter: Imprint Academic.

Mouffe, C. (2013) *Hegemony, Radical Democracy and the Political*, Martin, J. (ed.), Oxford: Routledge.

Natarajan, S. (1962) *A Century of Social Reforms in India*, 2nd ed., Delhi: Asia Publishing House.

Oakeshott, M. (1975) *On Human Conduct*, Oxford: Clarendon Press.

O'Sullivan, N. (2002) Why read Oakeshott?, *Social Science and Public Policy Society*, **39** (3), pp. 71–74.

O'Sullivan, N. (2012) in Franco, P. & Marsh, L. (eds.) *A Companion to Michael Oakeshott*, University Park, PA: Penn State University Press.

Panikkar, K.N. (1990) Culture and consciousness in modern India: A historical perspective, *Social Scientist*, **18** (4), pp. 3–32.

Parekh, B. (1979) The political philosophy of Michael Oakeshott, *British Journal of Political Science*, **9** (4), October, pp. 481–506.

Parekh, B. (1995) Oakeshott's theory of civil association, review essay, *Ethics*, **106** (1), October, pp. 158–186.

Rorty, R. (1993) *Contingency, Irony and Solidarity*, New York: Cambridge University Press.

Index

Adorno, Theodor W. 147, 156
Ancient Rome 42, 48-49, 50-52, 55, 116
Arendt, Hannah 5, 96
Aristotle 23, 75, 109, 125, 127
Aron, Raymond 99, 102
Augustine, St. 1, 10, 125

Berlin, Isaiah 96, 99, 102
Blackburn, Simon 149
Bosanquet, Bernard 16, 130, 181
Boswell, James 67
Bradley, F.H. 181
Burke, Edmund 100, 103

Carlyle, Thomas 100
Cecil, Lord Hugh 101
Chabod, Federico 144
Chinese tradition 15, 161, 166-167, 170-172, 174-178 (see also: Tradition)
Cicero 42, 51-54
Civil association 3-5, 8, 10, 13-18, 20-21, 24, 27-30, 41, 55, 63, 65-66, 69-70, 90, 93-97, 102, 107, 116-117, 119-120, 130, 133, 142, 153-157, 162-163, 177, 183-193 (see also: Civil condition, Civil society, Civility)
Civil condition, The 25, 69-70, 93, 112
Civil society 7, 153, 171
Civility 30-31, 174, 177, 187
Civilization 1, 5, 18, 21-22, 35-36, 74, 82, 108, 110, 112, 124, 139, 165, 169-170, 178, 182
Coats, John 9
Collingwood, R.G. 11, 73-74, 78-86, 130
Coltman, Irene 7

Confucianism 15, 129, 132, 138, 160, 167-168, 170-172 (see also: Confucius)
Confucius 57, 63, 65, 171 (see also: Confucianism)
Democracy 8, 16, 18, 92, 108, 112-116, 119,142-144, 146-147, 149, 154-156, 160-162, 164-167, 170-171, 176-177, 183, 185 (see also: Liberal democracy)
Descartes, René 8, 91, 112, 137
Dilthey, Wilhelm 109

Enterprise 3, 15-17, 24, 28-29, 35, 39, 42, 60, 66, 70, 75, 93-94, 95-97, 107, 116, 130, 133, 135, 152-154, 164, 183-184, 186-190 (see also: Enterprise association)
Enterprise association 16, 24, 28-29, 35, 70, 93-97, 116, 130, 133, 135, 183-184, 189 (see also: Enterprise)
Ethics 12, 18, 64-65, 124, 126, 134-136

Feng, Qiu 173, 176
Feher, Ferenc 108
Franco, Paul 97, 102
Freeden, Michael 97
Fung, Edmund S.K. 163

Gadamer, Georg 11, 73-74, 81-88, 101, 109, 181
Gellner, Ernest 17
Geuss, Raymond 18
Godolphin, Francis 7
Godolphin, Sydney 7-8
Gray, John 155
Green, T.H. 16, 181

Haiguang, Yin 160-161, 164, 166
Hayek, Friedrich 15, 102, 104, 124, 134-136, 163-169, 172-173, 177
Hegel, Georg Wilhelm Friedrich 56, 73-74, 109, 126, 130, 134, 143, 157
Heidegger, Martin 88, 109, 149
History 5, 10-11, 16, 23-24, 34-35, 41-45, 47-52, 54, 62, 73-79, 82, 84, 88, 95-96, 101, 103, 108-109, 112, 116, 119, 123, 127, 130-131, 134, 137-138, 143-145, 152, 155, 157, 176, 181-182, 188, 190, 193 (see also: Roman history)
Historicity 11, 73, 143-144
Hobbes, Thomas 2-3, 6-8, 12-14, 20-21, 23-28, 32, 35, 39, 56, 61, 67-68, 74, 76-77, 115-120, 126, 143-145, 151
Hobhouse, L.T. 98-99
Hobson, J.A. 98
Hogg, Quintin 101, 103, 155
Honig, Bonnie 147, 151
Horkheimer, Max 156
Huizinga, Johan 18, 156
Hume, David 149

Jisheng, Yang 165
Johnson, Samuel 67
Junning, Liu 172-173
Justice 6-7, 14, 16, 27, 29-30, 64, 66, 166, 183, 185, 189

Kant, Immanuel 8, 56, 61, 64, 67, 128, 148
Kennington, Richard 148
Keynes, John Maynard 68
Kidd, Benjamin 100
Kojève, Alexandre 152
Koselleck, Reinhart 13, 107-112, 114-120

Legend 4-5, 34, 41-52, 54-55, 110
Lenin, Vladimir 167
Letwin, Shirley 25-27
Liberal democracy 18, 107, 112, 114, 144, 156 (see also: Democracy)
Liberalism 96, 98-102, 111-116, 160-163, 165-166, 170, 172-175, 177-178

Liberty 35, 38, 66, 98-99, 102-104, 126, 156, 164-166, 189
Livy 42, 49, 51-54
Locke, John 68, 143, 167

Machiavelli, Niccolò 34, 143-144
MacIntyre, Alasdair 124, 134, 136-137
Maimonides, Moses 125-126, 138
Mapel, D. 185
Marcuse, Herbert 147
Maritain, Jacques 101, 103
Marx, Karl 58, 65, 108, 120, 143, 181
Mill, John Stuart 67, 102, 104
Modernity 8, 10, 15, 51, 90-91, 99-100, 102-104, 123, 127-128, 138, 143-144, 147-149, 161, 163, 167, 177, 181
Montaigne, Michel de 57, 65, 127-128
Moralism 6, 57-58
Mouffe, Chantal 183-185
Müller, Jan-Werner 13
Muralt, Andre de 125-126, 138
Myth 1-6, 8, 10-12, 15, 17-18, 21-23, 29, 34-39, 41-43, 48, 52, 54-55, 109-111, 119, 143, 182

Naevius 53
Nietzsche, Friedrich 58, 68, 138, 143, 149

Ockham, William of 125-126
Ortega y Gasset, José 18, 156

Pippin, Robert 144, 148
Plato 74, 80, 82, 85, 87, 123, 126-128, 137, 139, 145-146, 148-150, 181
Pluralism 12-13, 98-99, 102, 104, 110, 114-115, 127, 144
Podoksik, Efraim 97, 102-103
Polanyi, Karl 169
Polybius 51
Popper, Karl 96, 99, 102
Purposive association 135, 183-185

Rationalism 9, 11, 22, 63, 90-92, 102, 110-112, 115-116, 120, 123-124, 129-130, 132, 136-138, 160, 163, 165-166, 168, 172, 175, 182
Rawls, John 68, 99, 101
Rickert, Heinrich 128

Roman 5, 42, 48-54, 139 (see also: Roman history)
Roman history 5, 50-53 (see also: Roman)
Romanticism 66, 68-69, 134
Romulus 43, 49-50, 53
Rorty, Richard 183, 185
Rousseau, Jean-Jacques 126, 143
Rule of law 2-3, 13-14, 16-17, 27, 59, 64, 67, 69, 93, 108, 112-113, 115-116, 119, 133, 135-136, 142, 145, 153, 155, 162, 166-167, 170-171, 175, 177, 185-187, 192
Rulun, Zhang 160, 166, 170

Sartre, Jean-Paul 10
Schmitt, Carl 13-14, 107-120, 151
Scotus, Duns 125, 138
Shils, Edward 171, 174-175
Society 3, 5, 7, 16, 26, 34, 42, 46-51, 54-55, 63, 87, 98-99, 104, 109, 112, 114-116, 133, 146-147, 149, 151-154, 156, 162-164, 169, 171, 175, 183, 185, 191, 193
Socrates 62, 67
Spencer, Herbert 101

Spinoza, Benedict 4, 20, 22, 24-29, 36, 39, 62
Strauss, Leo 11, 73-74, 81-82, 84-88, 101, 103, 124, 134, 137-139, 142-152, 156
Tacitus 51
Taylor, Charles 124, 134-136
Thomas, St. 75
Tradition 3, 5-6, 11-12, 15-16, 32, 43, 47, 53, 58, 64-66, 74, 82-83, 90, 92-94, 100-101, 103-104, 108, 112, 116, 136, 144, 147, 161-163, 166-167, 170-178, 181-183, 187, 190 (see also: Chinese tradition, Western tradition)
Treitschke, Heinrich von 100
Trotsky, Leon 165, 167
Tseng, Roy 97
Tudor, Henry 52-53

Virgil 51

Weber, Max 96-97, 99, 109, 172
Western tradition 17, 83, 92, 101, 103, 144 (see also: Tradition)

Yu-Sheng, Lin 166

www.ingramcontent.com/pod-product-compliance
Lightning Source LLC
Chambersburg PA
CBHW031710230426
43668CB00006B/173